UNDERSTANDING CONSUMPTION

Understanding Consumption

ANGUS DEATON

CLARENDON PRESS · OXFORD

1992

Oxford University Press, Walton Street, Oxford OX2 6DP

Oxford New York Toronto
Delhi Bombay Calcutta Madras Karachi
Kuala Lumpur Singapore Hong Kong Tokyo
Nairobi Dar es Salaam Cape Town
Melbourne Auckland Madrid

and associated companies in
Berlin Ibadan

Oxford is a trade mark of Oxford University Press

Published in the United States
by Oxford University Press Inc., New York

Library of Congress Cataloguing in Publication Data
Data available

ISBN 0-19-828759-3
ISBN 0-19-828824-7 (pbk)

Library of Congress Cataloging in Publication Data
Data available

ISBN 0-19-828759-3
ISBN 0-19-828824-7 (pbk)

Typeset by Angus Deaton

Printed in Great Britain
on acid-free paper by
Biddles Ltd, Guildford & King's Lynn

330 480

For Helge

Preface

This book is an expanded version of the Clarendon Lectures given in Oxford in May 1991; earlier versions were presented to the Network for Quantitative Economics in Rotterdam in May 1990, and to my *Empirical Modelling* course in Princeton over a number of years. In Oxford, there were three one-hour lectures, and although the book is faithful to the structure of my verbal presentation, many of the details have been filled in, and there is additional material to which only passing reference was made in the lectures. Many of those in the Oxford audience were graduate students, and the lectures were presented at a level designed to be comprehensible to them as well as to advanced (British) undergraduates. The emphasis is on the development of intuition rather than on the mathematics underlying the results, and on stylized facts rather than on formal econometric methodology. The book has more mathematics and more econometrics than the lectures, but I have attempted to retain the original level of accessibility. I hope that my professional colleagues will be as tolerant of the informality as were the Oxford faculty who attended the lectures.

Attempts by economists to understand the saving and consumption patterns of households have generated some of the best science in economics. For more than fifty years, there has been serious empirical and theoretical activity, and the two strands have never been long separated as has happened in so many other branches of economics. Research has drawn microeconomists interested in household behavior, as well as macroeconomists, for whom the behavior of aggregate consumption has always occupied a central role in explaining aggregate fluctuations. Econometricians have also made distinguished contributions, and there has been a steady flow of new methodology from those working on saving and consumption. Nor have policy concerns ever been far from the surface. The relationships between saving and business cycles, saving and growth, saving and competitiveness, and saving and welfare have been hotly and continually debated. It is hard to think of economic issues that are more important than the accumulation of capital, and the means by which citizens, either individually or collectively, make provision for their futures. All of this has produced an unusually rich brew, with aromas that attract almost all types of economist. Especially over the last fifteen years, and in particular since Hall's (1978) paper on the stochastic implications of forward-looking behavior, there has been a great flurry of activity. This activity paralleled and took off from the earlier explosion of the 1950s, which saw the development of the then 'new' theories of the consumption function, particularly the life-cycle theory of Modigliani and Brumberg (1954, 1979), which is the basis for essentially all modern research on consumption and saving.

In these chapters I try to tell the story of the most recent burst of research. I do not know whether now is the best time to try, or whether the best results are just around the corner, perhaps in a working paper of which I am unaware. But the story as it now stands is a good one; a great deal has been learnt that we did not know before, about methodology, about the evidence, and about the substance of the issues. So the tale is worth telling, even at the risk that the conclusions will be transparently wrong only a year or two from now. Indeed, the time can hardly be worse than when John Muellbauer and I wrote the consumption chapter of *Economics and Consumer Behavior* in 1978; we had read Hall's paper and discussed it in the book, but could not anticipate the outpouring of research that it was to engender. To some extent this book is my attempt to bring that chapter up to date, and to assess how much we have learned in the last fifteen years.

I have not been a neutral participant in the debate, so that even if it were possible to write a balanced, impartial survey, I am in a poor position to do so. Instead, I have tried to present a coherent account, fully conscious that the interpretations are my own, and that there are many who hold different views. The literature on consumption and saving is so large that the risk of missing something really important is unusually high, and I apologize in advance to those whose contributions have been neglected. There are also important areas that I have consciously and deliberately omitted. I have little to say about durables, and even less about labor supply. Each of these topics deserves a chapter, but these are lectures, not a comprehensive text, and the boundaries must be drawn somewhere. Life-cycle models of labor supply have remained a largely separate research topic, and I am relatively comfortable discussing consumption on the assumption that labor income is outside the agent's control. Durables are another matter, and recent work by Bertola and Caballero (1990) and others on non-convex and asymmetric adjustment costs has at last provided the foundations for coherent attempts to interpret the data. This work may ultimately have a profound effect on the study of consumption as a whole, for non-durables as well as durables, and I have excluded it, not for lack of relevance, but because of the lengthening of the book that would be required to do justice to this very different material.

Instead, I have emphasized the interplay between the micro and the macro, between the studies of cross-sections and panels, on the one hand,

and aggregate time-series on the other. Although the central Chapters 3 and 4 are concerned almost exclusively with representative agent models applied to aggregate data, an emphasis that mirrors the balance of the literature, I have come to believe that such studies are of limited value, and that what we have learned from them is more methodological than substantive. Representative agents have two great failings; they know too much, and they live too long. An aggregate of individuals with finite lives, and with limited and heterogeneous information is not likely to behave like the single individual of the textbook. We are likely to learn more about aggregate consumption by looking at microeconomic behavior, and by thinking seriously about aggregation from the bottom up. Chapters 5 and 6 are concerned with work that has been directed towards at least some aspect of this task.

The book is perhaps not long enough to require any guide beyond the table of contents. Even so, different readers will be interested in different parts of the story, so that some map might be useful. Chapter 1 is a reasonably comprehensive guide to the theory, and as such goes into more detail than is required for the main arguments in the subsequent substantive chapters. Section 1 presents a simple model of intertemporal choice that covers (only) the basics. The first few subsections of Section 3, on the evolution of consumption in an uncertain world, and Section 4, on aggregation, could not easily be skipped without losing the thread of the book as a whole. Section 2 can be dipped into at choice. Chapter 2 is about saving, growth, and interest, and is the least technical chapter of the book. Chapters 3 and 4 discuss the permanent income hypothesis, and largely follow the macroeconomists' approach to aggregate consumption, focusing on issues of time-series and dynamics. Chapter 5 is largely a review of empirical work using microeconomic data on household behavior. It also attempts to build some bridges between this microeconomic research and the macroeconomic analysis of the pervious two chapters. Chapter 6 is more technical than the others, although the broad thrust of the argument ought to be apparent even if the mathematics are skipped. It is also the most speculative, and covers recent research into precautionary saving and the effects of imperfect credit markets. A brief Chapter 7 tries to step back from the detail of the research, however fascinating, and to summarize how much we understand about consumption, how much we have learned in recent years, and how much we have yet to learn. There are still many important facts of saving and consumption behavior for which understanding remains elusive.

In writing this book, I have had support from the Center of International Studies at Princeton, from the Lynde and Harry Bradley Foundation of Milwaukee, and from the World Bank, who supported my work on savings in LDCs, some of which is reported here. I am grateful to both institutions. I also thank the Department of Applied Economics and Churchill College in Cambridge for their hospitality during my sabbatical year in 1990–1, and to Princeton University, for their generous sabbatical policy, and more generally, for providing me with such splendid colleagues and the world's best academic environment.

I have received help from a large number of people, not least several classes of Princeton graduate students who have worked through similar material over the last five years, and some of whom have made important contributions of their own. I have learned a great deal from their challenges and questions, and from their splendid refusal to take anything for granted. I also was delighted to receive so many and so extensive comments on the draft that was circulated in the Fall of 1991. I am grateful to Orazio Attanasio, Samuel Bentolila, Tim Besley, Alan Blinder, Kristin Butcher, John Campbell, David Card, Kevin Carey, Chris Carroll, Stanley Fischer, Marjorie Flavin, Luigi Guiso, Fumio Hayashi, Larry Kotlikoff, Guy Laroque, Annamaria Lusardi, John Muellbauer, Greg Mankiw, Christina Paxson, Steve Pischke, Jon Skinner, Larry Summers, Guglielmo Weber, and Steve Zeldes, all of whom helped me rewrite and rethink. I have not adopted all of the suggestions, but I have used most of them, and some have caused me to make very substantial changes, both to the text and to my way of thinking. I owe a major debt to all those who gave me their time so unsparingly.

Angus Deaton

July 1992
Princeton

Contents

CHAPTER 1

Theoretical Foundations

This book is about consumption and saving, at the level of the individual, or at least the household, and at the level of the economy as a whole. The title, *Understanding Consumption*, is chosen to highlight the approach that I intend to take. The ultimate aim is to develop a coherent theoretical description of individual behavior, a description that is based on the usual suppositions about human greed and rationality, and that can account for the variety of empirical evidence, including the evidence from both aggregate and individual behavior. This is an uncontroversial objective, but a good deal of the work on consumption does not subscribe to it. Especially for those whose main concern has been the *prediction* of aggregate consumption, theoretical foundations have been of secondary concern compared with the ability to fit the aggregate data and to give accurate predictions outside the fitted sample. While we might reasonably hope that understanding might lead to good predictions, the search for coherent foundations may not always be the most direct way to discover useful empirical regularities.

The decision of how much to consume is a decision about spending money now as opposed to retaining it to finance future consumption, for some specific purpose, or for some general unspecified contingency in the future. The appropriate basis for a theory of consumption is therefore the theory of intertemporal choice, which formalizes the trade-offs between present and future consumption. The simplest possible version is that found in the elementary textbooks, where the consumer, living in a two-period world of complete certainty, chooses how much to spend today and how much to spend tomorrow. More realistic formulations can be thought of as elaborations on this basic theme, so I use it as a base point from which to mount more interesting expeditions. Section 1 rehearses this familiar material, and shows how it can be extended to model the way in which consumption evolves over the life cycle. This model provides a basic theoretical framework for the book, albeit in a stripped-down form. The rest of the chapter fleshes out the theory, starting with the specification of preferences, in Section 2, and moving on, in Section 3, to the predictions of the theory for the behavior of consumption. Section 4 is a first look at a theme that recurs throughout the book; what does the microeconomic theory of consumption behavior imply for the macroeconomic aggregates of consumption and saving?

1.1 A simple model of intertemporal choice and the life cycle

In the simplest possible case, there is a single consumer who has preferences defined over consumption in two periods, 1 and 2. As usual, tastes are represented by a utility function

$$u = \upsilon(c_1, c_2) \tag{1.1}$$

which the consumer maximizes subject to the opportunities that are available. There is a single asset, of which the consumer possesses an amount A_1 at the beginning of period 1, and which earns an interest rate r_2 on funds held over from period 1 into period 2. There is no requirement that holdings of assets be positive, so that the consumer can borrow or lend as much as desired, but the world is assumed to come to an end after period 2, and the consumer is not permitted to be in debt at the end of the world. If we also abstract from bequest motives, and assume that the consumer always prefers more to less, then assets will be zero at the end of period 2. The consumer also receives 'labor income' y_1 and y_2 in each of the two periods; this is separate from any (positive or negative) income flows earned from holding the asset. The stock of assets evolves from one period to the next according to

$$A_2 = (1 + r_2)(A_1 + y_1 - c_1). \tag{1.2}$$

Since assets will be zero at the end of period 2, consumption in period 2 will be the sum of A_2 and y_2, so that $A_2 = c_2 - y_2$. If we use this to substitute for A_2 in equation (2) above, we obtain the intertemporal budget constraint

$$c_1 + \frac{c_2}{1 + r_2} = A_1 + y_1 + \frac{y_2}{1 + r_2}. \tag{1.3}$$

The maximization of the utility function (1) subject to the budget constraint (3) is the canonical intertemporal choice problem. Because it is in the standard form of consumer demand analysis, the maximization of utility subject to a linear budget constraint with parametric prices, we can bring to bear all the standard apparatus of consumer choice theory. In particular, the discount factor $(1 + r_2)^{-1}$ is the price of consumption tomorrow relative to consumption today, while the role of initial assets and of the discounted present value of labor incomes is that of 'income' or total expenditure in the standard problem. The effects of assets, income, and interest rates can then be analyzed using the standard tools of demand analysis.

Such an approach readily yields the following results which I note for future reference:

(*i*) An increase in the interest rate r_2 (*a*) makes future consumption cheaper relative to current consumption, the substitution effect, (*b*) permits more second-period consumption with the same total resources and without cutting first-period consumption, the income effect, and (*c*) if y_2 is positive, reduces the present discounted value of total life-time resources, the 'human capital' effect. Effects (*a*) and (*c*) act so as to cut current consumption, while (*b*) works so as to increase it. For consumption over all goods and services together, it seems implausible that the substitution effect should be very large, but in any case the direction of the effect of interest rates on consumption is not predictable on theoretical grounds. For example, it is a simple exercise to show that if, for parameter $\rho > 0$, the utility function is $(1-\rho)^{-1}(c_1^{1-\rho} + c_2^{1-\rho})$, then the direction of the effect of the interest rate on current consumption depends on the size of the parameter ρ.

(*ii*) Increases in labor income, now or in the future, act so as to increase consumption. The size of the effect of changes in current income on current consumption depends on how future income is linked to current income. Where there is no uncertainty, this is hardly an issue, but in richer and more realistic models, it will be necessary to deal with the way in which expectations of the future are affected by current events.

Many periods and the life cycle

The basic idea of the life-cycle model is to apply ideas of intertemporal allocation to explain the way in which consumption evolves with age over the life-span of individuals and households. The theory extends the two-period 'today versus tomorrow' model to many periods or ages, with consumers choosing when to spend their lifetime resources according to their needs and tastes. As in the two-period model, consumption is financed from life-time earnings or from inherited assets, and consumers use capital markets to decouple the time-pattern of earnings and assets from the desired pattern of consumption. As always, choice is governed by a set of intertemporal preferences, which in their most general form, might be written

$$u = V(c_1, c_2, c_3, \ldots, c_T), \tag{1.4}$$

where periods 1 through T are the years of life, so that as the consumer ages and chooses each year's level of consumption, he or she 'fills in' the blanks in the life-cycle utility function (4).

The preferences represented by (4) allow unlimited patterns of complementarity and substitutability between consumption levels in different periods, and such a specification is too general for most purposes. I shall discuss various special cases in this book, but by far the most widely used assumption is that preferences are *intertemporally additive*, or *strongly intertemporally separable*, in which case (4) takes the special form

$$u = \upsilon_1(c_1) + \upsilon_2(c_2) + \ldots + \upsilon_T(c_T), \qquad (1.5)$$

where the individual period 'subutility' or 'felicity' functions $\upsilon_t(c_t)$ are increasing and concave in their single arguments. With or without separability, utility is maximized subject to a lifetime budget constraint that is the obvious generalization of (3),

$$\sum_1^T \frac{c_t}{(1+r)^t} = A_1 + \sum_1^T \frac{y_t}{(1+r)^t}. \qquad (1.6)$$

Note that I am holding the real interest rate constant over time, largely to avoid the notation involved in dealing with multiple discount factors, and that, for the moment, I am still working in an imaginary environment in which there is no uncertainty.

The combination of additive utility in (5) and the budget constraint (6) yields an elegant and useful characterization of life-cycle behavior, a characterization first exploited by Heckman (1971, 1974) and by Ghez and Becker (1975). The first-order condition for maximizing (5) subject to (6) can be written

$$\lambda_t(c_t) = \upsilon'_t(c_t) = \mu(1+r)^{-t}, \qquad (1.7)$$

where I have defined $\lambda_t(c_t)$, a monotone decreasing function, as the marginal utility of consumption in period t, and where μ is the Lagrange multiplier for the lifetime budget constraint. The point to note about (7) is that the muliplier μ, because it applies to the lifetime constraint, is constant over time, and that the marginal utility of consumption is a function only of current consumption. Hence, (7) characterizes the evolution of consumption over time, or over the life cycle, in terms of the real interest rate r and the marginal utility functions $\lambda_t(c_t)$.

Lifetime consumption profiles

Suppose that the variation with age of the functions $\upsilon_t(c_t)$ can be captured by writing

$$\upsilon_t(c_t) = (1+\delta)^{-t}\upsilon(c_t, z_t), \tag{1.8}$$

where z_t are variables that affect the desirability of consumption at different points in the life cycle, household demographic structure being perhaps the most obvious, and δ is the rate of time-preference. If the z_t variables do not change, utility in the future is discounted to the present at rate δ. In this case, the first-order condition becomes

$$\lambda(c_t, z_t) = \mu\left(\frac{1+\delta}{1+r}\right)^t, \tag{1.9}$$

an equation which has a number of useful implications.

First, note the role of the 'taste shifters' z_t. Suppose that $r = \delta$ so that the right-hand side of (9) is constant. If there are particular periods in the life cycle where the z_t variables make the *marginal* utility of consumption high, then, since the marginal utility function is decreasing in its first argument, consumption in that period must also be high. This simple story provides a reasonable explanation for a number of life-cycle phenomena. When there are more people in the family, the marginal utility of additional expenditure will be higher, so that the life-cycle pattern of household consumption can be expected to have the same general shape as the life-cycle pattern of household size, rising to middle age, and declining thereafter. Low consumption of the elderly might also be attributed to the fact that marginal utility of expenditure is low in old age, see for example, Börsch-Supan and Stahl (1991). It might also be the case that consumption and leisure are substitutes, so that, even if we are correct in our assumption that hours worked are exogenously given, the marginal utility of consumption will be high when hours worked are at their highest. This is another reason why consumption might be higher in middle age, see Thurow (1969) and Heckman (1974).

The second implication of (9) concerns the behavior of consumption in response to the real interest rate. Note first that if z_t is constant, consumption will be growing or declining with age according to whether the real interest rate is greater or less than the rate of time-preference. If the incentive to wait overcomes impatience, it pays to postpone consumption, and to let it grow with age. Note that this says nothing about the effect of the interest rate on the *level* of consumption; a higher interest rate will correspond to a consumption profile that rises more steeply with age, but the position of that profile also responds to the interest rate, so that, just as in the simple two-period model, we cannot deduce whether consumption in any given period goes up or down. A more precise characterization of consumption growth can be obtained by differentiating (9) with respect to time, holding z_t constant. If we assume that r and δ are small enough, then denoting a time-derivative by a superimposed dot,

$$\frac{\dot{c}_t}{c_t} = \frac{-\upsilon'_t}{c_t \upsilon''_t}(r - \delta), \tag{1.10}$$

so that the *magnitude* of the response of consumption growth to the incentive $r - \delta$ is (minus) the reciprocal of the elasticity of the marginal utility of consumption. This quantity is known as the intertemporal elasticity of substitution and depends (inversely) on the curvature of the felicity functions $\upsilon(c_t)$. If the marginal utility of consumption is very sensitive to small changes in consumption, consumers are unwilling to change their consumption much to take advantage of intertemporal incentives since the profile of marginal utility can be matched to changed interest rates with little change in consumption. Note that if the felicity functions take the isoelastic form

$$\upsilon(c_t) = (1-\rho)^{-1}c_t^{1-\rho} \tag{1.11}$$

for parameter $\rho > 0$, then the elasticity of the marginal utility of consumption is $-\rho$ and the intertemporal elasticity of substitution is ρ^{-1}.

The curvature of the utility function plays an important role in consumer theory in general since it controls attitudes towards risk, and indeed the standard Arrow–Pratt coefficient of relative risk-aversion is defined as the elasticity of the marginal utility of consumption, which is the parameter ρ in the special case (11). In the next section, once uncertainty has been introduced, I shall return to this relationship between risk-aversion and the willingness to substitute over time.

1.2 On intertemporal preferences

Many of the basic insights of the theory of intertemporal choice are contained in the simplest case with no uncertainty, and with preferences additively separable over time. Even so, we shall need a more sophisticated treatment at various points in the book, and this section and the next provide a somewhat deeper look at preferences and at the choices that they imply. In this section, I consider five issues. First, I look at the concept of consumption, and how it comes about that people can be thought of as having preferences, not over individual goods and services, but over some appropriately defined aggregate of goods. Second, I consider an issue that often occurs in practice, especially when only limited data are available; whether it is valid to apply intertemporal choice theory to a subset of consumption, such as food or non-durables? Third, I briefly discuss questions of dynamic or time-inconsistency, whether in the absence of uncertainty, new information, or changes in preferences, people might want to change their previously made plans when they reach the times at which those plans must be implemented. Fourth, I return to the issue of intertemporal separability, and look at some useful preference structures that recognize that the effects of consumption in one period are likely to persist into later periods. Finally, I discuss the role of uncertainty, and in particular the relationship between expected utility theory and the intertemporal separability of preferences.

Consumption as an aggregate of commodities

For the purposes of this book, and in almost all of the literature on intertemporal choice, decisions are made with respect to 'consumption,' usually defined, as it is in the national income and product accounts, as a constant price aggregate of expenditures on a long list of goods and services. From a theoretical perspective, the ultimate objects of consumer choice are these individual goods and services, not the aggregates, and in this section I discuss various ways that allow us to pass from one to the other. The theoretical results used here are based on those in Gorman (1959).

A general starting-point is to work with the life-cycle utility function (4), but to replace the consumption aggregates c_t by *vectors* q_t, with dimension large enough to capture all the richness of variety and product differentiation that exists in reality. I shall confine myself to a restricted version of this, in which there is *weak* separability between periods, so that life-time utility can be written

$$V\left(u_1(q_1), u_2(q_2), \ldots, u_T(q_T)\right). \tag{1.12}$$

We can translate (12) from goods into money by replacing each of the sub-utility functions by the corresponding *indirect* subutility functions. As usual, these are defined by

$$\psi_t(x_t, p_t) = \max_{q_t}\left(u_t(q_t); \text{ s.t. } p_t \cdot q_t = x_t\right). \tag{1.13}$$

where p_t is the vector of prices at t, and x_t is whatever total expenditure is allocated to period t. Substitution of (13) into (12) gives a lifetime utility function defined on the prices and expenditure levels in each of the T periods. The maximization of this function is already a substantial simplification over the maximization of the original function (12), since the choice is only over the levels of expenditure in each period, and not over the myriad elements of each consumption vector. The problem is further simplified if preferences are intertemporally additive and take, for example, the form (8), so that utility can be written

$$u = \sum_1^T (1+\delta)^{-t}\psi(x_t, p_t, z_t). \tag{1.14}$$

For many purposes, (14) is enough, and indeed the only difference between this utility function and one in terms of consumption aggregates is that the allocation is done with respect to *money* expenditures, not *real* expenditures, with the individual prices appearing explicitly, instead of being implicit in the deflation from money to real expenditures.

It is possible to come closer to the conventional treatment if further restrictions are placed on preferences. The simplest and most elegant approach is to assume that the felicity or subutility functions $u_t(q_t)$ are homothetic. In this case—see Deaton and Muellbauer (1980: 142-4)—the indirect subutility functions have a single argument, total expenditure deflated by a price index, so that

$$\psi_t(x_t, p_t) = \upsilon_t(x_t / \pi_t(p_t)), \tag{1.15}$$

where $\pi_t(p_t)$ is a concave linearly homogeneous scalar function of the prices p_t, in other words, a price index. Hence, if the consumption aggregate c_t is *defined* as $x_t / \pi_t(p_t)$, substitution of (15) into (12) gives what we want, a 'standard' utility function defined over consumption aggregates. There are two practical problems with this approach. First, the data on consumption do not come in this form, and second, homothetic subutility is rejected by the empirical evidence. The former is probably not much of a problem, at least for time-series data where prices are relatively collinear, so that different price indices tend to be very similar. The latter is much more serious; homothetic subutility implies that the within-period Engel curves for goods are straight lines through the origin, so that all goods have identical unit elasticities. The supposition that there are neither luxuries nor necessities contradicts both common sense and more than a hundred years of empirical research.

A different approach is to generalize the felicity functions (15) and write

$$\psi_t(x_t, p_t) = \upsilon_t\left(x_t/\pi_t(p_t)\right) + \gamma_t(p_t),$$ (1.16)

where $\gamma_t(p_t)$ is a second concave, linearly homogeneous function. For the general preferences (12), the specification (16) is not useful, but if inter-temporal utility is additive, and if we define c_t as before, the utility function can be written

$$u = \sum_1^T \upsilon_t(c_t) + \sum_1^T \gamma_t(p_t).$$ (1.17)

Since the second term on the right-hand side of (17) appears additively, it has no consequences for the choice of the period consumption aggregates, so that maximization of (17) generates the same results as maximization of the first term alone, which is the conventional procedure. Of course, changes in the γ_t terms have consequences for welfare that would typically be (incorrectly) ignored by the standard treatment of consumption as an aggregate, but in many applications the measurement of welfare is not an issue. Furthermore, it is easy to check that (16), often referred to as 'generalized Gorman polar-form preferences,' are consistent with a wide range of non-linear Engel curves, and that the γ_t indices can be recovered from examination of within-period demand functions. A number of studies have explicitly followed this approach, see Anderson (1979), Browning (1989), and Blundell, Browning, and Meghir (1991).

A final approach to commodity aggregation avoids the need to restrict preferences, but works with utility-dependent price indices. For each sub-utility function, let $c_t(u_t, p_t)$ be the corresponding cost or expenditure function, defined as the minimum amount of money needed to attain felicity u_t at prices p_t. With only minimal abuse of notation, define the consumption aggregates by

$$c_t = c_t(u_t, p_0),$$ (1.18)

where p_0 is some baseline set of prices. By this definition, the consumption aggregate is a 'money-metric' measure of subutility; it is the constant price cost of obtaining the subutility generated by period t's bundle of goods and services. Corresponding to these quantity indices are price indices, defined by the true cost-of-living index numbers

$$P_t = P(p_t, p_0, u_t) = c_t(u_t, p_t)/c_t(u_t, p_0). \qquad (1.19)$$

Since the felicity levels satisfy $u_t = \psi_t(c_t, p_0)$, the intertemporal utility function (12) is also a function of each of the consumption aggregates, and since the product of the consumption aggregate and the price index (19) is total expenditure x_t, the standard budget constraint (6) continues to hold.

This last is perhaps the most satisfactory approach to commodity aggregation for practical application, and although price indices will rarely come with the utility dependence required by (19), standard consumption measures, which are typically constant-price values of bundles of goods and services, as well as their associated implicit price deflators, will often provide a close approximation to the theoretical concepts. Of course, none of the methods discussed here is completely satisfactory, and none can be relied upon to work in all conceivable situations. However, I do not believe that the treatment of consumption as a real aggregate is a major problem for the analysis that follows, or that commodity aggregation is responsible for any of the empirical puzzles with which I shall be concerned.

Intertemporal preferences and components of consumption

There is another issue that is closely related to commodity aggregation but which is possibly more serious in practice, and less easily resolved in theory. The commodity aggregate defined in the previous subsection contains all goods and services that generate felicity in each period. However, data are sometimes available only for a subset of consumption, for example for food, while in other cases researchers wish to avoid the special issues that arise in dealing with durable goods, and define consumption to be the total of non-durable goods and services, including neither purchases of durables nor any estimate of their user cost. As is usually the case in demand analysis, there are separability conditions that justify these procedures, but in the context of intertemporal choice these conditions are quite severe. To illustrate, suppose that intraperiod preferences are separable between two groups of goods, so that

$$\upsilon_t(q_t) = u_t\big(\phi_{1t}(q_{1t}), \phi_{2t}(q_{2t})\big), \tag{1.20}$$

and we make one of the further assumptions discussed in the previous sub-section so that we have *two* consumption aggregates, c_{1t} and c_{2t}. Even so, it will generally be the case that the intertemporal choices for either of these aggregates will depend on the choices for the other one. Indeed, perhaps the most straightforward empirical procedure is to recognize the dependence explicitly, and to make, for example, the demand for non-durable consumption a function of the durable goods owned by the household, with the endogeneity of the latter dealt with by instrumenting with respect to the price of durables.

If intraperiod separability is strengthened to intraperiod additivity, if intertemporal preferences are taken to be additively separable, and if, to simplify, we take both commodity groups to be homothetic, the intertemporal utility function takes the form

$$u = \sum_{1}^{T} u_t\big(\upsilon_{1t}(c_{1t}) + \upsilon_{2t}(c_{2t})\big). \tag{1.21}$$

This problem will only split into two separate problems if the u_t functions are identity functions so that intertemporal utility becomes a double sum, over both goods and periods,

$$u = \sum_{t=1}^{T}\sum_{i=1}^{n} \upsilon_{it}(c_{it}), \tag{1.22}$$

where I have generalized to allow n aggregates in each period. Note that double additivity imposes more structure than either additivity within periods or additivity across periods, both of which are satisfied by the weaker structure (21). Note also that, even without the additional requirements, within-period additivity is itself a strong assumption; it rules out inferior goods and complementary goods, it forces an approximate proportionality between income and own-price elasticities, and it is typically rejected on the evidence, see Deaton (1974).

If (22) is correct, the consequences of additivity are extended to all goods in all periods. All aspects of the behavior of each good, income elasticities, price elasticities, and intertemporal elasticities, are controlled by the shape of each felicity function, and more specifically by its curvature.

These implications forge links between phenomena that would usually be considered to be quite disparate. For example, as noted by Atkeson and Ogaki (1990), and as is easily checked from the first-order conditions for maximization, a version of (10) holds for each good separately. Hence, if f stands for food, or indeed any other good, the growth rate of food expenditure should satisfy

$$\dot{c}_{ft}/c_{ft} = \sigma_{ft}(r-\delta), \qquad (1.23)$$

where σ_{ft} is the reciprocal of the elasticity of the marginal felicity of food. Since the ratio of the growth rate of food to the growth rate of total expenditure is equal to the expenditure elasticity of food, the Engel elasticity, (10) and (23) together imply that

$$\varepsilon_f = \sigma_f \sigma^{-1}, \qquad (1.24)$$

where σ is the intertemporal elasticity of substitution of consumption as a whole, defined as the multiplier of $r-\delta$ in (10). Hence, if it is true that the rate of growth of food consumption is the same in rich and poor countries, then (23) implies that σ_f is also the same. But the empirical evidence shows that the expenditure elasticity of food is higher in poor countries than in rich ones, so that, by (24), the intertemporal elasticity of substitution σ must be lower in poor countries. Atkeson and Ogaki suggest that this greater unwillingness to respond to intertemporal incentives can perhaps explain why poor countries would save less than rich countries. While the argument can be challenged at a number of points, it illustrates very well the power and restrictiveness of the assumptions that are required to justify the application of intertemporal optimization theory to only a subset of consumption.

Intertemporally consistent choices

I have presented the lifetime consumption plan as if it were made at the beginning of life, with the consumer doing no more thereafter than following the predestined plan. The artificiality of the construct is obvious as soon as we admit uncertainty and, in reality, it will always make sense to postpone decisions as long as possible so as to take advantage of new information as it evolves. Of course, even under certainty, it would be possible to replan each period, taking previous decisions as given, and maximizing anew over the choices that are still available. It should be obvious that such an exercise should not lead to any change of plans; in the absence of new information, an optimal plan is an optimal plan whether looked at from age 1, age 20, or age 100. However, there is a strand in the literature dating back to Strotz (1956), which claims that standard models of intertemporal choice can generate dynamic inconsistencies, so that consumers may even make plans for the future when they know that they will not want to follow them when the future comes. Indeed, there are many actual cases where people apparently take steps to precommit themselves to a course of action, especially when they believe that they will be incapable of making sound judgements at some later date. But, as was recognized in the literature quite soon after Strotz's paper, these are cases where preferences change or where people alternate between mutually inconsistent preferences, and cannot arise if intertemporal choices are made according to the standard axioms of consumer choice. However, following the work of Kydland and Prescott (1977) and Calvo (1979), the problem of dynamic inconsistency has reappeared in connection with the design of macroeconomic policy, and this literature has perhaps had the effect of resurrecting the Strotz misunderstanding. I review the issue briefly here, partly to avoid confusion, but also because working through the argument is itself a useful exercise. For a fuller treatment, see Deaton and Muellbauer (1980: 340–3).

The basic issue can be seen in the context of the general lifetime utility function (4). Write the general intertemporal problem as one of maximizing

$$V(c_1, c_2, .., c_{t-1}, c_t, .., c_T) \tag{1.25}$$

subject to the general constraint

$$G(c_1, c_2, .., c_{t-1}, c_t, .., c_T) = 0. \tag{1.26}$$

Suppose that the optimal consumption policy involves setting consumption in period t to be c_t^*. Consider then the 'new' problem, to choose consumption levels c_t through c_T so as to maximize

$$V(c_1^*, c_2^*, .., c_{t-1}^*, c_t, .., c_T) \tag{1.27}$$

subject to the constraint (with previous consumption levels now fixed) that

$$G(c_1^*, c_2^*, ..., c_{t-1}^*, c_t, ..., c_T) = 0. \qquad (1.28)$$

It is obvious that the solution of this new problem gives the same consumption levels from t onwards as were given in the solution to the original problem. Provided that the consumer has actually implemented the optimal plan up to date t, and provided that neither the objective function nor the constraints change, there can be no dynamic inconsistency. Replanning simply reconfirms the original plan.

How then can there be any misunderstanding? Paradoxically, the problem arises from simplifying and from working with the intertemporally additive special case (5). Consider the time t replanning exercise when preferences are additive, and when the felicity functions take the form (8). Substituting into (27), the consumer will choose consumption levels from t on so as to maximize

$$\sum_{k=1}^{t-1} (1+\delta)^{-k} \upsilon(c_k^*) + \sum_{k=t}^{T} (1+\delta)^{-k} \upsilon(c_k). \qquad (1.29)$$

The first sum in (29) contains predetermined levels of consumption, so that dropping it has no effect on the choice of the remaining consumption levels. Furthermore, multiplying the remaining term by $(1+\delta)^t$ cannot affect the optimal solution, so that the consumer might just as well maximize the linear transformation of (29),

$$\sum_{k=t}^{T} (1+\delta)^{t-k} \upsilon(c_k). \qquad (1.30)$$

Many researchers studying intertemporal choice would start with the maximization of this function, and not with the maximization of the original lifetime utility function. The analysis here shows that such a procedure will give the right answer, although it is important to recognize that, at best, (30) only represents a fragment of lifetime preferences, albeit that fragment that is 'live' or 'active' for current decision-making. The confusion arises when this distinction is forgotten, and the fragment (30) is taken as representing preferences.

To see how a problem might arise, consider the 'generalization' of (30)

$$\sum_{k=t}^{T} d(t-k) \upsilon(c_k), \qquad (1.31)$$

where $d(t-k)$ is a 'generalized' discount factor, depending only on the distance between the present and the time-period for which plans are being made. In some contexts, this might be a sensible utility function, but it turns out that, for a single agent's choice of consumption over time, (31) cannot be linked back into a consistent set of lifetime preferences unless it is of the form (30). It may look like a suitable maximand, but its maximization involves changing preferences unless the discount factors have the standard form. The easiest way to see this is to note that, unless preferences or constraints change, the existence of lifetime preferences implies that the marginal rates of substitution between any two periods should not change with the calendar date from which the periods are viewed. But this is not the case for (31), which gives a marginal rate of substitution between two periods s and s', both greater than t, of

$$\frac{d(s-t)\upsilon(c_s)}{d(s'-t)\upsilon(c_{s'})}. \tag{1.32}$$

For general discount factors, (32) varies with t, so that these 'preferences' have the odd feature that the relative attractiveness of consumption at, say, ages 50 and 51, is different for a 44-year-old consumer than for a 45-year old consumer, so that the latter, at age 45, will wish to unravel the plans made a year earlier, even though nothing has changed, and no new information has become available. This is not only dynamic inconsistency, it is irrationality. The utility function (31) is consistent with the existence of unchanging lifetime preferences if, and only if, (32) is independent of t. It is not hard to show that this will be the case if, and only if, the discount factors take the standard form $(1+\delta)^{-t}$, as indeed was shown by Strotz in his original paper.

As we shall see, the presence of uncertainty will make consumers wish to recompute their plans as they get older, and if the future does not turn out as expected, they will sometimes wish that they had behaved differently. But such revisions have everything to do with uncertainty, and nothing at all to do with inconsistency, nor with the need to precommit behavior.

Time and the structure of preferences

The utility function (5) is *intertemporally additive*; it is the sum of felicity functions, one for each period. Additivity is not always assumed in studies of consumption and saving, and many of the most important insights can be obtained without it. However, the assumption is widely used, particularly in more formal econometric investigations. Additivity means that the marginal rate of substitution between any two periods is independent of the level of consumption in any other period. In consequence, it does not allow for goods whose effects last over time, or whose desirability is enhanced by use. Additivity rules out phenomena such as habit formation, or the existence of goods such as treats or holidays, where the benefits persist beyond the act of consumption.

While it is hard to find anyone who would defend the literal truth of the additivity assumption, it is not clear on theoretical grounds that it is seriously misleading for an aggregate of commodities (real consumption) with preferences defined over the quarterly or annual frequencies that are usual in empirical work. The severity of the assumption is also its strength; it imposes a great deal of structure on the allocation process, structure that can be used to organize the data. If and when paradoxes arise, the consequences of its relaxation can be investigated.

If additivity is abandoned, something is required in its place. The non-separable utility (4) is much too general, and imposes no structure on the relationship between consumption in different periods. Something closer to additivity is required, something less strong but still with a great deal of structure. There are several useful possibilities. One is to allow the period felicity functions to depend not only on current consumption, but also on consumption in periods prior to t, perhaps just in $t-1$. For reference I record one such form:

$$u = \sum_{t}^{T} \upsilon_\tau(c_\tau, c_{\tau-1}, \ldots, c_{\tau-\gamma}),$$
(1.33)

where γ is the number of lags to be included, often only one.

An alternative draws an analogy with durable goods, and makes felicity depend on a 'stock' or 'state' variable S_t, say, which might represent the stock of durable goods, or more vaguely, a psychological stock of habits or of preference 'capital' the presence of which affects the utility to be obtained from current consumption. The state variable itself evolves with current consumption. For example, write preferences as

$$u = \sum_{t}^{T} \upsilon_\tau(c_\tau, S_\tau)$$
(1.34)

with the evolution of stocks governed by

$$S_{t+1} = (1-\theta)S_t + c_{t+1},$$
(1.35)

where θ can be thought of as a depreciation parameter. Stocks or habits wear off over time, but grow with consumption. In the simplest form of (34), the felicity functions are $\upsilon_t(\alpha c_t - \beta S_t)$, with $\alpha \geq 0$. If β is positive, stocks detract from the utility of consumption (habits), while if β is negative, stocks add to utility (durable goods.) In the habit case, the higher is previous consumption, the bigger the habit, and the higher must be the current level of consumption to deliver the same effect. Note that (33) and (34) can be thought of as moving-average versus autoregressive represent-ations of intertemporal preference dependence. The latter in particular has a long history in applied demand analysis, for example Houthakker and Taylor (1970), Phlips (1974, pt. 2), Spinnewyn (1981), and most recently Becker and Murphy (1988). It is perhaps less obvious that such specifica-tions are appropriate for the aggregate of goods that is real consumption, but they nevertheless provide a useful alternative against which to test the intertemporally additive specification.

The moving-average and autoregressive representations of preference dependence are far from being the only ones. Heaton (1990) has proposed a model in which there are both stocks of goods and stocks of habits. Felicity is a function of the stocks S_t, defined according to (35), while habits are built up from consuming the flows associated with the stocks. This formulation has the attractive feature that consumption expenditures that are close in time are substitutes, since they both contribute to the same stock of durables, while expenditures some distance apart will be comple-ments, since the past consumption has built up habits that call for greater amounts of the good in the present. Another non-separable formulation was originally suggested by Uzawa (1968), and has recently been the subject of an elegant development by Obstfeld (1990). The idea here is that the rate at which utility is discounted through time, or the rate of time-preference, is itself a function of past consumption behavior. We can accommodate this by writing the felicity functions in the form

$$\upsilon_t = \prod_1^t \left(1 + h(c_\tau)\right)^{-1} \upsilon(c_t) \tag{1.36}$$

with preferences given, as usual, by the sum of the υ_t. The function $h(c)$ is concave in consumption, and is either increasing or decreasing depend-ing on whether impatience is augmented or diminished by consumption.

As the argument develops, I shall return to the consequences for behavior of various forms of intertemporal dependence in preferences.

Uncertainty, additivity, and expected utility

One of the distinguishing features of recent research on consumption has been the way in which a coherent account of uncertainty has been introduced into the analysis. When the permanent income and life-cycle theories of consumption were developed in the 1950s, all the participants recognized the importance of uncertainty, of expectations, and that there would be a need to replan in the face of new information. Indeed the recognition of a precautionary demand for saving goes back at least as far as Keynes, and Friedman (1957) made the propensity to spend out of permanent income a decreasing function of income uncertainty. Nevertheless, the apparatus required for a formal treatment of uncertainty did not exist. Papers by Samuelson (1969) and Merton (1969) pioneered the use of stochastic dynamic programming in solving life-cycle problems, but the routine treatment of uncertainty has only become standard in the last decade or so.

The standard approach, as in the rest of economics, is to replace utility by expected utility so that equation (5) is replaced by

$$u = E_t\left(\sum_t^T v_\tau(c_\tau)\right) = E\left(\sum_t^T v_\tau(c_\tau) \mid I_t\right), \tag{1.37}$$

where the second version emphasizes that the expectation at time t, E_t, is to be interpreted as a mathematical expectation, conditional on I_t, the information available at time t. Although the consumption level in each period is chosen by the consumer, he or she will not make final choices for future periods until those periods arrive. Information about prices, incomes, and yields on various assets will become available as time passes, so there is no point in committing future consumption any sooner than is necessary. Indeed, precommitment would close off the option of changing plans, an option that will usually be valuable. In consequence, at time t, future consumption levels are uncertain, and the maximization of expected utility as in (37) is the appropriate rule for a rational consumer.

To fix ideas, suppose that there are a finite number of states of nature, indexed by $s = 1, 2, \ldots, S$. Viewed from time t, alternative futures fan out in a tree structure, with each s labelling a complete future through the tree, from t to T. If the probability associated with each of these futures is π_s, then the expected utility in (38) can be rewritten as

$$u = \sum_{s=1}^{S} \sum_{\tau=t}^{T} \pi_s v_\tau(c_{\tau s}) \tag{1.38}$$

so that expected utility theory and intertemporal separability together induce a *doubly* additive form for preferences. (Note the relationship with the double additivity in the discussion of within-period and between-period additivity on p. 11 above, although here the additivity is over *states* and periods, not *goods* and periods.) The double additivity of (38) puts a great deal of structure on preferences over states and consumption levels, perhaps too much. Indeed (38) is certainly not the *only* utility function that is consistent both with expected utility theory and with the original certainty preferences (5).

Consider the alternative utility function:

$$ u = \sum_{s=1}^{S} \pi_s F_s \left(\sum_{\tau=t}^{T} \upsilon_\tau(c_{\tau s}) \right), \tag{1.39} $$

where $F_s(.)$ is a monotone-increasing function. Under certainty, with π_s unity for some s, (39) is simply a monotone-increasing function of an additive function and thus represents intertemporally additive preferences. There is also no conflict with the axioms of the theory of choice under uncertainty, since utility is the expected value of utility over the various states. However, as is easily checked from calculating marginal rates of substitution, (39) will imply very different behavior from (38). In (39) the *MRS* between $c_{\tau s}$ and $c_{\tau' s'}$ depends on the consumption levels in states s and s' in all the other periods, so that we might have legitimate doubts as to whether (39) is really an appropriate representation of intertemporal additivity under uncertainty. Indeed, such dependencies seem better handled by working with the habit or durable-good models in an uncertain environment. But the basic point remains that the standard doubly additive utility function, (37) or (38), is not the only possible choice.

Recent literature has focused on a different generalization of the preferences represented by (37). As we have already seen on p. 6, intertemporally additive preferences have the effect of forging an inverse link between the extent to which the consumer is prepared to substitute between periods, the intertemporal elasticity of substitution, and attitudes towards risk, as measured by the coefficient of relative risk-aversion. If behavior comes from the maximization of doubly additive expected utility functions like (37), agents who are risk-averse will be unresponsive to intertemporal incentives, while those who are willing to reallocate their consumption in response to incentives for doing so will also display relatively little aversion towards risk. *The simultaneous additivity induced by intertemporal additivity and expected utility implies that the degree of intertemporal substitutability is inversely related to the degree of risk-aversion.*

To some economists it is obvious that risk-aversion and intertemporal substitution are independent aspects of consumer preferences, so that any formulation that confounds them is incorrect; such a case has been argued, for example, by Hall (1989) and Weil (1990). Such a view is made attractive by empirical evidence on the relationship between consumption and asset prices that can perhaps be more readily explained if risk-aversion and intertemporal substitutability are freed of any link. Others, who wish to use intertemporal additivity, but who do not wish to reject the axioms of expected utility theory, have no choice but to accept the link between them. Indeed, time and uncertainty are so intimately connected that (at least to this writer) there is strong intuitive support for a relationship between attitudes towards risk and attitudes towards substitution. In an uncertain world, the substitution of future consumption for current consumption inevitably increases exposure to risk, and those who are willing to contemplate the former must be willing to face the latter.

Risk-aversion can be untied from intertemporal substitution in several different ways. The route that has been adopted in the recent literature is to abandon expected utility theory, and to endow consumers with preferences that violate the axioms of choice under uncertainty. There are some good arguments for such a strategy. First, there is a good deal of evidence, experimental and otherwise, that the axioms of choice are frequently violated by the actual choices that people make in uncertain situations. Second, decision theorists have developed different non-expected utility models of choice, at least partly in response to the experimental evidence, and some of these can be used to generate simple, empirically useful models that break the restriction between risk-aversion and intertemporal substitutability. Third, and more specifically, Kreps and Porteus (1978) have developed decision rules for consumers who are not indifferent to the *time* at which uncertainty is resolved, so that, for example, they may have a preference for early resolution over late resolution, even in cases where the expected utility would be the same. This theory has been developed into an applicable form in papers by Epstein and Zin (1989, 1991) and they and Attanasio and Weber (1989) use the results to interpret the US and British evidence on consumption and asset prices.

This is an impressive line of research, but I shall not follow it further in this book. Instead, I adopt the alternative strategy of trying to reconcile the evidence with expected utility theory. In spite of the experimental evidence, the axioms of choice and the structure that they impose on the empirical evidence are not things to be abandoned lightly. Of course, such choices of research strategy are ultimately matters of taste. Even so, if the primary motivation comes from the indigestibility of the link between risk-aversion and intertemporal substitution, then the abandonment of expected utility seems a high price to pay, especially given the availability of what is surely a more palatable alternative, which is to abandon intertemporal additivity. The assumption has little more to commend it than convenience, and the exploration of habits and intertemporal dependence would seem to be a natural avenue of generalization before taking the more drastic step of removing one of the pillars of economic analysis. Besides, as I shall argue below, temporal dependence can account for at least some of the evidence that has been cited in favor of non-expected utility specifications. I therefore adopt the utility function (37) as my basic working specification, but will from time to time consider generalizations that allow for temporal dependence. However, both preference dependence and non-expected utility theory are currently very active areas of research, and it may well turn out that my choice is the wrong one.

1.3 Intertemporal choice

This section combines preferences and constraints to look further at the evolution of consumption over time for a consumer making optimal intertemporal choices. I start with a more detailed specification of the *means* by which people can transfer money from one period to another, here a menu of risky assets. If asset and debt transactions are not limited in any way, purchases and sales of these assets allow consumers to tailor the time path of their consumption to their needs and preferences, unconstrained by the time-path of their earnings. The first subsection extends the simple intertemporal optimality condition (7), and shows how, at least in principle, the theory of intertemporal choice under uncertainty unifies the theories of consumption and of asset pricing. The second subsection looks at the evolution of consumption, and discusses martingales, random-walks, and the influence of precautionary motives. I then return to temporal dependence in preferences, and work through a simple case to show how the life-cycle pattern of consumption is altered when current felicity is affected by previous levels of consumption. Finally, I consider what happens to consumption if we suppose that there are 'complete' markets, in which consumers can buy state-contingent assets for all possible states of nature, so providing insurance for their consumption by spreading risk over many different individuals.

Risky assets and intertemporal optimality

Given the desire to allocate expenditure over time, there are a wide range of assets available that provide the means. They differ in yields, in riskiness, and in the ease with which they can be liquidated, and the agent must choose between consuming now and investing in some or all of them to provide for future consumption. Assets also provide insurance; different assets have different pay-offs in different states of the world, so that a judicious portfolio of securities can help protect future levels of consumption. However, unless there are assets tailored to all relevant states of the world, so that asset markets are 'complete,' there will be some contingencies for which consumers cannot insure. This is the relevant case in practice, and it is the case on which I focus here.

Suppose that, at the beginning of period t the consumer possesses financial wealth (assets) with total real value A_t. In the same period, he or she also receives real *labor* income y_t. As its name suggests, this income excludes the income from assets, rents, dividends, interest, and the like. In the theory of consumption, much hinges on maintaining the distinction between labor and capital income; the latter is the result of previous investment decisions, and is therefore part of what we are trying to explain. I follow the tradition in the consumption function literature of treating y_t as outside of the control of the agent. While this trivializes the treatment of labor supply, it allows us to focus on another major topic of interest, which is how agents handle the consumption consequences of unanticipated shocks to income, for example unemployment for an industrial worker, or a poor harvest for a farmer. Capital income, by contrast, depends on the asset and portfolio choice of the consumer, and is therefore at least partly under the agent's control.

The sum of assets and labor income is to be allocated between consumption c_t, and a menu of assets. Write N_{it} for the real expenditure on each of n assets, $i = 1, \ldots, n$. Before the beginning of period $t + 1$, each of these is increased by a factor $1 + r_{it+1}$ representing real capital gains, interest, and dividends. The yields r_{it+1} are generally not known in period t, although one or more of them may be. The budget constraint between t and $t+1$ can therefore be characterized by the two equations

$$c_t + \Sigma_i N_{it} = y_t + A_t,$$

$$A_{t+1} = \Sigma_i (1 + r_{it+1}) N_{it}. \tag{1.40}$$

Together with preferences, and some condition to tie down the terminal level of assets, equation (40) determines behavior.

For much of this book, I shall be concerned less with portfolio choice than with consumption and saving. It is therefore frequently convenient to work with a single asset A_t, with real interest rate r_t, in which case equation (40) can be collapsed into the simpler asset evolution equation

$$A_{t+1} = (1 + r_{t+1})(A_t + y_t - c_t). \tag{1.41}$$

There are several different ways of deriving conditions on consumption implied by preferences and the budget constraint. Perhaps the most intuitive is to adopt the standard approach in dynamic programs of solving the last period first, and then working backwards to the beginning. In the last period, there is no choice; in the absence of a bequest motive, assets and any labor income will be spent on consumption. The value of subutility in the last period is thus given as a function of assets carried into the period, and this value function also defines the marginal value for assets carried into the last period. In the second last period, there is a choice between consumption in $T-1$, and holding assets for their expected value in T, the value and marginal value of which has already been established. Solving this two-period problem yields new value and marginal value functions for assets carried into period $T-1$, so that the next two-period problem will be between consumption in $T-2$, and assets carried into $T-1$, for consumption in the last two periods. In this way, through a series of two-period problems, we eventually reach the decision period, period t.

Working with the utility function (37), write current utility, the expected sum of current and future felicities, as $V_t(A_t)$ which is the value function for the problem. Of course, current utility is a function of things other than A_t, most obviously labor income, but also of any current variables that condition the expectation of future incomes. However, it is the level of assets that allows the consumer to transfer resources between periods, and

I temporarily suppress the other arguments. From the budget constraint (40), consumption can be written as $y_t + A_t - \Sigma N_{it}$, so that the value functions for successive periods must satisfy the recursive equation

$$V_t(A_t) = \max_N \left(\upsilon_t(y_t + A_t - \Sigma N_i) + E_t V_{t+1}\left(\Sigma(1 + r_{it+1})N_i \right) \right). \qquad (1.42)$$

The value of assets at time t is the best that can be obtained by trading off between current consumption and future consumption by choosing how much to spend together with a portfolio of assets. The expectation operator reflects the uncertainty about future yields and labor income; note also that the next period's value function $V_{t+1}(.)$ also implicitly contains expectations about random variables further into the future. Indeed, equation (42) with $t + 1$ substituted for t could be used to substitute for the value function on the right, and so on until we reach an extensive representation of the whole decision problem that the consumer is going solve, age by age, as he or she moves through the life cycle.

Equation (42) can be used to derive implications about the behavior of consumption. First, there are n equations that come from the first-order maximization conditions for the assets. These are

$$\upsilon_t'(c_t) = E_t \left((1 + r_{it+1}) V_{t+1}'(A_{t+1}) \right). \qquad (1.43)$$

The marginal felicity of consumption today should equal the marginal value of money tomorrow, taking into account that money saved today will be worth more tomorrow, at least if yields are positive. There is also a link between the marginal value of assets, the life-time marginal utility of money, and the marginal felicity of consumption. Differentiate (42) with respect to assets A_t, and use the envelope theorem (that it is possible to differentiate through the right-hand side of (42), ignoring the effects of changes in A_t on the optimal values of N):

$$V_t'(A_t) = \upsilon_t'(c_t), \qquad (1.44)$$

so that the marginal utility of money and the marginal felicity of consumption coincide, and we can talk about them interchangeably. It is the marginal utility of money, the utility price of money, or the reciprocal of the money price of utility, that is the common 'price' that links the periods and guarantees the efficiency of the intertemporal allocation. Use (44) to substitute in (43) to write

$$\lambda_t(c_t) \equiv \upsilon_t'(c_t) = E_t \big((1+r_{it+1})\lambda_{t+1}(c_{t+1}) \big), \tag{1.45}$$

where $\lambda_t(c)$, as before, is the marginal utility of consumption.

Consumption and portfolio choice must be so arranged that (45) holds for *all* assets; conditional on consumption choices, the equation offers a theory of asset prices, while, conditional on asset prices, it offers a theory of consumption. However, note the strength of the assumptions required to establish the result. There are no transactions costs here, nor are there any restrictions on short sales. Indeed (45) will typically involve *negative* holdings of some assets by some consumers, so that the equation can only be safely applied to those assets that can be sold short by households. Depending on how (45) aggregates across agents, and aggregation will be much complicated by any prohibition on short sales, there will typically be testable implications for the yields on assets and the relationships between them, for example for the term-structure of interest rates. While it is certainly true that some consumers have liabilities of one sort or another, it is far from clear that it will always be possible for an individual to issue bonds or treasury bills, for example, and there may be limits on the consumer's ability to borrow at all, an issue to which I shall return in Section 2 of Chapter 6. As far as consumption is concerned, (45) is a straightforward generalization of the condition that the marginal rate of substitution should equal relative price. If there were no uncertainty, and if there were only one asset with real interest rate r_{t+1}, the ratios of marginal utilities in the two periods, $\lambda_t / \lambda_{t+1}$, would be set equal to the relative price of consumption in the two periods, $1 + r_{t+1}$ –see the simple example at the beginning of this chapter. The intertemporal optimality condition, in its simple form—marginal rate of substitution equals the relative price—or somewhat less simple form—the 'Euler equation' (45)—lies at the heart of much of the recent work on consumption, on saving, and on asset pricing.

The evolution of consumption

The intertemporal optimization conditions, together with the budget constraint, tell us how the consumption levels of an optimizing household will evolve over the life cycle. Equation (45) links consumption in periods t and $t+1$, and so defines a (stochastic) difference equation that governs the behavior of consumption over time. This evolution is shaped by preferences, the functions λ_t and λ_{t+1}, by the yields on assets, and by unanticipated events. If expectations are fulfilled, in the sense that the realization of the right-hand side of (45) is equal to its expectation, then *only* yields and preferences determine the evolution of consumption. This is perhaps the most important insight of the life-cycle hypothesis, that the evolution of consumption is *not* determined by income, that consumption patterns are shaped by tastes and by life-cycle needs, and not by the temporal pattern of life-cycle labor income. Given the ability to borrow and lend, anticipated changes in incomes have no effect on consumption; if income is low in early life, but is anticipated to be higher later, there is no need to delay higher consumption because any borrowing incurred now can be repaid later. Of course, consumption is not predicted to be constant over life. Some needs are located at specific times in the life cycle; most children cannot be sent to college in early infancy, nor will the provision of heat to a young adult guarantee that he or she will be warm in old age. All of which are reasons why the felicity functions and the marginal felicity functions must be indexed on age. Moreover, interest rates govern the relative price of consumption in different periods, and consumers have an incentive to postpone consumption when returns are high. But unless the patterns of preferences and yields mimic the patterns of labor income, there is no reason for consumption to track income over the life cycle. More precisely, *in the absence of uncertainty*, there is no reason for consumption to track income. The expectation term in (45) complicates the analysis a good deal, and although the presence of uncertainty does not provide any *general* reason to tie consumption to income, we shall meet cases where it does so.

The simplest, and most dramatic case of (45) comes from assuming that, apart from discounting, the felicity functions are independent of age—see equation (8) without the z_t variables. If the real interest rate is constant and equal to the rate of time-preference δ, (45) becomes

$$\lambda(c_t) = E_t \lambda(c_{t+1}). \tag{1.46}$$

The stochastic process governing marginal utility is a *martingale*; this period's expectation of next period's marginal utility is equal to the current value of marginal utility, as indeed are the current expectations of all future values of marginal utility. If the expectation is fulfilled, consumption will be constant from t to $t+1$. Alternatively, consider the case where the felicity functions are quadratic so that the marginal felicity functions are linear. The expectation goes through the function, and the marginal felicity of consumption is equal to the marginal felicity of expected consumption. It is as if expected consumption were known with certainty, and hence the 'certainty equivalence' label that is often applied to quadratic utility. In this case, consumption itself follows a martingale, and can be written in either of the two forms:

$$E_t(c_{t+1}) = c_t \qquad (1.47)$$

$$c_{t+1} = c_t + u_{t+1}, \qquad (1.48)$$

where u_{t+1} is an *innovation* or martingale difference. It is the difference between the realization and the one-period-ahead expectation of consumption, and as such is orthogonal to any variable that was used in predicting c_{t+1}. Note that this says nothing about the *variance* of u_{t+1}, and in particular, there is no presumption that it be constant. In consequence, equation (48) is not (strictly) a random-walk, although the term is often used to describe it. The distinction is of more than technical importance; the distribution of consumption changes could be 'heavy-tailed' under (48) whereas the occasional appearance of large outliers would be a reason to reject a random-walk.

These martingale models of consumption are simply stochastic generalizations of the simplest or 'stripped-down' life-cycle model, in which consumption is constant over life, with variations in income offset by appropriate asset transactions. Of course, income still plays a role in determining consumption. The *level* at which consumption is initially set depends on lifetime resources, determined at least in part by current and future levels of labor income. Furthermore, the innovation u_{t+1} will reflect *unanticipated* changes in income; if income changes in a way that was not previously anticipated, a new lifetime level of consumption is warranted, so that current and expected future levels of consumption will change. In consequence, the proposition that consumption follows a martingale does not preclude a correlation between changes in consumption and changes in current labor income. It does however require that changes in consumption be orthogonal to lagged changes in income, at least if these are known to the consumer prior to the current period.

The martingale models of consumption follow from (41) only under very special assumptions, and these special assumptions rule out potentially important phenomena. To see some of these, rewrite (41) in the form

$$E_t\left(\frac{(1+r_{t+1})\lambda_{t+1}(c_{t+1})}{\lambda_t(c_t)}\right) = 1, \tag{1.49}$$

where I have again specialized to the case of a single asset. If we ignore the expectation, consumption will be higher in $t+1$ than in t if, at constant consumption, marginal utility in $t+1$ would be higher than in t. Since the marginal felicity functions are declining in the level of consumption, (49) also implies that, if taste factors are not an issue, so that the λ's are the same in the two periods, consumption will be growing most rapidly between periods where the interest rate or reward for waiting is highest. In the special case where the felicity functions change only through discounting by the rate of time-preference, equation (8), (49) takes the form

$$E_t\left(\frac{(1+r_{t+1})\lambda(c_{t+1})}{(1+\delta)\lambda(c_t)}\right) = 1 \tag{1.50}$$

so that, under certainty, we have again the result that consumption will be growing when the interest rate is greater than the rate of time-preference, and declining when the interest rate is less than the rate of time-preference.

Such simple results cannot be derived in the general case where interest rates and consumption are stochastic. In special cases, for example when felicity functions are quadratic and the real interest rate is non-stochastic, they will hold exactly. Otherwise, the convexity or concavity of the marginal felicity function matters, as does the covariance between the interest rate and the marginal utility of money. Note also that these relatively unambiguous conclusions about the effects of interest rates on consumption and saving are results about the way in which consumption evolves over an anticipated life-cycle path. Over such a trajectory, there are incentives to allocate consumption to where it is cheapest, so that interest rates have an unambiguous effect. However, interest rates, like labor incomes, also exert an influence on the *level* of the path, and unanticipated changes in interest rates, like unanticipated changes in labor incomes, will move the path up and down. In consequence, the theory of this chapter provides no general result on the effects of changes in interest rates on current consumption, and certainly says nothing that contradicts the conclusions of the elementary model from which I began.

One final consequence of (49) is of some importance. Suppose that the real interest rate is non-stochastic, and consider the effects of an increase in uncertainty about future consumption, in the sense that, at time t, there is a mean-preserving increase in the spread of the distribution of c_{t+1}, perhaps because the general economic environment is seen as more uncertain. Given that the interest rate is fixed, the effect on current consumption depends on what the additional uncertainty does to the marginal utility of next period's consumption. In the certainty equivalence case, where the felicity functions are quadratic and the marginal felicity functions linear, there will be no effect, because the mean of marginal felicity is simply the marginal felicity of mean consumption, which I have assumed to be unchanged. There is therefore no reason for current consumption to change.

However, if $\lambda_{t+1}(c_{t+1})$ is *convex*, a mean-preserving increase in risk will *increase* marginal utility, so that current consumption will have to *decrease* in order to bring the current marginal utility back into equality. Conversely, if $\lambda_{t+1}(c_{t+1})$ is *concave*, an increase in risk will *increase* current consumption. Convexity of marginal utility therefore provides a rationalization for the *precautionary* demand for saving, whereby an increase in future uncertainty increases saving to provide for the now wider range of possible contingencies. More generally, young consumers, early in the life cycle, are likely to spend less and save more than would be the case for those whose preferences do not suggest caution. Indeed, the constant consumption, or martingale models (47) and (48), were derived under the assumption of quadratic felicity, an assumption that explicitly excludes precautionary saving. Linear marginal felicity, although analytically convenient, is not consistent with the existence of a precautionary motive. For that reason, there has been a trend in recent work away from the simple models towards those where the precautionary demand for saving is taken seriously; I shall return to this issue in detail when I discuss precautionary saving in the first section of Chapter 6.

Consumption evolution with temporal dependence

It is useful to look briefly at the way in which the foregoing analysis is altered when we drop the assumption that preferences are intertemporally additive. The main insights of the life-cycle model remain, but we have a richer menu of consumption profiles from which to choose. Typically, the first-order stochastic difference equations that characterize behavior in the separable case are replaced by higher-order equations, and these generally have more complicated solutions.

I follow the development of Hayashi (1985*b*) and Muellbauer (1988) and look at some special cases that are of interest in their own right and that develop an intuition for the sort of phenomena to expect. In particular, consider the 'autoregressive' model of (34) and (35) specialized to

$$u = E_t \sum_{\tau=t}^{T} \upsilon_\tau (\alpha c_\tau + \beta S_\tau), \qquad (1.51)$$

where, repeating equation (35), S_t is a stock or state variable satisfying the difference equation

$$S_{t+1} = (1-\theta)S_t + c_{t+1}. \qquad (1.52)$$

The parameters must clearly satisfy the restrictions that $\alpha \geq 0$ and $0 \leq \theta \leq 1$. For the marginal felicity of current consumption to be positive, we also require that $\alpha + \beta > 0$. Finally, consider the steady-state case where consumption is a constant c, so that by (52), $S = c/\theta$, and the argument of the felicity function is $(\alpha + \beta/\theta)c$. Since this must be increasing in c, we need also need $\alpha\theta + \beta > 0$.

Within these constraints, there is a wide range of possible parameter values, and the model includes a number of important cases. If $\alpha = 0$, and $\beta > 0$, the state variable can be interpreted as the stock of a durable good, which generates utility through a proportional service flow. The stock depreciates at rate θ, and is augmented by purchases c_t. If α is positive and β is negative, the model is one of habit formation, in which the stock of habits, S_t, is increased by consumption. The larger the habit, the less the pleasure from a given amount of consumption, and the larger must be purchases to generate the same benefit. If we reparametrize the model, writing $\beta = -\gamma/(1-\theta)$ and $\alpha = 1-\beta$, then set the depreciation parameter $\theta = 0$, we reach the simple habit model in which felicity depends positively on current consumption, and negatively on lagged consumption:

$$u = E_t \sum_{\tau=t}^{T} \upsilon_\tau (c_\tau - \gamma c_{\tau-1}). \qquad (1.53)$$

In all of these models, it is assumed that the consumer is entirely aware of the effects of current consumption on future felicity, so that current choices are made with a view to their future consequences. Of course, one could also consider 'myopic' agents who do not look ahead, who are constantly surprised by the effects of their own actions, and who constantly regret their own past decisions. But this is not the case I examine here.

The maximization conditions for (51) can be derived in much the same way as in the additive case. However, we must now explicitly recognize the dependence of the value of the program, not only on assets, but also on the stock inherited from the last period. Hence, if (52) is substituted into (51), we can write utility in the recursive form

$$V_t(A_t, S_{t-1}) = \max_N \big(\upsilon_t \big((\alpha + \beta)(y_t + A_t - N) + \beta(1-\theta)S_{t-1} \big)$$

$$+ E_t V_{t+1} \big((1 + r_{t+1})N, (1-\theta)S_{t-1} + y_t + A_t - N \big) \big), \qquad (1.54)$$

where I have used the fact that consumption is $y - A - N$, and I have again specialized to a single asset. Note that the value function in $t+1$, like that in t, depends on the updated value of the stock. From (54), three equations can be derived, a first-order maximization condition with respect to N, and the two 'envelope' conditions with respect to the two arguments of the value function. It so happens that these equations can be much simplified for the case where the real interest rate is constant, and the assumption is good value for my current, illustrative purposes.

The first-order condition is

$$(\alpha + \beta)\lambda_t = R E_t V_{t+1,1} - E_t V_{t+1,2}, \qquad (1.55)$$

where $V_{t+1,1}$ and $V_{t+1,2}$ are the partial derivatives of V_{t+1} with respect to its first and second arguments respectively, R is the interest factor $1+r$, and, as before, λ_t is the instantaneous marginal utility or felicity. The derivative of the value function with respect to assets gives the marginal utility of wealth,

$$V_{t,1} = (\alpha + \beta)\lambda_t + E_t V_{t+1,2} \qquad (1.56)$$

while the derivative with respect to the lagged stock is

$$V_{t,2} = \beta(1-\theta)\lambda_t + (1-\theta)E_t V_{t+1,2}. \qquad (1.57)$$

These conditions are readily interpreted. Equation (57) records the benefits ($\beta > 0$) or costs ($\beta < 0$) of entering period t with one more unit of stocks or habits; there is an immediate effect on current felicity, which echoes into the future provided the depreciation rate is less than one. Equation (57) shows that the marginal utility of wealth is the marginal felicity of consumption together with the stock effects that the current purchase will bring in the future. Equation (55) balances the marginal felicity of consumption now, including the stock effects, against the benefits of saving the money.

If (57) is substituted into (56), we have equations for both derivatives of the value function in terms of marginal utility, so that both can be substituted out of the first-order condition (51). This gives the second-order difference equation

$$(\alpha+\beta)\lambda_t - (\alpha(1-\theta) + R(\alpha+\beta))E_t\lambda_{t+1} + \alpha(1-\theta)RE_t\lambda_{t+2} = 0. \quad (1.58)$$

This equation is written more simply using the forward shift operator F, with $Fx_t \equiv x_{t+1}$, so that (58) can be factored into

$$(\alpha+\beta-\alpha(1-\theta)E_tF)(1 - RE_tF)\lambda_t = 0. \quad (1.59)$$

One solution to this equation is the familiar one,

$$\lambda_t = RE_t\lambda_{t+1} = E_t(1+r)\lambda_{t+1} \quad (1.60)$$

which corresponds to the second root in (59). The other root is unstable because $\beta + \alpha\theta > 0$. If T is infinite, this solution can be ruled out by the transversality condition; optimal intertemporal allocation prohibits the expectation of the marginal utility of consumption tending to infinity. For finite T, we know that assets must be zero at the end of T, a condition that can be used to show that the root is unimportant provided T is far enough in the future, see again Hayashi (1985*b*).

The solution (60) is a remarkably simple one and allows us to extend the analysis of consumption evolution under intertemporal additivity to these non-separable cases. To illustrate, consider the case where preferences are quadratic and there is a fixed real rate of interest equal to the rate of time-preference. If preferences are intertemporally additive, these are the assumptions that imply that consumption is a martingale, equations (47) and (48). In the current case, we have instead of (48)

$$\alpha c_{t+1} + \beta S_{t+1} = \alpha c_t + \beta S_t + u_{t+1} \quad (1.61)$$

so that, if we use (52) to substitute for stocks in (61), we reach

$$(\alpha + \beta)\Delta c_{t+1} = \alpha(1 - \theta)\Delta c_t + u_{t+1} - (1 - \theta) u_t. \qquad (1.62)$$

where Δc_{t+1} is the *first difference* of consumption $c_{t+1} - c_t$, and u_{t+1}, as before, is an innovation. The unit root in consumption remains, but the change in consumption is no longer serially uncorrelated as is the case when preferences are intertemporally additive.

The case where $\alpha = 0$, so that only stocks appear in the felicity functions, was first analyzed in this way by Mankiw (1982), although the basic model for durable goods goes back at least as far as Stone and Rowe (1957, 1958) and Nerlove (1957). With $\alpha = 0$, the lagged first-difference of consumption plays no part in (62), so that the durability modifies the original martingale result by replacing the innovation by a moving average of the current and first-lagged innovations. When β is negative, habits are important. The simplest case is where we adopt the parametrization of the simple habit model and use (53) with felicity depending on consumption and lagged consumption, so that (62) becomes

$$\Delta c_{t+1} = \gamma \Delta c_t + u_{t+1} \qquad (1.63)$$

so that the first difference of consumption is autoregressive.

As far as life-cycle planning is concerned, consumption is no longer expected to be constant, instead the consumer plans for $\alpha c_t + \beta S_t$ to be constant at k, say, so that, eliminating the state variable using (52), planned consumption will satisfy the difference equation

$$c_t = \frac{\alpha(1 - \theta)}{\alpha + \beta} c_{t-1} + \frac{\theta k}{\alpha + \beta}. \qquad (1.64)$$

Since $\beta + \alpha\theta > 0$, the coefficient on lagged consumption is less than unity, and the difference equation is stable, so that consumption will eventually asymptote to the constant value $\theta k/(\beta + \alpha\theta)$. Whether consumption increases or decreases to this asymptote depends on the initial 'endowment' of the state variable S_t, and on the sign of β. If we suppose that the state variable is initially zero, then consumption will decrease throughout life if $\beta > 0$, the durable-goods case, and increase if $\beta < 0$, the habits case. This is most easily seen by noting that, in either case, S_t is a weighted average of past consumption, and that $\alpha c_t + \beta S_t$ remains constant over the plan. Hence, if $\beta > 0$ consumption must decrease as the stock accumulates, while if $\beta < 0$, consumption must continually increase so as to offset the negative effects of the ever-increasing stock of habits. Habits, like prudence, provide a reason to postpone consumption. Put differently, consumption becomes cheaper with age, because the habits that will be engendered by consumption have less time left to do their damage. By contrast, if consumption benefits are durable, consumption by the young is doubly blessed, yielding both immediate and continuing benefits. Other cases are possible if people begin life with stocks of durables, or if their upbringing endows them with habits, see Becker (1991).

It is worth emphasizing that these models deal with only one of the many phenomena associated with durable goods. In particular, many (although not all) durable goods come in large, lumpy, and expensive units; buying prices are frequently higher than selling prices, and both purchases and sales involve fixed transactions costs. Successful modelling of durable purchases, at the individual level, or in aggregate, must deal seriously with the consequences of these non-convexities—see in particular the papers by Grossman and Laroque (1990) and Bertola and Caballero (1990). In general, consumers will not make smooth adjustments, but will wait until their stocks of durables are some way from their optimum, and then make a discrete purchase or sale. The analysis here does not address these questions, but is designed more to explore the limited durability of non-durables, and to recognize that consumption may induce non-separabilities over time because of habits, or because the benefits of consumption take time to wear off. Simple models of durability and habit formation are worth exploring because of their insights into the consequences of non-additive preferences.

Consumption, insurance, and complete markets

In the presence of uncertainty and risk, plans will not be fulfilled. Even for identical consumers, with identical initial inheritances, and identical prospects, there will be different lifetime consumption profiles *ex post*. Some people will be lucky, getting good draws of income, or favorable investment opportunities, while others get the bad draws, and hence lower consumption levels. Indeed, the effects of uncertainty will be cumulative over time, with consumption trajectories typically diverging, even for a group of initially identical consumers. That this is the case is most obvious in the random-walk case (48). If the distribution across individuals of consumption innovations is independent of consumption levels, it follows immediately that the cross-sectional variance of consumption is increasing over time. More generally, from (46), if the distribution of marginal utility innovations is independent of levels of marginal utility, individual marginal utilities will drift apart through time. Since consumption is a monotone function of marginal utility, consumption levels will also diverge. Since people are generally averse to risk, this situation offers scope for improvement. Consumers in the same initial situation should be able to agree at the outset to share their good and bad fortune, and the spreading of risk will improve *expected* utility for all of them. Such risk-spreading can be decentralized if markets are 'complete,' in the sense that each state of nature can be insured against by buying (or selling) the appropriate security.

The simplest case is where there is a complete set of 'Arrow securities,' each of which promises a unit return if state s occurs in period t, against payment now of a price p_{st}, with the prices determined in competitive security markets. Each consumer can then make his or her life-cycle consumption plan at the beginning of life, the 'master' plan in this case consisting of a set of contingency plans, each detailing what consumption will be in each possible state of the world, from birth to death. With complete markets, such plans can be effectively implemented, since it is possible, by buying and selling the Arrow securities, to guarantee that the plan will be fulfilled, at least in the sense that, given the states that actually occur, consumption in those states will be exactly according to the initial contingency plan.

To see the implications, start from the intertemporal utility function (38), reproduced here as

$$u^h = \sum_{s=1}^{S} \sum_{\tau=t}^{T} \pi_s \upsilon_\tau(c_{\tau s}^h), \tag{1.65}$$

where the h superscripts refer to an individual (household), and where it is assumed—and, as we shall see, the assumption is important—that the probabilities of the states are the same for all consumers. Since a unit of consumption in state s at time t can be bought in period 1 for $p_{st}(1+r)^{-t}$, the lifetime budget constraint is

$$\sum_{s=1}^{S} \sum_{t=1}^{T} p_{st} c_{st}^h (1+r)^{-t} = A_1^h + \sum_{s=1}^{S} \sum_{t=1}^{T} p_{st} y_{st}^h (1+r)^{-t}, \tag{1.66}$$

where y_{st}^h is labor income in period t and state s, the contingent claim to which has a value in the first period of $p_{st} y_{st}^h (1+r)^{-t}$. Unlike the dynamic programming that is required in the usual case, the existence of the market in contingent claims allows the problem to be written as the maximization of expected utility subject to an expected value budget constraint. The first-order optimization condition for (65) subject to (66) is

$$\lambda_t(c_{st}^h) = \theta^h \left(\frac{1+\delta}{1+r}\right)^t \frac{p_{st}}{\pi_s},$$ (1.67)

where θ^h is the Lagrange multiplier for individual h. If we use s to label the state that actually occurs in t, then equation (67) will hold with actual consumption c_t replacing contingent consumption c_{st}.

The notable feature of equation (67) is the way in which individual marginal utilities move in lock step. Marginal utilities differ from consumer to consumer, and vary over time, just as in the case when markets are incomplete. However, the *ratio* of marginal utilities for any two consumers, h and k, say, is the constant θ^h/θ^k, which does not change over time. This is what happens if all risk is pooled. Some consumers are (lifetime) richer than others, and they will have lower marginal utility of consumption, and thus higher consumption, throughout life. Uncertainty still remains, since which state will occur in each period is not revealed ahead of time, with the result that each person's marginal utility of consumption is not constant. But there is no reason for the resolution of uncertainty to cause one person's marginal utility to rise while another falls, because each person's expected utility can be increased *ex ante* by agreeing to pool the risk. Suppose for example that the felicity functions are isoelastic as in equation (11), so that, allowing for time-varying taste factors z_t as in (8), marginal utility is given by $\lambda(c_t) = f(z_t)c_t^{-\rho}$ for some function $f(z_t)$. Substituting in (67) gives, after taking logarithms,

$$\ln c_t^h = -\rho^{-1}(\ln\theta^h - \ln f(z_t) + \ln\mu_t),$$ (1.68)

where μ_t is independent of h and is defined by comparison with (67). In this case, apart from changes in taste variables z_t, the rate of growth of consumption is the same for everyone who is covered by the market for contingent claims.

It is an important consequence of perfect insurance that there will be proportionality of the marginal utility of consumption across different individuals. However, there are only a limited number of cases where we might expect to observe the result, since in practice, many important events cannot be insured, either directly, or by holding a suitable portfolio of existing assets. Moral hazard is one obvious problem. Many events are at least partially under the control of the individual who is affected, so that insurers may not be able to protect themselves against what is effectively fraud. As a practical matter, observation suggests that many potential insurance markets are absent, and further that it is evidently false—even without recourse to the data—that the consumption levels of all individuals move in parallel. Indeed, the term 'complete markets' is itself sometimes misleading, since it suggests that 'completeness' is the normal case, and that markets will usually pool risks. In fact, full risk pooling is only likely to occur among close-knit groups of individuals where people can be monitored, or are fully trusted by one another. But even small families know that there are problems associated with protecting everyone against all the consequences of their own actions.

1.4 On the aggregation of individual behavior

The link between microeconomic and macroeconomic behavior is something to which I shall return at many points in this book, but it is useful to give some preliminary consideration to the main issues. All of the analysis so far applies to single individuals, or at best to a single household viewed as an integrated decision-making unit. Nevertheless, interest in consumption and saving is not confined to those who work on microeconomics. The behavior of aggregate consumption has always been of central importance to macroeconomists, and that centrality has survived in one form or another through the many changes of focus in macroeconomic theory over the last half century. Consumption is a large share of gross domestic product, and it is impossible to understand the transmission of economic fluctuations, or the way in which such fluctuations can be moderated, without an understanding of the determinants of aggregate consumption. Indeed, one of the major concerns of research in the 1950s on life-cycle and permanent income theories of consumption was to analyze how consumption could be expected to respond to fiscal policies.

Much of the recent macroeconomic literature on aggregate consumption adopts the theory discussed in this chapter, more or less without modification, to provide working models for a 'representative agent.' Aggregate consumption is treated as if it had been generated by the decision processes of a single agent. It is possible to regard such an assumption as a convenient fiction; empirical analysis requires structure, and the source of that structure is a matter of secondary importance, provided always that the implications are thoroughly tested on the data. I have some sympathy with this position, although it puts a great deal of responsibility on the econometric analysis, and it requires that the econometric tests be powerful enough in practice to separate right from wrong. However, unless there is some reason to suppose that the microeconomic structure *ought* to aggregate up to the macro level, the strategy is arbitrary and hardly brings great intellectual satisfaction. Why this theory rather than some other? At the microeconomic level, greed and consistency provide well-tried axiomatic foundations for behavior, but there is generally no reason to suppose that such axioms are useful for a fictional representative agent. Representative agents, by doing away with aggregation, also rule out the possibility that aggregation will be useful, itself an aid to understanding. Aggregation is not always a nuisance; it can also be a fruitful source of hypotheses about aggregate behavior.

Do the models in this chapter support a representative agent interpretation of the aggregate data? If not, what are their implications for aggregate behavior, and especially for the behavior of aggregate consumption over time? Start from equation (45), rewritten to distinguish each household h:

$$(1+r_{it+1})\lambda_{t+1}^{h}(c_{t+1}^{h}) = \lambda_{t}^{h}(c_{t}^{h}) + u_{it+1}^{h}, \qquad (1.69)$$

where, as before, u_{it+1}^{h} is the difference between the realization and its expectation. Note again that (69), which comes from the first-order condition of dynamic optimization, assumes an interior solution, so that the equation will only hold for those assets that can be held both short or long by households, or if short sales are not allowed, for those assets that all households wish to hold in positive quantities. For the representative agent model to apply, we should like to have a relationship of the form:

$$(1+r_{it+1})\lambda_{t+1}(c_{t+1}) = \lambda_{t}(c_{t}) + u_{it+1} \qquad (1.70)$$

for some suitably defined macro function $\lambda(.)$ and consumption aggregate c_{t}, preferably average consumption.

As is usual in aggregation theory, functional form is a part of the story; what are the restrictions that have to be placed on individual preferences to allow the derivation of the aggregate (70)? However, there are two additional issues that are specific to intertemporal choice under uncertainty.

First, while it may be reasonable to suppose that all agents face the same parametric prices and interest rates, it is not reasonable to impose homogeneity of information. Each consumer knows things that other consumers do not know, if only about his or her own future, so that the innovations in (69) are each conditioned on different information sets. Aggregation must recognize the heterogeneity of individual information, and (70), with its aggregate innovations, can only make sense with respect to some suitable aggregate information set.

The second issue is to do with the passage of time. In general, the people in the population will not be the same in $t+1$ as in t; some people alive in t will be dead in $t+1$ and those people born in $t+1$ are unborn in t. The consequences of finite lives are harder to deal with than either of the other two topics, and so it is convenient to discuss functional form and heterogeneous information first, under the temporary assumption that no one ever dies, or (only marginally) more realistically, that households are 'dynasties' that live for ever. I also assume that there is no population growth, so that there is a constant and finite population of households. I shall return to reality below.

Suppose that the marginal felicity functions are the same for all households, and that either consumers are permitted to hold negative amounts of the ith asset, or, if not, that all consumers hold the asset in positive amounts. Then it is easy to show that (70) will hold with $c_t = \tilde{c}_t$, where $\tilde{c}_t$ is defined by

$$\tilde{c}_t = \lambda_t^{-1}\left(\frac{1}{H}\sum_h \lambda_t(c_t^h)\right), \tag{1.71}$$

where H is the total number of households. If the $\lambda(.)$ functions are linear, then $\tilde{c}_t = \bar{c}_t$, mean consumption, while $\tilde{c}_t$ is greater or less than the mean as $\lambda(.)$ is concave or convex respectively. The ratio of the two quantities can be regarded as a measure of inequality in the cross-section distribution of consumption. In consequence, if this measure of dispersion remains constant over time, c_t and $\tilde{c}_t$ will move in parallel, something that typically will be sufficient to support econometric analysis based on the means. Of course, if the cross-sectional distribution of consumption is changing over time, aggregation requires linearity of the $\lambda(.)$ functions. Grossman and Shiller (1982) show that under suitable assumptions on the evolution of returns, linearity is effectively satisfied if the time-intervals are sufficiently fine, but the result may not provide much reassurance for studies using quarterly or annual data. Note too that it will often be possible to weaken the requirement that preferences be identical. For example, in the linear case, it is sufficient that the derivatives of marginal felicity with respect to consumption be uncorrelated with the consumption levels themselves, and appropriately defined (but still limited) variability can also be allowed in the non-linear case.

The stochastic term u_{it+1} in (70) is simply the average of the individual martingale differences, and there is nothing in the microeconomic theory that guarantees that it will be orthogonal to lagged *macroeconomic* variables. In particular, because of the cross-sectional covariance terms, the orthogonality of lagged household-level variables to the individual differences does not guarantee the orthogonality of the averages. Indeed, there are good reasons to suppose that the covariances are non-zero; for example, some unanticipated event may effect all poor people one way, and all rich people another. However, the aggregate (70) will mimic the stochastic properties of the individual equations if the macroeconomic variables are included in individual's information sets, so that each lagged macro variable is orthogonal to *each* of the micro shocks, again see Grossman and Shiller. Such an assumption is perhaps plausible, since individuals certainly have public access to such variables. Even so, there is no guarantee that they will actually use such information. For example, it is typically the case that macroeconomic changes in income have very little explanatory power for individual income changes, so there may be little value to individual consumers of finding out about aggregate data, always supposing that they understand how to extract from them the information that is relevant to their own futures. If they do not, the aggregate shocks may well be predictable by lagged macroeconomic variables, even if individuals are behaving according to the theory.

It should not be surprising that the difficulties with information are absent in the case of complete markets, because markets in contingent claims effectively aggregate the heterogeneous individual information. With complete markets, the individual marginal utilities satisfy, from equations (67) and (68),

$$(1+r_{it+1})\lambda_{t+1}^h(c_{t+1}^h) = \theta^h\mu_t, \tag{1.72}$$

where μ_t is the same for all agents. If (72) is averaged over all agents, we obtain immediately an aggregate equivalent

$$(1+r_{it+1})\lambda_{t+1}(\tilde{c}_{t+1}) = \bar{\theta}\mu_t, \tag{1.73}$$

where $\tilde{c}_t$ is again defined by (71). The parallel movement of consumption in the special case of (68) provides an even more obvious example; if each individual's consumption grows at the same rate, so does the aggregate of their consumptions.

Clearly then, aggregation may or may not fail, although it is fair to say that, given infinite lives or household dynasties, there exist assumptions under which aggregation will go through, and an aggregate intertemporal condition will hold that looks very much like the microeconomic efficiency conditions. However, aggregate behavior will not look like individual behavior if the marginal felicity functions are not linear, or if information heterogeneity is not dispelled either by the existence of complete markets —a very tall order indeed—or by individuals knowing about the aggregate economy and understanding its implications for their own futures. As I shall argue in Chapter 5, exploring the consequences of the failure of these assumptions is useful in interpreting the empirical evidence.

Once it is recognized that neither individuals nor households live for ever, there are even more serious problems. A simple example illustrates their nature. Suppose that there is no uncertainty, that the marginal felicity functions take the isoelastic form $\lambda(c) = c^{-\rho}$ where ρ is the coefficient of relative risk-aversion, that there is a single asset with constant real interest rate r, and that preferences take the 'discounting' form (8). The allocation condition (9) implies that

$$\ln c_{t+1}^h - \ln c_t^h = \frac{1}{\rho} \ln\left(\frac{1+r}{1+\delta}\right). \tag{1.74}$$

Suppose that $r > \delta$ so that, for every household that exists in both t and $t+1$, consumption is growing. If the aggregate economy is stationary, so that labor income is constant over time, the lifetime trajectory for different households will be the same, with young households consuming little, and old, about-to-die households consuming most, with T years of consumption growth between them and the youngest cohorts. In such an economy, aggregate consumption is also stationary. Although consumption is growing for every household that exists in both periods, the high consumption of the about-to-die households is constantly being replaced by the low consumption of the newborn households, so that the average is constant. If $r < \delta$ the same argument goes through; individual consumption is falling, but the aggregate is constant. Nor is the result special to the particular assumptions used here; Blanchard (1985) derives similar results under uncertainty, where individuals have a constant hazard of dying. In an economy with finitely lived agents, there is no conformity between the behavior of individual consumption and its aggregate. In particular, there is no general reason why the relationship between consumption growth and real interest rates for individual households should carry through to the aggregate.

These problems are somewhat more tractable when individual consumption follows the martingale process (48). This case requires linearity of the marginal felicity functions, and so satisfies the functional form aggregation condition, and it also requires that $r = \delta$ so that the growth and decline issues of the previous paragraph do not arise. Hence, provided macro variables are included in the individual information sets, and provided there is no growth in the economy, so that the dying households are replaced by look-alike young ones, aggregate consumption will also follow a martingale, at least approximately. The result is not exact, because the difference in consumption between the newly born and the newly dead will depend on the income history of the latter, so that this component of the consumption change is predictable.

If there is productivity growth in the economy, young workers will have higher lifetime resources than old workers. All generations plan to have constant consumption over life, so that, with new information becoming available, each person's consumption will follow a martingale from one period to the next, as will the averages for all cohorts who are alive in both periods. However, the initial consumption of the newly born will now be higher than the final consumption of those who have just died. For example, if productivity growth produces a linear increase of g per cohort in labor income, the consumption of the newly born will be (only) approximately (because of the surprises throughout the lives of the old) an amount gT greater than those who are T years ahead of them and have just died. But the new cohort is a fraction T^{-1} of the total population, so that average consumption satisfies the approximation

$$c_{t+1} \simeq g + c_t + u_{t+1}. \tag{1.75}$$

The drift in productivity is transmitted to aggregate consumption, even though there is no drift in any individual's consumption.

I shall return to aggregation issues at various points in the chapters that follow, in Chapter 2.2 on the effects of interest rates on aggregate consumption, and in Chapter 5.2, where I shall explore further and more precisely the aggregation of the martingale model. For the moment, the point to remember is that, unless we are prepared to assume that households live for ever, only the martingale version of the model is likely to aggregate to anything like its microeconomic form. If one is prepared to swallow the assumption of infinite dynasties, the prospects are better, and the further assumptions required to ensure aggregation are perhaps more readily digestible. Even here, however, it is important to think hard about differences in what people know, and how those differences affect their behavior.

CHAPTER 2

Consumption, Growth, and Interest

That there should be a positive relationship between productivity growth and the ratio of savings to income in the aggregate economy is an early and justly celebrated prediction of the life-cycle hypothesis. Although various theories of economic growth also predict that saving (or investment) and growth should be positively related, the life-cycle model is unique among models of consumer behavior in predicting a causal relationship that runs from faster growth to greater household saving. The result is not implied by the permanent income theory of consumption nor by the earlier and less sophisticated models that postulated a simple relationship between income and outlay. The growth-to-saving prediction offers a possible explanation for the fact that virtually all developed economies have experienced simultaneous falls in the rate of productivity growth and in national saving rates during the 1970s and 1980s. In Section 2.1, I discuss the basis in life-cycle theory for the growth–saving relationship, and look at some of the recent international evidence. While there seems little doubt that growth and saving are indeed linked, it cannot be established that life-cycle saving is the cause.

The effect of interest rates on saving, discussed in Section 2.2, has always been a central issue in political economy. Aggregate saving and capital accumulation are society's provision for the future, so that, for many people, failures or distortions in saving behavior are seen as compromising the welfare of future generations. There is also a commonly held view that identifies saving with growth, regarding both as measures of a country's economic performance. If interest rates have an effect on saving, then there is a direct link between policy, particularly monetary and fiscal policy, and economic performance. There are many versions of the story: taxation of capital income lowers real interest rates and stifles the incentive to save; taxation of capital income distorts saving and generates deadweight losses; financial 'repression' in developing countries lowers returns, depresses saving, and retards growth. All such arguments depend on the existence of a positive response of saving to higher interest rates. The theory of Chapter 1, while relevant to these questions, hardly suggests a definitive answer, so that much hinges on the empirical evidence. However, the interpretation of the data is not straightforward, particularly once we recognize the importance of the aggregation from microeconomic theory to macroeconomic data.

2.1 Saving and growth

That saving will be generated as a result of productivity growth is an insight that comes from even the simplest model of life-cycle saving and consumption, so that such a model is a good place from which to begin. Armed with the basic ideas, I discuss various elaborations of the model, and their likely effects on its predictions. I then turn to the empirical evidence, and to its implications, both for the relationship between saving and growth, and for the life-cycle model itself.

The stripped-down life-cycle model

Begin by considering the simplest version of the life-cycle model without uncertainty, where the only change in income is when the consumer retires from work, and where consumption is constant over life. This can be formally justified using the theory of Chapter 1, or we can simply assert, along with Modigliani (1986), 'the self-evident proposition that the representative consumer will choose to consume at a reasonably stable rate, close to his anticipated average life consumption,' a proposition that is a good deal more general than intertemporal additivity of preferences. Figure 2.1 illustrates this case, which Modigliani refers to as the 'stripped-down' version of the life-cycle model. Labor income is constant throughout the L (= 40) years of working life, at one unit per period, and then falls to zero through the R (= 10) years of retirement. The real interest rate is zero so that consumption is constant at $L/(L+R)$ per period, or 80% of income through the working life. Assets accumulate at $R/(R+L)$ (= 20%) of income per period, reaching a maximum of $RL/(R+L)$ (= 8) times income immediately before retirement. Throughout life, the average ratio of assets to labor income is $0.5R(L/(R+L))$ (= 4), the first of many such numbers that conform to reality (at least roughly) under even the simplest assumptions.

The stripped-down model predicts that both demographic and productivity growth will generate saving, and that without either there will be no net saving in the economy as a whole. Saving is done by young people, and dissaving by the old. If the population is stationary, and if the incomes of the young are the same as were the incomes of the old, saving and dissaving are equal and opposite. With productivity growth, the younger are richer than were their parents at the same age, their saving is on a larger scale than was that of their parents, and net saving is positive. The faster

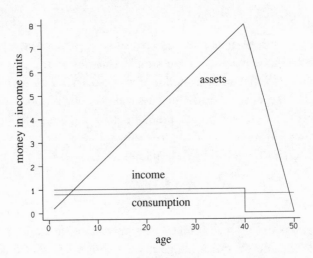

Figure 2.1: Consumption, income, and assets in the stripped-down life-cycle model

the growth, the higher the saving rate. Population growth works exactly the same way; if there are more young people than old people, their total saving outweighs the total dissaving by members of their parents' generation, so that once again there is positive saving in society as a whole.

If the rates of population and productivity growth are constant, and if the real interest rate is zero, the stripped-down model generates simple formulas for the relationship between saving rates and growth. Suppose that population is growing at rate n, and productivity at rate g, so that national income is growing at rate $n+g$. There are $n_0 e^{nt}$ consumers born at date t, and each has a *constant* income of $y_0 e^{gt}$ throughout life, so that productivity growth takes place between cohorts, but not within the lifetime of each individual. Just as in Figure 2.1, each person consumes a fraction $L/(R+L)$ of income per year. Hence at date t, total income is the income of all those born since $t-L$, while consumption is the consumption of those born since $t-R-L$. The aggregates are therefore given by

$$C = \int_{t-L-R}^{t} \frac{L}{L+R} y_0 e^{g\tau} n_0 e^{n\tau} d\tau, \quad Y = \int_{t-L}^{t} y_0 e^{g\tau} n_0 e^{n\tau} d\tau. \quad (2.1)$$

If we compute the integrals, the consumption to income ratio is given by

$$\frac{C}{Y} = \frac{L}{L+R} \frac{1 - \exp(-(g+n)(L+R))}{1 - \exp(-(g+n)L)}. \quad (2.2)$$

Given the assumptions, equation (2) can be used to investigate the behavior of the saving ratio as the growth rates change. Note first that the two growth rates, of population and productivity growth, do not appear separately in (2), but only as the sum $n + g$, so that it is only *aggregate* growth that matters for the saving ratio, not whether it is population growth at constant per capita income, or income growth in a stationary population. For given work and retirement spans, (2) implies that saving is zero if growth is zero and that saving is a concave increasing function of the growth rate of aggregate income. The formula generates realistic saving rates at realistic growth rates; for $L = 40$ and $R = 10$, as in Figure 2.1, the saving rate rises from zero at zero growth, to 4.5% at 1% growth, 8.2% at 2%, 11.1% at 3%, and 15.1% at 5%. The slope of the saving-growth relationship is $R/2$ at the origin, and for the (40,10) combination for (R, L) is an easily remembered figure of 2, so that if growth increases from, say, 3.5 to 4.5%, the saving ratio will increase by 2 percentage points.

Complications to the basic model

These back-of-the-envelope calculations suggest that even the stripped-down model generates the sorts of results and predictions that are well worth checking out against the data. However, we must first examine how many of the qualitative results are basic features of the life-cycle model, and how many are artefacts of the very special and clearly unrealistic assumptions of the stripped-down model, particularly the assumptions that income is constant until retirement, and that interest rates are zero.

The introduction of a positive interest rate does a great deal to complicate the algebra, because we now have to keep track of capital income as well as labor income, but the main features are not seriously affected. Positive real interest rates will tip consumption paths downwards in the early years and upwards in old age, as agents adjust their intertemporal paths to the intertemporal incentives. But this only implies that the young will save relatively more, and it is the saving of the young that is the fulcrum upon which the growth effects operate.

More serious consequences follow from the recognition that labor incomes are not constant throughout the working life. Even in occupations where there is very little training, and productivity depends on brawn rather than brain, incomes typically start out at low levels, increasing with age before eventually declining. The longer the period of training, and the greater the return to human capital, the later is the peak, but there is nearly always some period of income growth at the beginning of the life cycle. Hence, if consumption is constant over life, it is possible that young consumers may want to *borrow*, not save, in the early years of their careers, especially if they are in occupations where the educational and training period is long. If so, then at rapid enough growth rates, additional growth will *decrease* saving, as higher growth rates magnify early borrowing relative to later repayment.

Of course, positive interest rates, the precautionary motive, restrictions on borrowing, or the effects of habits may act so as to restrain early consumption, so that young people with hump-shaped income profiles may not wish to borrow, or be able to do so. However, it must also be recognized that productivity growth may generate income growth *within* individual life cycles, and not just across them. If so, and if consumers anticipate real growth, as surely they must, there is again an incentive to borrow against that growth, and the borrowing will be larger the larger is the growth rate. The general point is that growth will increase aggregate saving if life-cycle saving occurs at earlier ages than life-cycle dissaving. The arguments above suggest that such a result is far from automatic, but it is nevertheless plausible, and will be the case even if there is only modest saving in late middle age, followed by dissaving after retirement.

The dependence of the saving ratio on total growth, and not on how it is divided between population and productivity growth, is another result that does not survive more realistic modelling. The stripped-down model recognizes old age, but not childhood. Workers spring from the womb, tools in hand, and immediately begin accumulating wealth for their retirement. If instead, they are born as dependent children into the households of those who are in the early years of their own working life, there is a further reason to expect consumption to be high and saving low in the first years of the working life. The presence of children, by placing an additional burden on young workers, may precipitate borrowing in the early years of the life cycle, and again reverse the postulated effect of productivity growth on saving. Faster population growth, if long enough maintained, increases the ratio of workers to the retired, but it also increases the ratio of children to workers, so that the net effect on saving is not necessarily positive, nor is there any longer a simple link between the effects of population and productivity growth. The stripped-down model is suggestive, but many of its predictions depend on its special structure.

The empirical evidence

The qualifications to the stripped-down model should only warn us that, as a matter of theory, there is no simple relation between national saving rates and growth; they should certainly not discourage us from looking at the evidence, nor from trying to interpret it in terms of the life-cycle story. Indeed, empirical studies have repeatedly shown that there is indeed a positive relationship across countries between saving rates and growth rates of national income. The relationship is clearest among the more developed countries, but the positive correlation also exists in a somewhat weaker form among less developed economies. Figure 2.2 shows a typical scatter diagram using data from (version 5 of) the Penn World Tables, see Summers and Heston (1991). There are 120 countries in the scatter, which plots the average value over the years 1981 through 1985 of the national 'saving ratio,' defined as 100 minus the percentage share of consumption in gross domestic product versus the average rate of growth of real GDP from 1965 to 1980. The slope of the regression line through these points is 1.34 with a standard error of 0.33, close enough to the prediction of the stripped-down model. Similar scatters can be generated using other data sets such as the annual data in the *World Development Report*, World Bank (annual)—see for example Deaton (1990). Of course, there are other possible explanations for these results; the share of investment in GDP is positively correlated across countries with the share of saving in GDP—see Feldstein and Horioka (1980)—and virtually all growth models predict that growth should respond to the share of investment. But this does not detract from the fact that the prediction of the life-cycle model is supported both qualitatively and quantitatively.

The clearest and most up-to-date survey of the cross-country evidence is by Modigliani (1990), who looks at OECD data from twenty-one developed countries from 1961 through 1987 (Canada, the US, Japan, Australia, Austria, Belgium, Denmark, Finland, France, Germany, Greece, Iceland, Ireland, Italy, The Netherlands, Norway, Portugal, Spain, Sweden, Switzerland, and the UK), and, in a separate exercise, at data from eighty-five developing countries from 1982 to 1988, provided from (a revised version) of Aghevli *et al.* (1990). The OECD data show a marked reduction in both saving and growth rates from the 1960s through to the 1980s; Table 2.1 shows the averages over the twenty-one countries by the three 'decades' 1961–70, 1971–80, 1981–7. As Modigliani emphasizes, the

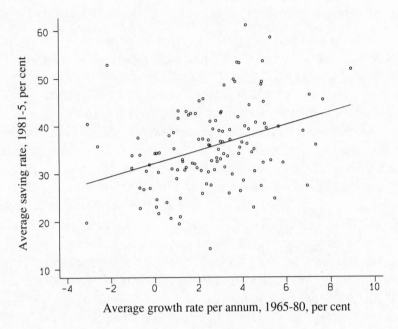

Figure 2.2: Cross-country saving and income growth: 120 countries from the
Penn World Tables, Summers and Heston (1991)

change is widespread over these countries. Only in Portugal, where it was
constant, was there no decline in the saving rate between the 1960s and
1970s and only in Switzerland and Norway was there an increase from the
1970s to the 1980s. Moreover, the 6.3 point drop in the saving ratio for a
2.5 point drop in growth rates is close to the 2 for 1 effect that comes out
of the simple stripped-down model. Modigliani treats the decades as sample points and estimates by ordinary least squares a pooled regression over
countries and periods:

$$\frac{s}{y} = 0.06 + 1.81 g_{-1} \qquad \bar{R}^2 = 0.37, \; s.e. = 0.041, \qquad (2.3)$$
$$\quad (4.2) \quad (6.1)$$

where the figures in brackets are t-values. The growth coefficient is well
determined and close to the value predicted from the simple theory.
(Modigliani presents regressions containing a number of other variables,
but the coefficient on growth is robust and remains within the range
suggested by the model.)

Table 2.1: Saving and growth in twenty-one developed countries, 1961–1987. (averages in percentages)

	Growth	National saving rate
1961–70	4.9	16.6
1971–80	3.4	15.3
1981–7	2.4	10.3

Source: Modigliani (1990)

For the eighty-five less developed countries, a comparable regression is

$$\frac{s}{y} = 0.068 + \underset{(5.5)}{1.30\,g} + \underset{(1.3)}{0.17\,active} + .. \quad \bar{R}^{2} = 0.59 \atop s.e. = 0.0549 \qquad (2.4)$$

where *active* is the proportion of the population aged 15–64, and there are other regressors (results not shown) for the reciprocal of the level of national income, the terms of trade (both significant and both negative), and a dummy for whether the country has a debt-servicing problem (significant and positive.) The demographic variable is not well determined, perhaps not surprisingly given the theoretical arguments, and this sort of finding is typical of the literature. Although there are some studies and some equations that find an influence of population growth or demographic effects, the results are typically not robust and there is no consensus on the direction of the effect on saving—see Gersovitz (1988) for a survey. However, the growth variable enters as predicted, and is again both well determined and in the range suggested by the theory. For the poorer countries, increases in the *level* of national income also appear to enhance saving, perhaps because saving for old age is unnecessary in the early stages of economic development.

These results would seem to provide a striking endorsement of the theoretical predictions of the simplest, stripped-down life-cycle model. Whatever the selection of countries, growth and saving are positively linked, and the much discussed recent reduction of saving rates in the developed countries can be attributed, along with much else, to the slow-down in productivity growth that began in the early 1970s.

Contradictory evidence?

In some ways, it is surprising that the evidence is quite so favorable. The predictions of the stripped-down life-cycle model owe as much to the simplifying assumptions as to the more basic supposition that consumers make sensible life-cycle plans. Hence the very success of the predictions suggests that other factors might be at work. Even in Modigliani's results, there is some hint that all is not well. Regressions of differences in saving ratios from one decade to the next show a weaker and less significant effect of changes in growth rates than did the earlier level on level regressions. Undoubtedly some of the change is attributable to the smaller sample size in these differenced regressions, although one might also suspect the influence of country-specific fixed effects that are removed by the differencing. If fixed effects are important, the cross-sectional results will attribute to growth what are in reality long-established differences between countries that are correlated with growth in the cross-section. As a result the cross-sectional results will not be consistent with the response of saving to the slow-down in productivity. In fact, this turns out not to be a problem. The inclusion of country dummies into (3) reduces the growth coefficient to approximately 1.5, with a t-value of 4.1, which, although showing some effect in the direction predicted, hardly suggests that country fixed effects are a major source of error.

Other evidence comes from following through the life-cycle explanation of saving and growth, and checking, not just the final result, that national saving rates should respond to national growth rates, but also the intermediate implications for the cross-sectional behavior of consumption and saving. If saving occurs at earlier stages in the life cycle than does dissaving, then increased growth, by magnifying the scale of activities of relatively younger consumers, will generate additional saving. So the life-cycle explanation for the cross-country relationship between saving and growth can only be correct if there is evidence for at least some 'hump' saving in the cross-section. Of course we do not have evidence for all the countries that appear in the cross-section regressions. But for the countries where there are data, and we shall see several examples below, it is typically the case that consumption and income are much more closely associated than is the case in stylized diagrams like Figure 2.1. The typical hump-shaped profile of income is closely matched by a corresponding hump-shaped profile of consumption, so that the smoothing of consumption over the life cycle, sometimes referred to as long-term or 'low-frequency' smoothing, if it takes place at all, takes place only on a limited scale. Life-cycle saving, when it occurs, takes place in middle or late middle age, not long prior to retirement. Whether there is saving among the young, or dissaving among the old, is something that varies from data set to data set, and has been the subject of a good deal of controversy.

These findings have implications, not only for the relationship between saving and growth, but also for the question of how much of total wealth can be accounted for by life-cycle saving. In particular, Kotlikoff and Summers (1981) have argued that the cross-sectional evidence for the US which follows the general pattern described above, does not generate enough life-cycle saving to justify the common belief since Tobin (1967) that this form of saving can at least approximately account for total wealth holdings in the US, a belief that again owes much to the stripped-down model of Figure 2.1. These topics have been the source of much discussion—see in particular Modigliani (1988) and Kotlikoff (1988)—but it would probably be fair to conclude that the observation of apparently widespread 'tracking' of income by consumption has led to a downward revaluation of the likely fraction of wealth that can be attributed to life-cycle saving, both in the US and elsewhere. As for saving and growth, if life-cycle saving means saving in late middle age followed by limited dissaving in retirement, then increased growth can be expected to generate increased saving. But the evidence for dissaving in retirement is at best mixed, and if, in addition, there is borrowing by young consumers, the life-cycle effects of growth may be to magnify borrowing, not saving.

Growth and the age-profile of consumption

What is to me the most persuasive evidence against the life-cycle interpretation of the cross-country relationship between growth and saving comes from cross-country comparisons of cross-sections of consumption and income. The idea comes from Carroll and Summers (1991). Consider two otherwise identical economies, one of which has had no income growth for a very long time, while the other has been growing steadily for an equally long time. In each we collect household survey data and compute consumption age-profiles, graphs of consumption against the age of the household head. In the no-growth economy, young consumers have on average the same lifetime resources as their parents and grandparents, while in the expanding economy, children are richer over their lifetimes than were their parents, and much richer than were their grandparents. In the absence of growth, the life-cycle consumption age-profile can take any shape at all, depending on needs and tastes over the life cycle; the argument does not require that there is a preference for constant consumption over life. However, in the growing economy, the ratio of the lifetime resources of the young to that of the old must be greater than in the stagnant economy, so that, since consumption is determined by lifetime resources, the consumption age-profile must be relatively tipped towards the young in the more rapidly growing economy. According to life-cycle theory, consumption depends on lifetime resources, not on current resources, and in rapidly growing economies the life-time resources of the young are larger relative to those of their parents and grandparents than is the case in a more slowly growing economy.

Carroll and Summers calculate age consumption profiles for the US in 1960, 1973, and 1985, for Japan in 1974 and 1979, and for various years for Canada, the UK, Denmark, and Norway. In spite of differences in growth experiences, the profiles are quite similar from one country to another. For the US and Japan, growth rates of real per capita GDP from 1960 to 1985 have been 2.1% per annum and 5.2% per annum respectively, so that if these rates were maintained indefinitely, a 25-year-old Japanese would be 12.5 times richer than his 75-year-old grandfather, whereas a 25-year-old American would be only 2.8 times richer than his grandfather. In spite of this, the Japanese consumption age-profile, although quite similar to the American, actually peaks slightly later, in direct contradiction to the theoretical prediction.

Similarly dramatic results can be obtained from examination of the consumption age-profiles in less developed countries. I illustrate using household survey data from Thailand, a rapidly growing economy, and Ivory Coast, which has experienced very little growth in the last quarter century. According to the Summers-Heston data, 1960 real national income per capita was 8% greater in Ivory Coast than in Thailand; by 1985, the Thai per capita income was twice that in Ivory Coast. The average annual growth rates over the period were 4.1% for Thailand and 0.9% for Ivory Coast, so that the corresponding ratios for lifetime resources of 25 to 50-year-olds are 7.11 times for Thailand and 1.64 times for Ivory Coast. Figures 2.3 and 2.4 show consumption age-profiles together with income-age profiles for the two countries. The Thai profiles are taken from the

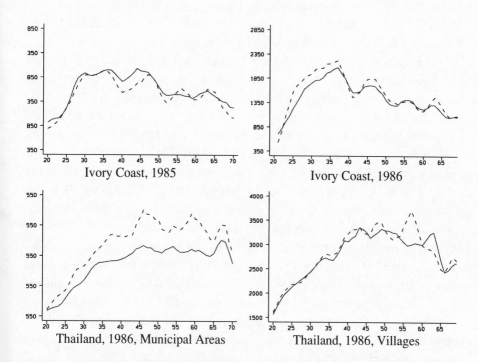

Figure 2.3: Age-profiles of income (broken lines) and consumption (solid lines), Ivory Coast 1985 and 1986, and Thailand 1986, urban and rural.

1986 Socioeconomic Survey, and are shown separately for municipal areas (urban) and villages (rural), and are averaged over 3,589 urban and 5,012 rural households. For Ivory Coast, the data are for the two years 1985 and 1986, and come from the Living Standards Surveys carried out jointly by the World Bank and the Government of Ivory Coast. The sample sizes are smaller than for Thailand, 1,600 households per year, so I have not attempted to show the rural and urban results separately. The graphs have been smoothed over age-groups, so that each point shows the average of consumption and income for the age and the two (Thailand) or three (Ivory Coast) ages on either side, with decreasing triangular weights. Hence, for example, average consumption at 30 years of age in Thailand is one-third of the mean for 30-year-olds, plus two-ninths of each of the means for 29- and 31-year-olds, plus one-ninth of the means for 28- and 32-year-olds. In principle, the Thai samples are large enough for one year averages to be sufficient, but in these data, as in many others from LDCs, people tend to round their ages to numbers ending in 5s and 0s, and the people who do so tend to have lower consumption and income than those who report non-rounded ages. Smoothing over five-year bands removes the irregularities that would otherwise be generated by such anomalies.

The Thai consumption age-profile peaks much later in the life cycle than does that for the Ivory Coast; Ivorian households reach their peak consumption levels when the head is aged around 35 years, while in Thailand, consumption continues to grow until at least age 45, and perhaps later. Once again, as in Carroll and Summers' comparison between the US and Japan, this is exactly the wrong way round. Thailand is growing much more rapidly than is Ivory Coast, and should have a consumption profile that is relatively tipped toward the young, whereas, in reality, it is the Ivorian profiles that peak at the younger ages. Of course, these comparisons of total household expenditure make no allowance for the different demographic compositions of households across the two countries. However, although household size is larger in Ivory Coast, maximum household size is attained at around the same age in the two countries, so that differences in the relationship between age and household size cannot by themselves explain the differences in the consumption age-profiles. Of course, total household size is only a crude measure of needs, but it seems unlikely that more sophisticated measures can account for the differences in the profiles.

One common reaction to these figures is to argue that it is unreasonable to suppose that tastes are the same in the two countries. It is certainly possible that the life-cycle model is true for each country separately, each with its different preferences. But it is not possible to make such arguments while maintaining that the life-cycle model is the explanation for the cross-country correlation between saving and growth. Without the assumption that the structure of intertemporal tastes is the same in different countries, the life-cycle story delivers no predictions about the effects of saving on growth in an international cross-section.

Does consumption track income too closely?

Where then are we left? There are two separate issues. The first is the validity or otherwise of the life-cycle explanation for the link between saving and growth, and the second is the validity of the life-cycle hypothesis itself. The cross-country evidence on consumption age-profiles makes it difficult to believe that the correlation between growth and saving is a consequence of hump-saving by youngish consumers saving for their old age. There is too little hump-saving and too little dissaving to make the story plausible. More importantly, consumption profiles for economies growing at different rates are not consistent with the basic hypothesis that consumption at all ages is determined by *lifetime* resources. But this does not by itself mean that the life-cycle hypothesis must be rejected. Inter-country taste-variation can be admitted, and other explanations sought for the correlation between saving and growth. There is no lack of contenders. There is a strong correlation between national saving rates and national in-vestment rates, so that we may simply be observing the relationship bet-ween investment and growth, either lagged as in (3), or current, as in (4). While the standard neoclassical Solow growth model does not predict a relationship between saving rates and growth in the long run, the dynamics of adjustment may be sufficiently slow for the cross-country correlations to be dominated by the transitional behavior, although see the counter-argu-ments in King and Rebelo (1989). Models such as that of Rebelo (1991) postulate that there are constant returns to a (broadly defined) concept of capital, and are therefore consistent with a positive relationship between the investment share and growth even in the long run. Alternatively, accounts of growth under increasing returns, for example Romer (1990), emphasize the role of preferences that embody a willingness to wait, and that allow countries to accumulate the human capital that is the decisive catalyst for growth. Countries with low rates of time-preference will have high saving and high growth, and vice versa, although the causality is neither directly from saving to growth, nor from growth to savings.

As far as the life-cycle hypothesis itself is concerned, there is certainly a sharp contrast between the life-cycle consumption and income profiles of the stripped-down model in Figure 2.1 and the actual paths for the US, or for Thailand and Ivory Coast as illustrated in Figures 2.3 and 2.4. I have already cited the findings of Kotlikoff and Summers (1981), who found lit-tle hump-saving in the US. Figures 2.3 and 2.4 show little evidence of saving at any age in either Ivory Coast or in rural Thailand, and while urban Thais do save over the life cycle, the heaviest savers are households headed by older heads. Deaton and Paxson (1992) look at households in Taiwan, one of the fastest growing and highest saving economies in the world. Although Taiwanese households save a great deal, there is once again very little that could be described as hump-saving. Households save at all ages, and if anything, the saving rate tends to *increase* with age. Ando and Kennickell (1987), after examining six sets of survey data from the US, conclude that 'most families save a relatively small portion of their income throughout the period of their active participation in the labor force, and after they retire, they dissave very little, keeping their assets more or less at the same level.' Other authors, Danziger *et al.* (1983) and Diamond and Hausman (1984) have not found the relationship between wealth and age that is predicted by hump-saving.

Perhaps most notably, Carroll and Summers (1991) use data from the US Consumer Expenditure Surveys of 1960–1 and 1972–3 to draw age-profiles of consumption and income for five educational groups and nine occupational groups. The patterns differ markedly from one group to an-other, although they are much more stable across time, and in each case the consumption profile is close to the income profile. Those who are in educational or occupational groups where income peaks late, in their late forties or early fifties, have consumption paths that also peak late, while those with little education and unskilled jobs have income and consumption profiles that peak early, that are flat, or that fall with age. Browning, Deaton, and Irish (1985), using British data, also find that consumption and income profiles are synchronized over the life cycle, both for manual and nonmanual workers. In the Michigan Panel Study of Income Dynamics, Lawrance (1991) finds that food consumption of poorer households rises less rapidly with age than does food consumption of richer households, a result that she interprets as showing that the rate of time-preference is inversely related to income, see equation (1.10). But poorer, less well-educated households also have less rapidly rising incomes, so that once again the evidence is consistent with consumption tracking income over the life cycle. These findings suggest a much closer association between con-sumption and income than might be thought to be compatible with the life-cycle hypothesis. While it is clear that a simple relationship between con-sumption and income is not a good alternative, if only because consump-tion is much smoother than income, these results suggest that it is worth considering hypotheses that link consumption and income over shorter periods than complete life cycles; I shall turn to this task in Chapter 6.

Even so, it should be admitted that with enough ingenuity, a good deal of this evidence can be made compatible with the life-cycle model, or in-deed with the theory of Chapter 1. One route is to look for factors that condition preferences and that are correlated with labor incomes over the life cycle. Children are one possibility, and family size and the expenditures that go with it tend to peak in middle or late middle age, at around the same time that family income peaks. Somewhat more heretically, preferences may be directly affected by income, if income and lifestyles come with particular types of jobs. Yet again, hours worked tend to follow labor income over the cycle, so that if consumption is a substitute for leisure, it would make sense to use consumption to compensate for the limited leisure opportunities of middle age. Such an explanation would hold whether or not the consumer chooses how many hours to work (although in either case the theory of Chapter 1 would have to be extended.) However, hours worked and wage rates also have their own life cycle and business cycle patterns, and it turns out that neither substitutability nor complementarity of leisure for goods can account for the co-movement of hours, wages, and consumption—see Browning, Deaton, and Irish (1985) for Britain, and Ando and Kennickell (1987) who report the same finding for the US. However, the precautionary and habit-formation models discussed in Chapter 1 would go some way to reconciling the theory with the evidence, since both tend to depress consumption early in life, when income is also low. Interest rates may play a similar role, and if real returns are higher in more rapidly growing economies, there may be a partial explanation for why consumption in rapidly growing economies does not more heavily favor the young. Some of these hypotheses have problems of their own, and none has the simple appeal of the direct link between consumption and income that is so characteristic of the data. However, a great deal more research remains to be done before we have the decisive evidence that would sharply discriminate these hypotheses one from the other, or indeed clearly invalidate the life-cycle hypothesis.

2.2 Saving and interest rates

The last decade has seen a renewal of interest in the empirical analysis of the relationship between consumption and asset returns. There has also been a change of focus, away from the traditional question of the effects of interest rates on saving, and towards the direct investigation of the intertemporal relationships discussed in Chapter 1. However, these studies are typically less concerned with the effects of returns on the shape of the intertemporal profile of consumption than with the implications for asset prices of their role in enabling agents to allocate consumption over time in an uncertain and risky environment. Before turning to this more modern literature, it is worth reviewing briefly the conclusions of the earlier work that tried to resolve the theoretical ambiguity by direct empirical analysis of the effects of interest rates on saving.

Traditional analyses of saving and interest

In the literature on the time-series consumption function, there are many studies where an interest rate is included in the model, along with income and other variables. There are also studies from cross-sections of countries that typically also incorporate the rate of growth effects discussed in the previous section. My reading of this literature is that the empirical results are as ambiguous as is the theory, or more positively, that the empirical results confirm the lack of invariance to time, place, and other variables that the theory predicts. Many of the studies have serious reproducibility problems, in that the results appear to depend on particular data sets, particular sample choices, particular specifications, or particular econometric techniques. For example, the widely cited study by Boskin (1978), which estimates a large response of saving to interest rates, uses data definitions that are far from standard, and the results do not recur in studies using more familiar data. Certainly, no one has generated the sort of robust finding that has commanded widespread assent among other researchers. Much of the difficulty reflects the fact that the amount of information in aggregate time-series data is rather low, so that it is generally difficult to measure precisely the effects of variables other than income, and to a lesser extent wealth.

The study by Blinder and Deaton (1985) can be used to document many of the problems. Reasonably precise estimates can be obtained for the effects on purchases of non-durables and services of current and lagged income, as well as, at least in this study, of the relative price of durable and non-durable goods, and of the change in wealth, a variable that is dominated by changes in the value of the stock market, and is essentially orthogonal to its own past and to other actual and potential regressors. Beyond that, there is a long list of other variables that might be included on theoretical grounds. Blinder and Deaton examine the effects of stocks of durable goods, of interest rates, of nominal inflation (see Deaton 1977), of government budget surpluses or deficits (Barro 1974), of temporary taxes, and of the timing of tax payments, and even this list hardly exhausts the possibilities. In some regressions, it is possible to find a negative effect on consumption of the three-month treasury bill rate, but the effect works only for *nominal* and not real rates, and the size of the coefficient is sensitive to the inclusion of other variables, particularly the relative price terms. The time-series data are probably incapable of providing sharp answers to how saving is affected by interest rates, at least if the question is posed in this form. It is not surprising, therefore, that recent time-series work has shifted towards a more limited agenda of much more sharply posed questions.

The difficulties with the cross-country studies are different in detail, but have much the same consequences. There are very severe data problems. Accounting practices are not always comparable across countries, particularly in such matters as the treatment of depreciation. Nor is it straightforward to choose a suitable measure of real asset returns that is widely available and comparably defined across countries. There are particular difficulties for developing countries, where official credit markets are frequently controlled, and where free markets may be either illegal or difficult to observe. As a result, there are many countries that report low, single-digit nominal interest rates, together with double- or treble-digit inflation rates. In such circumstances, a suitable choice of 'sample' can generate almost any desired result. Nevertheless, there are several cross-country studies in the literature, several of which estimate positive interest rate effects, see for example Fry (1987, ch. 2). Again, it is difficult to know what to make of these studies. Several have been challenged by other researchers, and in some cases the standard of econometric practice is not such as to inspire confidence in the correctness and reproducibility of the results.

For what it is worth, my own view of the empirical evidence is that saving is not much influenced by interest rates. Given the theoretical ambiguities, I do not find it surprising that clear results have not emerged from the analysis of the data, nor that different results can be obtained by looking at different data sets in different circumstances. However, there are many economists who would not accept such a position, who believe that saving is in truth very sensitive to changes in yields, and that the failure of econometric analysis to document that sensitivity comes from flaws in data, econometric procedure, or both. Others have convinced themselves of the same position on theoretical grounds.

Consider the following simplified example, where there is no uncertainty, the consumer has cash assets A_t, so that looking ahead T periods, there is a budget constraint

$$\sum_{i=1}^{T}(1+r)^{-i}c_{t+i} = W_t \equiv A_t + \sum_{i=1}^{T}(1+r)^{-i}y_{t+i}. \tag{2.5}$$

Suppose that lifetime resources W_t are allocated equally over the T periods in the sense that the discounted present value of consumption from each period $t+i$, $(1+r)^{-i}c_{t+i}$ gets a fraction $1/T$ of the total; since $(1+r)^{-i}$ is the 'price' of consumption in period $t+i$, such an allocation can be thought of as equal budget shares for each period. The discount factor (and thus the price) is unity in period t, so that consumption in period t is given by

$$c_t = \frac{1}{T}W_t. \tag{2.6}$$

I have deliberately derived (6) as a 'reasonable' spending rule, without reference to preferences, but it is easy to check that it is the optimal policy if preferences are isoelastic, (1.11), the rate of time-preference is zero, and the coefficient of relative risk aversion is unity; this is the log utility or Cobb–Douglas case. Equations (5) and (6) imply that consumption will fall and saving rise in response to an increase in interest rates. With initial cash assets A_t and the stream of labor incomes held constant, the discounted present value of the latter must fall as the interest rate rises, and thus so will consumption. Although the allocation of wealth across periods in this example is clearly special, the fact that a higher interest rate decreases the present value of wealth is not, and this 'human-wealth' effect will generally act so as to cut consumption. Indeed, it would seem to be a powerful general mechanism through which an increase in interest rates will increase saving at the expense of consumption.

Even so, the example is misleading as a general result; Cobb–Douglas preferences imply an intertemporal elasticity of unity which is large enough to ensure that substitution effects outweigh income effects, and which guarantees the result. The same budget constraint, together with a preference for equal consumption, generates a different outcome. Suppose that preferences are Leontief, with utility equal to the minimum consumption level in the life cycle. Such preferences, while admittedly extreme, have an intertemporal elasticity of substitution of zero, and ensure that consumption will be equal in all periods. Setting c_t in (5) to a constant, letting T tend to infinity,

$$c_t = \frac{r}{r+1}W_t = \frac{r}{r+1}\left(A_t + \frac{1+r}{r-g}y_t\right), \tag{2.7}$$

where the last equality is calculated for the case where labor income will grow at a constant rate $g<r$ from y_t. In this model, if assets are positive, consumption responds *positively* to the interest rate when g is less than or equal to zero, though the effect will change sign as g increases and the human-wealth effect becomes large. When growth is low or negative, consumers will start by saving, so that higher interest rates will make them better off and increase their consumption. With growth positive, consumers start off as borrowers, and higher interest rates decrease consumption.

These simple examples show that the effect of interest rates on consumption (and saving) will be large only when consumption plans call for large positive or negative asset positions at some point in life. But we have already seen in the previous section that much of the evidence suggests that consumption and income track one another fairly closely over the life cycle, so that few consumers ever accumulate many assets or liabilities. In such a world, the effect of changes in interest rates on saving rates cannot be large. One must therefore be skeptical of simple theoretical examples that predict a large response of saving to interest rates, particularly when the examples are based on Cobb–Douglas preferences, or on plausible but undocumented assumptions about the time-paths of future labor incomes. Skepticism should also be shown towards the results from computable general equilibrium models that adopt Cobb–Douglas preferences. In such models, 'findings' of high interest rate effects, or of major distortions associated with the taxation of capital income, are not findings at all, but assumptions, and should be treated as such.

Note finally that all of this theoretical discussion applies only to the case of a single agent facing a parametric real interest rate, and cannot be directly extended to the aggregate economy, partly because of aggregation difficulties, but also because, at the aggregate, the interest rate cannot be treated as an exogenous variable. I shall return to these questions below.

Interest rates and intertemporal substitution

Although the theory is ambiguous in its predictions about the *total* effect of interest rates on saving, it is much clearer in its prediction that the consumption path over the life cycle should be tailored to take advantage of expected real interest rates. If the real interest rate between t and $t+1$ is abnormally high, and if the rate has been foreseen, so that the whole life-cycle path has already been adjusted to take account of whatever income effects there might be, then there is an additional incentive to postpone consumption in t in favor of $t+1$. These effects take a particularly simple form when preferences are additive, there is a constant rate of time-preference, and the felicity functions are isoelastic, so that the intertemporal optimization condition takes the form, cf. (1.50),

$$c_t^{-\rho} = E_t\left(\frac{1+r_{t+1}}{1+\delta}c_{t+1}^{-\rho}\right). \tag{2.8}$$

As we shall see, it is possible to use (8) as an estimating equation, but it is nevertheless useful to rewrite it in other forms. In particular, if there were no uncertainty we could remove the expectation operator and take logarithms, so that

$$\Delta \ln c_{t+1} = \rho^{-1}(r_{t+1} - \delta) \tag{2.9}$$

provided r_{t+1} and δ are small enough to justify the approximation. Equation (9) shows the evolution of *planned* consumption in response to *anticipated* real interest rates, with the elasticity of intertemporal substitution equal to the reciprocal of the coefficient of relative risk-aversion ρ.

Accommodating uncertainty complicates (9) only slightly. Making the same approximation, equation (8) can be rewritten in the form

$$E_t \exp\left[-\rho\left(\Delta \ln c_{t+1} - \rho^{-1}(r_{t+1} - \delta)\right)\right] = 1. \tag{2.10}$$

If we assume that $\ln c_{t+1}$ and r_{t+1} are joint normally distributed, an assumption that would require appropriate distributional restrictions on the exogenous processes, then we can take the expectation explicitly and obtain a recognizable generalization of (9),

$$E_t \Delta \ln c_{t+1} = \rho^{-1}(E_t r_{t+1} - \delta) + \frac{1}{2}\rho\,\omega_t^2. \tag{2.11}$$

where ω_t^2 is the time t variance

$$\omega_t^2 = \mathrm{var}_t(\Delta \ln c_{t+1} - \rho^{-1}r_{t+1}). \tag{2.12}$$

According to (11) and (12), the rate of growth of consumption responds to the *expected* real rate of return according to the elasticity of substitution, much as in the certainty version (9), but there is an additional component of consumption growth that is larger the larger is risk-aversion (the smaller is the elasticity of substitution) and the larger is uncertainty as measured by ω_t^2. This last term is the contribution of the precautionary motive, postponing consumption in the face of uncertainty, and thus increasing its rate of growth.

Representative agents and intertemporal substitution

Considerable effort has been devoted in recent years to testing these equations against the aggregate data on consumption and various real rates, presumably, but not always explicitly, on the supposition that consumers live for ever, that all consumers hold positive or negative quantities of the asset whose yield is being used, and that the distribution of consumption in the cross-section is sufficiently stable to allow aggregation through the isoelastic marginal felicity functions (see Chapter 1.4 above.) The flavor of the results can be seen from a few simple calculations using the data from the Blinder and Deaton study discussed in the previous section. All data are for the US, are quarterly, and run from the third quarter of 1953 to the last quarter of 1984. The consumption figure is per capita and differs from the official National Income and Product Accounts estimate of consumption of non-durables and services in a number of ways, the most important of which is in its treatment of clothing and shoes as durable goods. The selection of a real interest rate is more problematic. We need the yield on an asset that is widely held, preferably by everyone who contributes to aggregate consumption. Although treasury bills are not widely held, their rates or those on similar assets are closely linked to those on the assets and liabilities that are more widely held by households. It is also necessary to allow for the effects of income tax. Taxes fall on *nominal* interest payments, so that the real return must be calculated by subtracting the inflation rate from the net-of-tax nominal rate, not by subtracting taxes from the real pre-tax rate. During periods of high inflation, such as the early 1970s, the correct procedure yields *negative* rates, even when the real pre-tax rate is positive. Of course, tax rates are not the same for all individuals, and Blinder and Deaton calculate the after-tax rate from the treasury bill rate by subtracting the tax rate implied by comparing yields of tax-free and non-tax-free AAA bonds. The real rate is computed by deducting from this nominal rate the rate of growth of the implicit price deflator of consumers' expenditure.

Even a cursory examination reveals difficulties in reconciling the data with equation (11). Ignore for the moment the term involving the variance ω_t^2, and compare unconditional expectations of the equation with sample means. Consumption growth was typically positive, and averaged (almost exactly) 0.5% per quarter over the period. The average real rate, by contrast, was *negative*, −0.06% per quarter over the period from the second quarter of 1953 to the fourth quarter of 1984. To reconcile these facts with (11), either the rate of time-preference must be *negative*, which is a far from the standard interpretation, or the intertemporal elasticity of substitution must be negative, which would violate concavity of the felicity functions and make nonsense of the model. Of course, the last term in (11) must be positive, and perhaps the precautionary motive is sufficient to predict actual consumption growth for the representative agent, see for example Caballero (1990b, 1991).

Even so, it is difficult to make the variance in (12) large enough, at least within the framework of a representative agent whose consumption is average aggregate consumption. The variance of the rate of growth of average consumption is 2.3×10^{-5}, that of the real rate is 2.8×10^{-5}, and the covariance is 0.5×10^{-5}. These figures can be used to calculate values of ω_t^2 for various possible values of the risk-aversion parameter ρ. However, unless we take *very* large values of ρ, the last term in (11) will not be large enough to explain the discrepancy between average consumption growth and negative real returns. For example, even when $\rho = 20$, which most people would consider absurd, the contribution of the precautionary motive to consumption growth is only 0.023% per quarter. The model would fit the facts better if, instead of working with the variance of average consumption, we worked with the average of the variances of individual consumption levels. In a world with idiosyncratic variation, individual consumption streams will be much less smooth than their mean, and the 'representative' consumption variance is presumably much larger than the variance of average consumption. Such an approach can be justified by explicitly aggregating (11) over different households, and holds out some hope for a model with precautionary saving, at least if aggregation is taken seriously. Of course, such an argument provides no support for a representative agent, whose consumption (and therefore consumption variance) corresponds to the macroeconomic aggregates.

There a number of other ways of checking the validity of the representative agent version of (11). More formal econometric analysis by Hansen and Singleton (1982) works directly with the Euler equation (8) and so avoids the approximation and distributional assumptions embodied in (11). To see how their method works, and how it relates to the above discussion, define the quantity z_{t+1} by

$$z_{t+1} = \frac{1+r_{t+1}}{1+\delta}c_{t+1}^{-\rho} - c_t^{-\rho}. \qquad (2.13)$$

According to the theory, any variable dated t or earlier, w_{tj}, say, that can be presumed to be in the representative agent's information set, must be orthogonal to z_{t+1}, so that, matching theoretical to sample analog, we should expect that

$$v_j = \frac{1}{T}\sum_{t=1}^{T} w_{tj}z_{t+1} = 0 \qquad (2.14)$$

for $j = 1, \ldots, J$, the total number of potential such instruments. Provided $J \geq 2$, and the z's are either taken to be stationary or transformed to be so, the two parameters ρ and δ can be estimated by minimizing some suitable quadratic form $v'\Omega v$, where Ω is a positive definite matrix. If in addition, we select $\Omega = [E(vv')]^{-1}$ or at least its sample analog, and if the orthogonality hypotheses are correct, the minimand will have an asymptotic χ^2 distribution with degrees of freedom equal to the number of over-identifying restrictions, J-2, and this can be used as a statistic to test the adequacy of the hypothesis.

Hansen and Singleton, again using data on consumption of non-durables and services, and using both treasury bill rates and the return on New York stock exchange stocks, find that the model must be rejected. As in the results given above, several of their models estimate negative values for the parameter ρ, and the values of their over-identification test statistics are frequently too large. One legitimate instrument for the Hansen–Singleton procedure is a constant, since its value is certainly known one period ahead. Hence one of the equations that is being used to estimate the parameters, and tested by the over-identification tests, is that the mean of z_{t+1} is zero, so that, substituting and taking a Taylor expansion, we require

$$T^{-1}\sum \rho\, c_{t+1}^{-\rho}\left(\rho^{-1}(r_{t+1}-\delta) - \Delta \ln c_{t+1} - \frac{(\rho+1)}{2}(\Delta \ln c_{t+1})^2 \right) = 0. \quad (2.15)$$

Satisfying (15) faces essentially the same difficulties as those generated by matching (11) to the data. The rate of growth of consumption has been too large relative to observed real interest rates, and its variance is too small;

whether we make informal comparisons of means, or construct formal econometric tests, the results are the same.

Another way of approaching the issue is to regress the rate of growth of consumption on expected real interest rates; this addresses the single issue of the correlation between consumption growth and real interest rates, leaving aside the question of whether the *mean* rate of growth of consumption can be matched to the right-hand side of (11). Campbell and Mankiw (1989) use US quarterly NIPA data on consumption from the first quarter of 1953 to the last quarter of 1986 together with real treasury bill rates to compute an OLS regression with a coefficient of 0.276 and standard error of 0.079; a similar result can be obtained for the Blinder and Deaton data, but that result is not robust to the inclusion of other variables in the regression. Campbell and Mankiw move from actual to expected real interest rates by instrumenting the regression using (four or six) lagged real interest rates, but the coefficient is hardly altered, although the standard error is raised by some 50%. However, in both these cases over-identification tests reject the assumption that lagged interest rates influence the rate of growth of consumption only through their role in predicting the contemporaneous expected rate. Hall (1988) uses long-run annual data, also for the US, and is careful to deal with the problems that occur from using data that are averaged over periods that may be longer than the decision period of a representative agent (see Chapter 3.2 below for further discussion.) He also finds little relation between the rate of growth of consumption and expected real rates. However, while Hall concludes from his evidence that the elasticity of substitution is small or even zero, Campbell and Mankiw adopt a position more akin to my own; that there is something seriously amiss with the model, sufficiently so that it is quite unsafe to make any inference about intertemporal substitution from representative agent models.

Other difficulties arise with the aggregate version of the Euler equation if we try to use it to explain the pattern of yields on different assets. Since there is a single representative agent, he or she can be safely presumed to hold all assets, so that (8) will hold for any two assets, i and j say. Hence, by subtraction

$$E_t\left\{(r_{it+1} - r_{jt+1})(1 + \Delta \ln c_{t+1})^{-\rho}\right\} = 0 \qquad (2.16)$$

so that, provided $\Delta \ln c_{t+1}$ is sufficiently small to allow the approximation, rearrangement gives

$$E_t r_{it+1} - E_t r_{jt+1} = \frac{\rho \, cov\left((r_{it+1} - r_{jt+1})\Delta \ln c_{t+1}\right)}{1 - \rho \, E_t \Delta \ln c_{t+1}}. \tag{2.17}$$

The problems with matching (17) to the data are similar to those with explaining the average rate of growth of consumption. For some pairs of assets, most notably common stocks and treasury bills, the difference in expected yields is large, historically some 6% real, whereas, given reasonable levels of the risk-aversion parameter, the expression on the right-hand side is small because consumption is smooth. This is the equity premium puzzle of Mehra and Prescott (1985), elaborated and extended in recent work by Hansen and Jagannathan (1991): given that consumption is not very variable, so that the living standard of the representative agent is at no great risk, why should he or she demand a large premium to hold risky assets? Once again, either risk-aversion is *very* large, or there is something wrong with the theory.

Some of these puzzles can potentially be removed by changing the specifications of preferences. If expected utility theory is abandoned, it is possible to maintain a form of intertemporal separability in which the intertemporal elasticity of substitution and the coefficient of relative risk-aversion are uncoupled—see in particular Epstein and Zin (1989). This allows us to choose a low substitution elasticity without committing ourselves to high risk-aversion, and such models have been implemented by Attanasio and Weber (1989) for British data and by Epstein and Zin (1991) for the US. The equity premium puzzle becomes somewhat less of a puzzle if preferences are modified to allow habit formation—see Constantinides (1990). For example, under the model of (1.53) where current felicity depends on $c_t - \gamma c_{t-1}$ rather than on c_t, the covariance in (17) involves not the rate of growth of consumption but the rate of growth of $c_t - \gamma c_{t-1}$, use equation (1.60) in place of (8). If habits are strong, this quantity could be very variable and very risky. The consumer obtains benefit not from all of consumption, but only from the excess once habits have been fed; habits, like a wife and children, provide hostages to fortune.

Even so, difficulties remain. Habits help increase the variability of what might be termed 'effective consumption,' but they do not help to increase the correlation between its rate of growth and real interest rates—see again Hansen and Jagannathan (1991). Other specifications can be considered, and the recent finance literature has devoted a good deal of attention to the explanation of asset returns along the lines of (17), but with preferences modified to allow for habits, or for leisure, or for both. This work is reviewed in Singleton (1990), who concludes, in accord with the evidence presented here:

'The results indicate that comovements in consumptions and various asset returns are not well described by a wide variety of representative agent models of asset price determination. There are several dimensions along which the models fit poorly. First, the average consumption growth rates were too large relative to average real asset returns during the postwar period in the US to be consistent with these theories. In addition, the serial correlations of the disturbances do not match those implied by the models. Because of the relatively small volatility of aggregate consumptions, the disturbances inherit the autocorrelation properties of the returns in the econometric equations.' (p. 622.)

Intertemporal substitution and aggregation

The main puzzle is not why these representative agent models do not account for the evidence, but why anyone ever thought that they might, given the absurdity of the aggregation assumptions that they require. While not all of the data can necessarily be reconciled with the microeconomic theory, many of the puzzles evaporate once the representative agent is discarded.

First, the fact that aggregate consumption is growing is surely no puzzle in an economy in which productivity is growing, or in which, as in the US over the last twenty years, labor force participation has been growing without a great deal of productivity growth. Even if the life-cycle model is true, and if individuals choose to have flat consumption profiles, aggregate consumption will grow from year to year because the young generation being 'born' has higher lifetime resources than the old generation that has just died. The difference between the two generations is just sufficient to ensure that consumption grows at the rate of productivity growth. While the rate of growth of individual consumption may (or may not) be determined by the difference between the rate of interest and the rate of time-preference, the supposition that *aggregate* consumption should grow over time because the real interest rate is greater than the rate of time-preference of a representative agent is surely something that does not deserve a moment's consideration. The real puzzle is that it should be treated in the literature as a serious hypothesis, worthy of the immense theoretical and empirical effort that it has received.

Second, the relationship between the rate of growth of consumption and the real rate of interest in a properly aggregated economy is as theoretically problematic as are the empirical results. Again, it is possible to generate almost any result under more or less plausible assumptions, and much depends on how the real interest rate is determined in the model. A very simple model, without any pretence to realism, illustrates the sort of things that can happen. Consider a simple economy with two overlapping generations. At any given time, there are two cohorts, young and old, who earn y while young, but consume in both periods. There is an international capital market with a fixed real rate of interest that is unaffected by anything that happens in the economy. There is no uncertainty and consumers have isoelastic preferences. Hence, if c_1 and c_2 are the consumption levels of the young and old respectively, we have

$$c_2 = \left(\frac{1+r}{1+\delta}\right)^{1/\rho} c_1 = \theta c_1, \tag{2.18}$$

with θ defined by the second equality. Aggregate consumption is the sum of the consumption of the young and the old, so that given (18) and the fact that the discounted present value of c_1 and c_2 is income y, we have

$$C = c_1 + c_2 = \frac{(1+r)(1+\theta)}{1+r+\theta} y. \tag{2.19}$$

Aggregate consumption is constant over time, because there is no productivity growth, although each generation's consumption changes from youth to old age if r is not equal to δ. Aggregate consumption is greater than aggregate labor income y, the difference being the interest (from abroad) on the retirement savings of the younger generation $y - c_1$. The country as a whole is a net lender on the international capital market,

What happens if the interest rate increases? Since θ is increasing in r, (19) implies that, once the new rate has been established, aggregate consumption will be higher, but once again constant. The behavior of consumption over the transition depends on whether the new interest rate applies to old saving. Suppose that it does, so that members of the older generation receive a windfall gain in their retirement, while the younger generation base their saving on the new, higher rate. Consumption in the transition is unambiguously higher than before the interest rate increase, and will be higher or lower than its the new equilibrium depending on whether ρ is greater or less than unity. Although there is temporary growth of consumption in response to the increase in the interest rate, this is no sort of victory for the theory of the representative agent. The elasticity of aggregate consumption with respect to the interest rate bears no simple relationship to the elasticity of substitution for the individual agents. Nor does the microeconomic relationship between the rate of growth of consumption and the level of the interest rate carry through to the aggregate data. Indeed, when the intertemporal elasticity of substitution is less than one, so that consumption overshoots in the transition, the response to the new higher interest rate is positive growth, followed by negative growth, followed by constancy.

This example can readily be modified to produce other results. Consumption responds positively to the interest rate because the country is a net lender. We could imagine an economy in which retirement precedes work, or with a good deal more realism, one in which there are three generations, the young, who borrow to finance consumption and child-rearing, the middle aged, who repay debts and accumulate for retirement, and the retired, who consume but do not work. Depending on the relative sizes of the effects, as in the life-cycle model discussed in Section 2.1 above, increased interest rates can permanently decrease consumption, not increase it. Further complications can (and should) be introduced by making the real interest rate endogenous in a properly specified growth model, but it is clear from the well-known complexities of overlapping-generations models, that along that route, there is no hope of mimicking the results by the behavior of an optimizing representative agent. Except under patently false assumptions, infinite life, or dynastic households that plan ahead for an infinite future, economic theory does not predict any simple relationship between consumption growth and the real rate of interest, so there can hardly be said to be any puzzle when the aggregate data show no such relationship. There is certainly no contradiction here between the theory and the data.

In a remarkable paper, Attanasio and Weber (1991) have looked at the individual data, and used their results to assess the importance of the aggregation issue for the difference between the microeconomic and macroeconomic estimates. Attanasio and Weber use the micro data from the British Family Expenditure Survey for the seventeen separate survey years 1970–86. They use the methodology introduced in Browning, Deaton, and Irish (1985) and Deaton (1985) to follow the cohort born between 1930 and 1940 through their randomly selected representatives in each of the seventeen surveys. Given any variable, consumption, the logarithm of consumption, or household size, a cohort mean is constructed for each of the sixty-eight quarters from 1970 to 1986. Since the cohort is aged from 30 to 40 at the beginning of the sample, and from 48 to 58 at the end, it should not have lost too many members to death or retirement. The resulting time-series is correctly aggregated; with the micro data, it is as straightforward (for example) to compute the mean of a logarithm as it is to compute the logarithm of the mean. It is also possible to aggregate 'incorrectly,' by taking the simple average of the whole survey, a time-series that itself provides a useful standard of comparison with the aggregates from the National Accounts. There is also a convenient and appropriate interest rate in Britain; deposits in building societies (savings and loan associations) are widely held, and the interest is untaxed for the vast majority of depositors.

Using the cohort 'correctly aggregated' means, the regression of consumption growth on the real interest rate, controlling for education, work status, numbers of adults, and numbers of children, yields a coefficient of 0.735 with a standard error of 0.236, a coefficient that corresponds to ρ^{-1} in equation (11) above. The expected rate of growth of income in the same regression has a coefficient that is not significantly different from zero. The aggregate data from the national income accounts, by contrast, yield an estimate for ρ^{-1} of 0.354 (0.131), which is closer to the figure of 0.265 (0.222) estimated from the averages of all of the survey data. In both these regressions, expected income growth enters with a significant and positive coefficient, as does the aggregate rate of productivity growth. Some of the difference can be explained by the effects of non-linearities in aggregation; the consumption series for both the averaged survey data and the national accounts are differences of the logarithms of averages rather than differences of the averages of logarithms. For the national accounts data, there is no remedy, but the survey averages can be recalculated to give an estimate of ρ^{-1} of 0.482 (0.142), which moves some way towards the estimate from the correctly aggregated cohort data. These results are clearly consistent with the belief that aggregation matters, that aggregate productivity growth should affect aggregate but not individual consumption growth, and that intertemporal elasticities of substitution estimated from representative agent models do not reveal actual intertemporal responses.

One of the problems in obtaining convincing microeconomic evidence on intertemporal substitution is that, although the samples may contain large numbers of households, the time-period of the analysis is typically relatively short, so that the range of variation of real interest rates is limited. Furthermore, rates only vary across periods and not across households, so that their effects cannot be distinguished from period dummies, which might be desirable on other grounds. One way round this problem would be to find data where there is regional variation in interest rates, or in rates of inflation, or possibly to use the fact that different individuals have different marginal tax rates, and, in principle, different inflation rates according to their specific consumption patterns, to construct individualized real rates for each household in the sample. The microeconomic data also tend to highlight the absurdity of assuming that everyone in the sample holds all of the assets in the economy. In the US, about a fifth of the consumption in the Consumer Expenditure Survey is accounted for by households who not only possess neither bonds nor equities, but who own no financial assets whatever, not even a saving or checking account. Indeed, Mankiw and Zeldes (1991) have used the 1984 data from the Panel Study of Income Dynamics to estimate that more than two-thirds of food consumption is accounted for by households that own no stock, and that at least some of the equity premium puzzle can be resolved if we look at the consumption of stockholders rather than the consumption of everyone.

A great deal of the microeconomic research remains to be done. There is no ideal data set for this work in the US: the PSID collects data only on food expenditures, a small (17%) and declining share of consumption in the US, and the Consumer Expenditure Survey, which runs on an annual basis only from 1980, is not a panel, and its design, which was optimized with a view to generating weights for the Consumer Price Index, makes it difficult to use for econometric analysis. The British Family Expenditure Survey data are better, but again it is not possible to track individual households over time. There are also substantial measurement errors, particularly in income, in these and other surveys, so that their econometric analysis is rarely straightforward. Even so, it seems unlikely that the microeconomic data will ever provide overwhelming support for simple models in which the evolution of consumption is determined only by the pattern of real interest rates. Section 2.1 documented some of the evidence for the tracking of income by consumption in the survey data. If this is indicative of a failure of the basic life-cycle model, then the role of interest rates, along with that of income, has to be rethought. If consumption is dissociated from income as the life-cycle model requires, then it is free to be determined by the pattern of tastes and real interest rates. But if there is some other factor that does not allow consumption to get too far from income or for too long, then the prima facie supposition must be that interest rates are not very important.

CHAPTER 3

Consumption and Permanent Income

Friedman's (1957) permanent income theory of consumption, like Modigliani and Brumberg's (1954, 1979) life-cycle hypothesis, is one of the lasting contributions of the 'new' consumption function literature of the 1950s. In the latter, consumption is determined by the value of lifetime resources; in the former, it is determined by permanent income, typically defined as average or expected income. If permanent income is taken to be the annuity value of lifetime resources, the two theories are very close, but Friedman did not commit himself to this interpretation. There are also important differences of emphasis between the two models. The permanent income theory has always been more concerned with the dynamic behavior of consumption, particularly over the short term and in relation to income, and has concerned itself little with the relationship between age, saving, and the creation of wealth. Much of the work that is reported in this chapter and the next comes from macroeconomists, whose primary concern has been how consumption responds to changes in income, and the role that consumption plays in transmitting fluctuations through the economy.

Whatever the definition of permanent income, we can immediately use the hypothesis to explain a number of stylized facts about consumption, and it is these that figure in the textbook treatments of consumption. First, since permanent income depends, not just on income in one year, but on income over a number of years, perhaps all of life, it is unlikely to fluctuate much in response to short-term fluctuations in income. Permanent income will be *smoother* than measured or current income, so that the theory is consistent with the observation that consumption is smoother than income. Second, over spans of many years permanent income will look much like measured income, so that, in the long run, consumption will be proportional to income.

Figure 3.1 illustrates the relative smoothness of consumption and income using the Blinder–Deaton data on consumption and labor income; much the same picture could be drawn using total income. Both consumption and labor income trend upward over time, but income fluctuates more about its trend than does consumption. The saving ratio is pro-cyclical, rising in the boom, and falling in the slump, so that consumption is to some extent protected against business-cycle fluctuations in income. In 1972 dollars, the standard deviation of consumption changes in Figure 3.1 is $12 per capita, while that of income at $28 is more than twice as much.

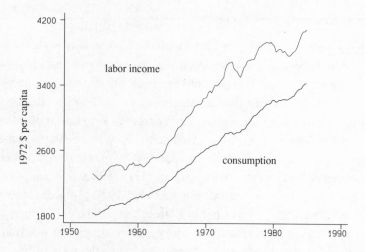

Figure 3.1: Consumption and labor income: US, 1953, Q2 to 1984, Q4

The long-run constancy of the consumption ratio in the US was a fact that was very much to the fore when the permanent income and life-cycle models were being first discussed. However, it is worth noting Friedman's own conclusion that the historical constancy in the US is the more or less accidental result of offsetting factors. Later research on historical data for other countries has also shown that the United States is not typical in its saving behavior, and that there are pronounced upward trends in the saving ratio with economic growth in several other countries—see in particular Maddison (1992).

The theory also delivers a range of other predictions whose consistency with the data was checked in the early literature. Tax-induced changes in household incomes will only change consumption to the extent that they change permanent incomes, so that some types of fiscal policy are likely to be much less effective than would be supposed from their effects on measured incomes. In the cross-section, the saving ratio should rise with income because the higher the income, the higher the fraction of income that is accounted for by temporary or transitory income, so the lower the ratio of permanent to measured income. The fact that, controlling for income, households headed by blacks have a higher saving ratio than those headed by whites is also consistent with the theory. Blacks' permanent incomes are lower than those of whites so that, if income is the same, the ratio of permanent to measured income is lower, and so is the consumption ratio.

Econometric consumption functions

None of these predictions is inconsistent with the life-cycle hypothesis, nor with other models of consumption, such as Duesenberry's earlier (1949) relative income hypothesis. Indeed, until the mid-1970s, macroeconomists tended not to draw very sharp distinctions between the theories, at least for the purposes of modelling the aggregate time-series on consumption and income. In the time-series work in Friedman's book, permanent income was treated as a weighted average of past levels of measured income, corrected for trend, and this sensible but *ad hoc* device was adopted in much of the subsequent literature. By the mid-1970s, macroeconomic model builders frequently cited either or both of the permanent income and life-cycle models as justification for an aggregate consumption function in which consumption was regressed on current and lagged values of income. Alternatively, and most commonly, consumption was taken to be a function of current income and lagged consumption, with the latter justified in terms of habit formation, slow adjustment, or by noting that such a formulation followed from representing permanent income as a declining geometric lag of income and taking consumption to be proportional to permanent income. Various measures of assets were also frequently included, either to better proxy permanent income, or to capture the effects of liquidity constraints. Given that these models seemed to fit the data well, and since the different theoretical models led to roughly similar estimating equations, there was a more or less satisfactory integration between theory and measurement. Good examples of the consumption function literature of this time can be found by looking at the descriptions of the various macroeconometric models, for example the paper by Suits and Sparks (1965) for the Brookings Quarterly Model in the volume edited by Duesenberry *et al.* (1965). Evans (1969, chs. 2 and 3) gives an unusually careful and thorough discussion of theory and estimation of consumption equations, again with macroeconometric modelling the main focus of the research. The papers by Stone and his co-authors, Stone and Rowe (1962) and Stone (1964, 1966, 1973) provide the equivalent best practice research for Britain, again focusing on the effects of lags of income and consumption, although these studies also consistently found an important role for government controls on credit.

Nevertheless, by the mid-1970s, serious problems were beginning to appear. Some of these were specific to the consumption function, but

others were general to macroeconomic practice. As often, empirical problems were to the fore, and just as the coexistence of inflation and unemployment spelt trouble for the neo-classical Keynesian synthesis of the day,
so too did the underprediction of consumption by the standard consumption
functions that had been regarded as the best-fitting and least troublesome
of all macroeconomic equations. One (entirely plausible) explanation was
poor empirical technique. By the mid-1970s, neither the estimation of consumption functions nor the building of large-scale Keynesian models was
a frontier activity in the profession, and the econometric problems that with
hindsight are evident were frequently ignored in the day-to-day production
of forecasts and policy analysis. It is a sobering undertaking to look back
at many of the macroeconomic models of the time, and note the (now) obvious time-series problems: spurious correlations between integrated regressors, high coefficients of determination coupled with low Durbin–Watson
statistics, and an almost complete lack of diagnostic testing.

The paper by Davidson *et al.* (1978) is a response to this situation. The
authors estimate a consumption function for the UK that essentially retains
the theoretical (or by today's standards *a*theoretical) foundations of the
consumption functions of the time, but repairs the econometric technique,
emphasizing the prevention of the sort of predictive failure that occurred in
the earlier models. This work has been updated at various intervals—Hendry and von Ungern-Sternberg (1981), Davidson and Hendry (1981)—and
although the models have been respecified with time, even the earlier
versions would not have suffered the failures of the popular models of the
1970s. Even so, the *economic* foundations of recent versions of this model,
in Muellbauer and Murphy (1990), or in the re-evaluation by Hendry,
Muellbauer, and Murphy (1990), are much more closely related to the
treatment in, say, Evans (1969), than to any of the recent work in the US.
In particular, the research agenda underlying this work remains the derivation of a stable predictive equation for use in macroeconometric modelling.
It is much less concerned with discovering a theoretically coherent model
of household behavior that is consistent with the macroeconomic and
microeconomic data.

The treatment of expectations

It was a different response to the macroeconomic problems of the 1970s
that dominated research on consumption functions in the US, and to a

considerable extent elsewhere. Lucas's (1976) famous critique used the consumption function as one of its examples, insisting that there was no reason to expect the stable lag structure between consumption and income that was routinely assumed in the literature. Consumption depends on expected future incomes, and the relationship between past and expected future incomes is not properly treated as an invariant feature of the economic environment, but will change whenever changes in policy or other events cause rational agents to change the way in which past incomes affect forecasts of future incomes. Without denying the importance of the critique for the conduct of economic policy, which was its main target, it is not clear why this particular issue should be viewed as any more pressing than the multitude of other possible specification errors in consumption functions. Indeed, as far as I am aware, the issue of changes in expectation formation has not been seriously addressed in subsequent consumption research. Nevertheless, Lucas's article permanently redirected attention towards the role of expectations in the determination of consumption. In particular, and along with much of the rest of macroeconomic research, there grew up a rational expectations research agenda in consumption. Consumption depends on expectations about income, so that it is not possible to model consumption without modelling income; indeed, if income is modelled simultaneously with consumption, the joint implications should be a rich source of restrictions for testing and for enhancing econometric efficiency. Most of this chapter is about the unfolding of this agenda.

3.1 A formal version of the permanent income hypothesis

This first section is largely preparatory, and lays the theoretical groundwork for discussing the empirical evidence. The permanent income hypothesis is taken to be the proposition that consumption is the annuity value of current financial and human wealth, a proposition that turns out to be a special case of the general theory of intertemporal choice as developed in Chapter 1. I first explore the relationship with the theory, and particularly the link between the permanent income hypothesis and the proposition that consumption should follow a martingale, (1.47) or (1.48). I then move on to the crucial question of how to model expectations and derive formulas for the change in permanent income in the case where labor income follows a linear autoregressive moving-average stochastic process. These formulas are what turns the theory into a set of propositions that can be confronted with the data.

Consumption and permanent income

There are many possible definitions of permanent income, and if we are to be precise, one must be selected. I work with a definition whereby permanent income is the annuity value of current financial and human wealth, and in which consumption is set equal to permanent income. Although there are passages in the book where Friedman explicitly dissociates himself from this interpretation, in later work, Friedman (1963), he is much more sympathetic, although he suggests that consumers may discount the future at rates that are a good deal higher than normal market rates. The annuity model also has the immense advantage of being consistent with the theory of Chapter 1, albeit under particular assumptions, so that this version of the permanent income theory can be brought within the general scope of the theory of intertemporal choice rather than being treated as a distinct theory. In particular, recall from Chapter 1 that if preferences are intertemporally separable, if felicity functions are quadratic, and there is a constant real interest rate r equal to the rate of time-preference δ, then consumption follows a martingale. Recalling (1.47), and applying the formula forward through time, we have for all t and k,

$$E_t c_{t+k} = c_t. \tag{3.1}$$

For a consumer who plans to die with no assets, and who will spend all assets and income in the last period of life, the realized consumption plan from t to T will satisfy, see (1.6):

$$\sum_{k=0}^{T-t} (1+r)^{-k} c_{t+k} = A_t + \sum_{k=0}^{T-t} (1+r)^{-k} y_{t+k}, \tag{3.2}$$

where, as before A_t is financial assets, y_t is labor income in period t, and T is the date of death. If T is infinite, the terminal zero-asset condition is replaced by the requirement that as t tends to infinity, the limit of $(1+r)^{-t}A_t$ be zero, a condition sometimes referred to as the 'no Ponzi game' condition (see e.g. Blanchard and Fischer 1989: p. 49).

Take expectations of (2) conditional on information available at time t, use the result of (1) that expected consumption is constant, and let T go to infinity to give

$$c_t = \frac{r}{1+r} A_t + \frac{r}{1+r} \sum_{k=0}^{\infty} (1+r)^{-k} E_t y_{t+k}. \qquad (3.3)$$

If T were taken to be finite, the annuity factors $r(1+r)^{-1}$ would have to be replaced by $r[(1+r) - (1+r)^{-T}]^{-1}$, but for the dynamic issues with which the permanent income model is mostly concerned, the distinction is not usually important, and the algebra of the infinite horizon model is much simpler. Of course, we still must take account of finite lives in thinking about aggregation, something to which I shall return in Chapter 5.3. Note too that the model as presented makes no requirement that consumption be non-negative. The ultimate source of the difficulty here is that quadratic felicity imposes no penalty for zero or negative consumption, and although one can imagine imposing the restriction on the optimization, the tractability of the model would be lost. However, by ignoring the restriction, we must beware of the possibility that the model can produce absurd predictions, some of which we shall encounter again in Chapter 6.1 below.

Equation (3) is what I shall take to be the permanent income hypothesis. This usage differs from some of the literature, which treats permanent income and life-cycle models as essentially equivalent, and applies the permanent income hypothesis label to any model derived from the theory of intertemporal choice. The assumptions that are required for (this version of) the permanent income hypothesis (infinite life, quadratic preferences, and a constant real interest rate equal to the rate of time-preference), are neither trivial nor plausible. However, there is also a sense in which the equation has a life of its own, a life that is independent of the general theory of choice. One might simply assert, at least as a working hypothesis, that consumption is the annuity value of human and non-human wealth. This is very much in the spirit of Friedman's original work, even though the definition of permanent income is not his. It is also very close to Modigliani's assertion that people have a preference for constant consumption, since that assumption, together with the budget constraint is what generates (3). Of course such a position requires us either to abandon intertemporal choice theory, or to accept the price of consistency, quadratic felicity, and the rest. Either way, we are ignoring the relationship between consumption growth and asset returns, although, given the discussion in Chapter 2.2, I find it hard to argue that this is a major drawback. What is probably much more important is the neglect of the precautionary motive for saving that is implicit in the permanent income hypothesis. A preference for constant consumption irrespective of future uncertainty is not compatible with a prudent behavior, and it is in this respect that the permanent income model seriously emasculates the basic theory of intertemporal allocation.

The PIH and the martingale property of consumption

The permanent income equation (3) can be used to gain a deeper understanding of the martingale property of consumption (1.47). Rewrite (3) in two different ways. First, use the asset evolution equation to substitute for A_t, so that

$$c_t = r(A_{t-1} + y_{t-1} - c_{t-1}) + \frac{r}{1+r} \sum_{k=0}^{\infty} (1+r)^{-k} E_t y_{t+k}. \tag{3.4}$$

Second, lag (3) one period, multiply through by $1+r$, and rearrange the income terms:

$$(1+r)c_{t-1} = rA_{t-1} + ry_{t-1} + \frac{r}{1+r} \sum_{k=0}^{\infty} (1+r)^{-k} E_{t-1} y_{t-k}. \tag{3.5}$$

Subtraction of (5) from (4) yields:

$$\Delta c_t = \frac{r}{1+r} \sum_{k=0}^{\infty} (1+r)^{-k} (E_t - E_{t-1}) y_{t+k}, \tag{3.6}$$

so that the change in consumption from $t-1$, to t, which is unpredictable at time $t-1$, is straightforwardly related to 'news' about income. New information at t will generally cause the consumer to revise previously held expectations about current and future labor income, so that the discounted present value of these expectations will itself change. This is the change in permanent income that is warranted by the news, and it is this that sets the change in consumption. The right-hand side of (6) is the innovation in the martingale process, but by writing it in terms of labor income, we can use any information that we might have about expected labor income to make inferences about what should happen to consumption.

The unpredictability of aggregate consumption growth was first tested in a seminal paper by Hall (1978). Hall used a representative agent model with isoelastic felicity functions, and derived (1.50), which characterizes the stochastic behavior of the marginal utility of money. Such a model does not lead to (6), but it has the similar prediction that, conditional on lagged consumption, variables lagged $t-1$ or earlier, and in particular lags of income, should not help predict consumption in period t.

It is difficult from today's perspective to recall the contemporary reaction to Hall's results. For twenty years, economists had been routinely estimating regressions of consumption on current and lagged values of income, and everyone understood that the different dynamics of the two series meant that at least some of the lags were important. Of course, Hall's regression differed from any of those previously estimated because current income was excluded; current income is correlated with the innovation to current income $(E_t - E_{t-1})y_t$ and so cannot be included when the orthogonality proposition is being tested. Nevertheless, few economists, including Hall himself, would have predicted his result, that the lagged income terms are not significant. In fact, Hall finally rejected the model, based on a finding that lagged stock-market values predicted consumption change. Even so, the 'news' in Hall's paper was the orthogonality of lagged income to consumption change, confirming the predictions of the permanent income hypothesis, and confounding the prior expectations of most of the profession.

Forming expectations about income

Suppose that we accept, for the moment, that, as predicted by the permanent income hypothesis, changes in aggregate consumption cannot be predicted by lags of income. But this is not the whole story. According to (6), the change in consumption ought to be the amount warranted by innovations in expectations about future labor income. If we know something about the process generating income, we ought to be able to check this prediction too.

One way to predict incomes is to model income as a stochastic process, and in particular a linear process, for which there exists a well-developed theory of estimation, inference, and prediction. Indeed, whatever method consumers actually use to predict their incomes, it is hard to argue that past values of income would not be an important part of the story. We therefore complete the permanent income model by adding to (3) an equation for income. Suppose, for the moment that y_t is a stationary ARMA process with mean μ, so that if z_t is the deviation from the mean, $y_t - \mu$ we write:

$$z_t - \alpha_1 z_{t-1} + \alpha_2 z_{t-2} + \ldots = \varepsilon_t + \beta_1 \varepsilon_{t-1} + \beta_2 \varepsilon_{t-2} + \ldots \qquad (3.7)$$

or, in a more economical notation

$$\alpha(L)z_t = \beta(L)\varepsilon_t, \qquad (3.8)$$

where $\alpha(L)$ and $\beta(L)$ are polynomials in the lag operator L and ε_t is a white-noise (serially uncorrelated) process, typically assumed to be Gaussian. In order that the process be stationary, the roots of the polynomial $\alpha(L)$ must lie outside the unit circle; the same condition on $\beta(L)$ guarantees that the moving average is invertible, so that it can be expressed in autoregressive form, without which the consumer would have no way of calculating the innovation from current and past values of income.

The way in which predictions are generated from these ARMA models is most easily seen if we start with a simple example. Suppose that z_t is an MA(1) process with parameter β, so that

$$(y_t - \mu) = \varepsilon_t + \beta\varepsilon_{t-1}. \qquad (3.9)$$

Since ε_t is white noise, it is the innovation or the 'news' about income in period t and it therefore governs all revisions to previous expectations. But period t's news is the lagged news in period $t+1$, so that good news now means, not only that the current period's income is higher than previously expected, but that next period's income expectations have to be revised too, upwards if β is positive, and downwards if β is negative. Since the moving average only has one lag, there is no reason to revise expectations about incomes further ahead, so that, given (9), we have

$$
\begin{aligned}
(E_t - E_{t-1})y_{t+k} &= \varepsilon_t & \text{if } k = 0 \\
&= \beta\varepsilon_t & \text{if } k = 1 \qquad (3.10) \\
&= 0 & \text{if } k > 1.
\end{aligned}
$$

This result can be substituted into the equation linking consumption changes to income innovations, (6), to give

$$\Delta c_t = \frac{r}{1+r}\left(1 + \frac{\beta}{1+r}\right)\varepsilon_t. \qquad (3.11)$$

From this example, it is straightforward to see what happens for any moving average, including the infinite-order case that is of particular importance since, by the Wold theorem, it can be used to represent a general stationary time-series. The first coefficient, β_1 determines $\beta_1\varepsilon_t$, which is the effect of the current innovation ε_t in period $t+1$, the second gives

$\beta_2 \varepsilon_t$ which is the change in the expectation of period $t+2$, and so on. Hence, if the income process is

$$y_t = \mu + \varepsilon_t + \sum_1^\infty \beta_k \varepsilon_{t-k} \qquad (3.12)$$

the warranted revision to consumption is

$$\Delta c_t = \frac{r}{1+r} \left(1 + \frac{\beta_1}{1+r} + \frac{\beta_2}{(1+r)^2} + \ldots + \right) \varepsilon_t = \frac{r}{1+r} \beta \left(\frac{1}{1+r} \right) \varepsilon_t, \qquad (3.13)$$

where the last term is the lag polynomial that defines the moving-average process, but evaluated at the discount factor $(1+r)^{-1}$. This formula gives us a very simple rule for evaluating consumption changes from the moving-average representation of a time-series; simply discount the moving-average terms, and add.

We can now easily derive the consumption formula when income is a general ARMA process, simply by converting the ARMA to its MA representation. From (8), the MA equivalent for z_t is simply $\alpha^{-1}(L)\beta(L)\varepsilon_t$ so that, if income is generated by (8), the warranted change in consumption is given by

$$\Delta c_t = \frac{r}{1+r} \frac{\beta\left(\dfrac{1}{1+r}\right)}{\alpha\left(\dfrac{1}{1+r}\right)} \varepsilon_t = \frac{r}{1+r} \frac{\sum\limits_0^\infty (1+r)^{-k}\beta_k}{\sum\limits_0^\infty (1+r)^{-k}\alpha_k} \varepsilon_t. \qquad (3.14)$$

where $\beta_0 = \alpha_0 = 1$. In principle then, once an ARMA process for income has been estimated, the change in consumption can be predicted and compared with the outcome.

These formulas show how innovations in labor income translate into changes in permanent income, and thus into changes in consumption. To the extent that the importance of the permanent income hypothesis lies in its prediction that changes in income only affect consumption in so far as they affect permanent income, these are central results, and it is worth developing the intuition behind them. The important point is that the effect of innovations in income on permanent income will be larger the more *persistent* are the effects of innovations in the labor income process. Strong persistence means that shocks in one period do not generate opposing reactions in subsequent periods that tend to cancel them, but have effects that continue or are magnified over time. Positive autocorrelation generates persistence: deviations from the mean in one direction tend to be succeeded by later deviations in the same direction, so that an innovation will have an effect that persists well beyond the period in which it occurs. To take a concrete example, if labor income is a first-order autoregressive process with parameter ρ, with $-1 < \rho < 1$ for stationarity, a unit innovation in income causes permanent income to change by $r(1+r-\rho)^{-1}$ which is monotonically increasing in ρ, and which approaches unity as ρ tends to its upper limit of unity. This last is the case where income follows a random-walk; the best predictor of future income is current income, and innovations are expected to persist for ever. A very different example is where income is a constant plus a moving average process with parameter -1, so that any innovation is reversed in the next period. In this case, the change in consumption is $r^2 (1+r)^{-2}$ which is the annuity value of a one-period interest-free loan. Of course, the autocorrelation or persistence can be 'located' in either the moving-average or the autoregressive part of the representation, but it is persistence that matters, as measured by the present discounted value of the sum of the coefficients in the moving-average representation. I shall return to this definition and to the measurement of persistence in Chapter 4.1.

3.2 The excess sensitivity of consumption

In this section, I look at some of the most important evidence against the proposition that the change in consumption is unpredictable. In particular, I review the work that uses the results of the previous section to test whether consumption responds to income in the way predicted by the permanent income hypothesis. The influential study here is that by Flavin (1981), which is my starting point for exploring the subsequent research.

Flavin's tests for excess sensitivity

The task of using the forecasting formulas and testing their implications was first taken up in an important paper by Flavin (1981). The null hypothesis considered in her paper is the truth of the permanent income hypothesis in the form (6), together with an autoregressive specification for the process governing labor income. Such a specification may be written as the two equations

$$\Delta c_t = \gamma + \theta \varepsilon_t$$
$$\alpha(L) y_t = \varepsilon_t.$$

(3.15)

where I have added a drift or productivity growth term γ to the consumption change equation, and where the parameter θ is the warranted change in consumption. If the model is correct, θ is given by applying (14), noting that the β polynomial in the numerator is simply unity in this case. Flavin works with an eighth-order specification of the lag on her quarterly data, but I shall work with a two-period specification here to keep the algebra simple; nothing substantive is lost by doing so.

The hypothesis with which Flavin works, the 'excess sensitivity' hypothesis, is a substantial generalization of (6), and allows consumption to respond to current and lagged changes in income by more or less than is required by the permanent income theory. The extended model is written in the form

$$\Delta c_t = \gamma + \beta_1 \Delta y_t + \beta_2 \Delta y_{t-1} + \theta \varepsilon_t + u_t$$
$$y_t = \alpha_0 + \alpha_1 y_{t-1} + \alpha_2 y_{t-2} + \varepsilon_t,$$

(3.16)

where β_1 and β_2 are the excess sensitivity parameters. The additional error term u_t is added to represent measurement error in consumption change, as well as the effects of information about permanent income that the consumer may have but that is not captured by the autoregressive specification of income. As we shall see below, there are better ways to incorporate superior information, so think of this term as pure measurement error. Flavin permits it to be correlated with ε_t, the innovation in the income process; as we shall see, this correlation has important consequences for identification of the model.

The interpretation of the β terms, the excess sensitivity parameters, has been subject to some confusion in the subsequent literature. Clearly, if the permanent income hypothesis is true, they should be zero. However, if β is non-zero, say positive, consumption responds to the change in income by more than the change in consumption that is warranted by the innovation in income. Note that this is *not* the same thing as saying that consumption is excessively sensitive to *innovations* in income. According to the excess sensitivity hypothesis, consumption responds even to *predictable* changes in income, changes for which the innovation is zero. Indeed, since the unpredictable component of income is already allowed for in the regressions, the effect that is being captured by the introduction of the actual income changes is the predictable component of income. The measurement of excess sensitivity is the measurement of the extent to which consumption responds to previously predictable changes in income.

Equations (16) form a two-equation simultaneous system in the change in consumption and the level of labor income. The income equation is already in reduced form, and the reduced form for consumption can be derived by substitution from the income equation. The result can be written in the form:

$$\Delta c_t = (\gamma + \beta_1 \alpha_0) + (\beta_2 - \beta_1(1 - \alpha_1))\Delta y_{t-1} - \beta_1(1 - \alpha_1 - \alpha_2)y_{t-2} + u_t + (\beta_1 + \theta)\varepsilon_t$$

$$y_t = \alpha_0 + \alpha_1 \Delta y_{t-1} + (\alpha_2 + \alpha_1) y_{t-2} + \varepsilon_t. \tag{3.17}$$

It is now easy to see that this system is exactly identified. The α parameters are identified from the income equation, and once these are known, the β parameters can be recovered from the consumption equation. Note too that, because u_t and ε_t are allowed to be correlated, the error structure of the system has an unrestricted variance covariance-matrix, so that the parameter θ cannot be recovered. Once the change in consumption is allowed to have a second innovation, whether attributed to measurement error or to superior information, we can no longer recover the response of consumption to the income innovation, nor check whether it conforms to the theoretical predictions. This is unfortunate, since θ is one of the parameters of greatest interest; however, I follow Flavin for the moment, and leave the topic for later discussion.

Equations (17) can still be estimated and checked for excess sensitivity. Indeed, since the system is exactly identified, and since the same right-hand side variables appear in both of the equations, full-information maximum-likelihood estimates is equivalent to ordinary least-squares regressions of each equation separately. But the first equation is the regression of the change in consumption on lags of income, here two, and in Flavin's case eight, so that the test for excess sensitivity is in principle the same as Hall's test for the orthogonality of consumption change to lagged incomes. Flavin, unlike Hall, restricts the coefficient of lagged consumption to be unity by working with the change in consumption, rather than its level, and provided this restriction is correct, as our version of the permanent income hypothesis implies, one might expect Flavin's test to be more efficient.

In practice, equations (17) cannot be estimated as they stand, or at least not without extending the theory as I have presented it. The immediate source of difficulty is that the autoregression for income, as well as the forecasting formulas, assume that income is a stationary process. In fact, as Figure 3.1 shows, labor income has a trend, and it would be absurd to try to model the series as a stationary process. I shall give a good deal of attention to this issue later in the chapter, and we shall see that the formulas can all be extended to handle the non-stationary case. However, Flavin's paper deals with the problem by fitting exponential time-trends to both consumption and income, and replacing consumption and income in the regressions by their residuals. Both the theoretical and econometric legitimacy of such a procedure are open to challenge, and I shall return to both issues later in the chapter.

Flavin uses data on non-durable goods consumption (excluding both durables and services) from the third quarter of 1949 to the first quarter of 1979 and estimates detrended versions of (17) with eight lags of income and eight excess sensitivity parameters in the consumption equation. She finds that twice the log likelihood for the system as a whole falls by 27.02 when the excess sensitivity parameters are excluded. If the permanent income hypothesis were true, this would be a random drawing from a χ^2 distribution with eight degrees of freedom; the probability associated with this is less than 0.5% The estimates for the first two β-coefficients are (with standard errors) 0.355 (0.275) and 0.071 (0.036), and those for the α's are 0.964 (0.092) and 0.069 (0.126). If we use these in equations (17), we see that the contradiction with the theory is most serious for the statistically significant β_2 coefficient, which links the change in consumption positively to the lagged *change* in income. The autoregression for income shows that the change in income is also positively predicted by last period's change in income, so that the excess sensitivity finding can be interpreted as a finding that consumption responds to *predictable* changes in income. Note that these findings are different from Hall's, who found no relationship between consumption and lagged income conditional on lagged consumption. The difference seems to be partly because of the choice of sample period; Hall's sample starts and finishes earlier, and inclusion of the immediate post-war data can have a considerable effect on the estimated income process (see also Nelson 1987). Flavin also includes more lags than Hall, and effectively restricts the coefficient on lagged consumption to be unity by working with the first difference of consumption.

The data from the Blinder and Deaton study can be used to generate findings that are very similar to Flavin's. With consumption and income separately detrended using data from the second quarter of 1953 to the fourth quarter of 1984, and with regressions run from the first quarter of 1954 to the first quarter of 1984, we have for consumption

$$\Delta c_t = 0.004 + 0.147 \Delta y_{t-1} - 0.004 y_{t-2}, \qquad (3.18)$$
$$(0.4) \quad (3.19) \qquad (0.47)$$

while the estimated income equation, rearranged so that Δy_t is the dependent variable is

$$\Delta y_t = 0.025 + 0.417 \Delta y_{t-1} - 0.025 y_{t-2}. \qquad (3.19)$$
$$(1.54) \quad (5.17) \qquad (1.56)$$

The F-statistic for the consumption change equation is 5.36, with an associated p-value under the null of 0.006, so that this and the t-statistic on the lagged income change term show excess sensitivity in much the same way as do Flavin's estimates. In spite of the rearrangement of terms, the income equation is of the same form as Flavin's (subtract lagged y from both sides), although the parameter estimates are somewhat different corresponding to the different sample periods. However, in both cases, the autoregressive parameters add to something very close to unity, so that, even after detrending, the income series is close to being non-stationary. Moreover, (19) shows very clearly how changes in income in one period predict changes in income the next, and (18) shows how those predictable changes affect consumption.

There are many possible reasons for this failure of the permanent income hypothesis, and I shall discuss several of them below. However, the most widely canvassed is that at least some consumers are unable to borrow as much as they would like. To see how this generates excess sensitivity, suppose that such a consumer receives new information that causes an upward revision to expectations about future incomes; the tenure review committee turns in a positive report, or the farmer sees that this year's crops are going to be much better than expected. The permanent income hypothesis calls for an upward revision of consumption now, without waiting for the additional income to materialize, something that the consumer may be able to implement if he or she has the funds to do so. But if cash is short, and if lenders will not advance credit without tangible and realizable collateral, the farmer and the assistant professor must wait until the income increase is actually received. When it is, their consumption will rise, in response to the previously predictable increase in income, and econometricians will observe excess sensitivity.

Excess sensitivity and non-stationary income

One possible explanation for Flavin's results is not that there is anything wrong with the theory, but that the econometric methodology biases the results towards rejection of the hypothesis. In particular, a good deal of attention has been given to Flavin's detrending procedure, and whether, from a purely econometric point of view, it is capable of generating spurious findings of excess sensitivity. The original point was made by Mankiw and Shapiro (1985), although the example given here is tailored more closely to what Flavin actually did.

Suppose that the permanent income hypothesis is true so that (15) is true. Income follows an autoregression, and consumption responds only to innovations in income. Suppose further that income follows the stochastic process:

$$\Delta y_t - \mu_g = \rho \, (\Delta y_{t-1} - \mu_g) + \varepsilon_t, \qquad (3.20)$$

Note that this is very close to the estimated process in (19), which was fitted to the *detrended* data. However, (19) is only just stationary around its trend; the roots of the polynomial $\alpha^{-1}(L)$ are 0.49 and 0.91. In (20), it is the *first difference* of labor income that is stationary, so that labor income itself is 'difference stationary' or integrated of order one. The root of 0.91 in (19) is replaced by a *unit* root, and the trend in income is attributed, partly to the drift term μ_g, and partly to the fact that integrated series, which depend on accumulations of white noise terms, typically exhibit behavior that, at least *ex post*, looks trendlike.

I have yet to discuss the appropriate forecasting rules and consumption formulas when income is non-stationary as in (20). However, suppose for the moment that consumption responds only to the innovation in labor income, so that the full model is (20) together with

$$\Delta c_t = \gamma + \theta \varepsilon_t \qquad (3.21)$$

for some (yet to be derived) quantity θ. An econometrician then runs a Flavin-type regression of the form:

$$\Delta c_t = \beta_0 + \beta_1 \Delta y_{t-1} + \beta_2 y_{t-2} + \beta_3 t + u_t, \qquad (3.22)$$

where t is a time-trend. The time-trend is present in order to mimic the detrending procedure used by Flavin. Although she detrended consumption and income before running the regression, the inclusion of a time-trend in the regression will have exactly the same effect; in general, a regression using detrended variables produces the same results as does a regression with the original variables together with a time-trend. In (21), the change in consumption, by construction, has no time-trend, so detrending can be expected to have no effect. Since the first difference of a time-trend is a constant, the first difference of a linearly detrended series differs only by a constant from the first difference of the original series. Hence, (22) will generate exactly the same coefficients on the lagged change in income and on income lagged twice as would Flavin's procedure had she used linear (as opposed to exponential) detrending.

To see what happens, consider the following Monte Carlo experiment. I used equation (20) to generate artificial labor income series of length 124 (the same as in the actual data) with the first two values set to be the actual income figures in the third and fourth quarters of 1953, using the actual estimates of μ_g and ρ, and with innovations independently and identically distributed as $N(0,\sigma^2)$ with σ set to the estimate of the equation standard error. The estimated equation is

$$\Delta y_t = 8.41 + 0.44 \Delta y_{t-1}; \quad \tilde{\sigma} = 25.3. \tag{3.23}$$
$$\qquad (3.3) \quad (5.4)$$

The change in consumption is set to its actual sample mean (13.1) plus the income innovation multiplied by θ. Although we do not yet know what value θ should be, it clearly makes no difference for these experiments, since θ only scales the consumption series and thus scales the coefficients in the experimental regression; it has no effect on the t-statistics or F-ratios. Hence θ was set to unity. I repeated the experiment 1,000 times with the results given in Table 3.1.

The table reports statistics from estimating equation (22), in particular, the t-statistics for excess sensitivity on each of the income variables, and the test for excess sensitivity as a whole, which is the F-test that both coefficients are jointly zero. Since the null hypothesis is correct, the results show that there is indeed an econometric problem. The overall F-test, which ought to reject 5% of the time, rejects 43% of the time, and the t-statistics on the individual coefficients, although not as far out of line, reject 14% and 21% of the time rather than the correct 5%. Clearly it is possible for the permanent income hypothesis to be true, with parameters

Table 3.1: Monte Carlo results for excess sensitivity tests

$|t(\Delta y_{t-1})|$	reject	$|t(y_{t-1})|$	reject	F	reject
1.04	0.14	1.33	0.21	3.51	0.43

Notes: The model is as defined in the text. Statistics are calculated from 1,000 replications. The first column is the average of the absolute values of the t-statistics on the lagged change in income, and the second is the fraction of times the coefficient would be adjudged to be significantly different from zero at 5%. Columns three and four give the same information for the t-statistics on income lagged twice. Columns five and six give the average F-statistic and rejection frequency for the test that both excess sensitivity parameters are zero.

very like those actually found in the data, and yet for excess sensitivity tests to reject it.

What is the source of the problem here, and why does a seemingly straightforward ordinary least-squares regression behave so badly? The source of the problem is the joint presence of the integrated regressor y_{t-2} and the time-trend on the right-hand side of the regression. Although the parameter estimates of the regression are consistent, the standard asymptotic theory of inference does not generally apply in the presence of integrated regressors, and the results in Table 3.1 show that the asymptotic failure is a real issue for the sort of samples encountered here.

Even so, these unit root problems cannot be used to account for the actual findings of excess sensitivity. First, the Monte Carlo results, although tailored to reflect the actual data, do not generate results that look like Flavin's. The estimated coefficients on the lagged change in income and income lagged twice are typically both *negative*, and there is no sign of the positive correlation between consumption changes and lagged income changes that are so strong a feature of the actual data, see (18). Second, there are several alternative excess sensitive tests that are immune to the unit root problems. For example, we can regress the change on consumption on the lagged change in income, to give

$$\Delta c_t = 11.39 + 0.121 \Delta y_{t-1}. \qquad (3.24)$$
$$\quad (9.7) \quad (3.2)$$

If the permanent income hypothesis is true, then both right-hand and left-hand side variables in this regression are stationary, the change in consumption because it is the first difference of a random-walk, and the change in income because income itself is assumed to be integrated of order one. So there are no difficulties in interpreting the t-statistics, and we have Flavin's result again, that changes in consumption are predictable by lagged changes in income, in contradiction of the hypothesis.

Another asymptotically valid procedure has been proposed by Stock and West (1988). Their version of the regression considered here is:

$$c_t = b_0 + b_1 c_{t-1} + b_2 \Delta y_{t-1}^d + b_3 y_{t-2}^d + u_t, \qquad (3.25)$$

where y_t^d is *disposable* income, which is labor income together with the income from assets. This is essentially the regression run by Hall in his original paper. Define saving, s_t, as the difference between disposable income and consumption

$$s_t \equiv y_t^d - c_t, \qquad (3.26)$$

then (25) can be rearranged to give

$$c_t = b_0 + (b_1 + b_3) c_{t-1} + (b_2 - b_3) \Delta y_{t-1}^d + b_3 s_{t-1}, \qquad (3.27)$$

As I shall explore in more detail in the next section, the permanent income hypothesis implies that saving is stationary, or in the language of time-series analysis, that consumption and *disposable* income are 'co-integrated'. Hence, under the truth of the hypothesis, the last two variables on the right hand side of (27) are stationary. Sims, Stock, and Watson (1990) show that, even in a regression with integrated regressors, like (25) and (27) where lagged consumption is integrated, and even if a time-trend is included, standard asymptotic theory can be applied to parameters that can be written as the coefficients on stationary variables. Inspection of (27) shows that b_2 and b_3 which are the excess sensitivity parameters, meet this criterion, because b_3 is the coefficient on saving and $b_2 - b_3$ is the coefficient on the change in disposable income, both of which are stationary. Hence, as far as those parameters are concerned, either (25) or (27) can be safely used to test excess sensitivity in the usual way. What we have here is the somewhat paradoxical situation where an attempt to improve efficiency, by imposing the *valid* restriction that lagged consumption has a unit coefficient, has the effect of changing the asymptotic distribution of the estimates. Stock and West use Monte Carlo experimentation to show that the technique seems to work well enough in practice for use with the usual sample sizes. This procedure gives the same results as before; the coefficient on the lagged change in disposable income is 0.12 (compare (24) above), with a t-value of 3.6, and twice-lagged disposable income is also significant with a coefficient of 0.088 (5.5). The overall F-test for excess sensitivity is 44.5, which is a very strong rejection.

Excess sensitivity and the timing of consumption

Although problems of unit root econometrics are not the cause of excess sensitivity, there are other possible explanations. One of these is based on the recognition that we have no grounds for supposing that the quarterly or annual data that we use for our calculations correspond to the periods over which consumers make their decisions. A particular difficulty arises if the data are averages over several decision periods.

Suppose, for example, that data are collected annually, but that agents make their decisions every six months. The recorded change in consumption Δc_t^* say, is related to the underlying consumption changes by

$$\Delta c_t^* = c_\tau + c_{\tau+1} - c_{\tau-1} - c_{\tau-2}$$
$$= \Delta c_{\tau+1} + 2\Delta c_\tau + \Delta c_{\tau-1}, \tag{3.28}$$

where I use the subscript τ to denote six-month periods, and where τ corresponds to the first half of the year t. The corresponding formula for the change in income from the previous period is

$$\Delta y_{t-1}^* = \Delta y_{\tau-1} + 2\Delta y_{\tau-2} + \Delta y_{\tau-3}, \tag{3.29}$$

since if τ corresponds to t, $\tau - 2$ must correspond to $t - 1$. If the permanent income hypothesis is true, then the consumption changes on the right-hand side of (28) will be innovations, uncorrelated with previous information, including previous changes in income. However, period $\tau - 1$ appears in both (28) and (29), so that since $\Delta y_{\tau-1}$ will generally be positively correlated with its own innovation, and since $\Delta c_{\tau-1}$ ought to be proportional to that innovation, there will be a positive correlation between the annual change in consumption and the previous year's change in income, as is found in the data. Of course, consumers may make their plans over any interval, and in the limit may do so continuously, revising their plans whenever new information creates a need to do so. But the basic point is the same, if the planning interval is shorter than the data interval, there will be a spurious positive correlation. Indeed, Christiano, Eichenbaum and Marshall (1991) find some mitigation of excess sensitivity once it is assumed that planning takes place continuously and the appropriate corrections are made to the estimates from the quarterly data.

Time-averaging problems induce spurious correlations for adjacent observations of a series that has been first-differenced; there is no overlap between differences two or more periods apart, between Δc_t and Δy_{t-2} or earlier changes. Hence, although the regression (24) may yield inconsistent estimates because Δy_{t-1} is spuriously correlated with Δc_t, Δy_{t-2} has no such problems, and can be used in place of the first lag, or used as an instrumental variable. Instrumentation by variables lagged two periods or earlier has the further advantage that it is then possible to allow for possible measurement error in consumption, or equivalently, for transitory consumption. If consumption satisfies the permanent income hypothesis, but is observed with an added white-noise error, the first difference of consumption will be the innovation in permanent income plus the first difference of the white-noise. But this generates a moving-average error, the lagged part of which could possibly be correlated with lagged income. Exactly the same story can be told about white-noise transitory consumption, which in many respects is equivalent to measurement error.

If (24) is re-estimated by instrumental variables, using both Δy_{t-2} and Δc_{t-2} as instruments (the latter will be discussed further in the next section, but note only that its double lag makes it a valid instrument), then we obtain

$$\Delta c_t = 10.63 + 0.174 \Delta y_{t-1}, \qquad (3.30)$$
$$(6.83) \quad (2.18)$$

so that, although the significance is reduced, as is to be expected from the instrumentation, there is still evidence of excess sensitivity once possible timing and transitory consumption problems have been taken into account. The positive correlation between consumption change and lagged income change cannot be explained by timing, nor by a moving-average error term generated either by transitory consumption or by measurement error.

Excess sensitivity could just as well (and perhaps more naturally) be tested by regressing the change in consumption on the *current* change in income, making use of the same technique as above, and estimating by instrumental variables using as instruments changes in consumption and income lagged at least twice. Such a regression corresponds to the model

$$\Delta c_t = \gamma + \beta E_{t-1} \Delta y_t + \theta \varepsilon_t, \qquad (3.31)$$

where β is the excess sensitivity of consumption to *predicted* income change, and which can be estimated by replacing the expected change by the actual change, and instrumenting by anything in the information set at time $t-1$. Excess sensitivity is tested, as usual, by the significance of β, and by making all the lagged variables appear only through the predicted change in income, it should be possible to obtain a powerful test, subject of course to the assumption that the instruments do in fact work this way. This assumption can be tested in turn by computing the over-identification test obtained from comparing the fit of (31) with that of an unrestricted least-squares regression of the change in consumption on all of the instrumental variables.

Because of the effects of time-averaging, it is necessary to lag the instruments one more period, but the estimation is essentially the original rational expectations methodology introduced by McCallum (1976). Campbell and Mankiw (1989, Table 1) estimate this version of the excess sensitivity model using various combinations of instruments selected from twice and more lagged consumption and income change and real and nominal interest rates. On their data, from 1953, Q1 to 1986, Q4, they again find excess sensitivity, and the result is robust to their choice of instruments. Campbell and Mankiw (1991) make the same calculations for six countries, the US (1953, Q1 to 1985, Q4), the UK (1957, Q2 to 1988, Q2), Canada (1972, Q1 to 1988, Q1), France (1972, Q1 to 1988, Q1), Japan (1972, Q2 to 1988, Q1), and Sweden (1972, Q2 to 1988, Q1). Their Table 2 shows that, with the exception of Japan, where their models fail to forecast either income or consumption, all the β's are positive and significantly different from zero. The excess sensitivity results for the US are repeated elsewhere; again except for Japan, changes in aggregate consumption are at least partly predictable by variables that predict income change. Similar results are obtained for Sweden, the US, Britain, Japan, Italy, Spain, and Greece in an independent study by Jappelli and Pagano (1989), who also draw attention to a cross-country correlation between the size of the excess sensitivity parameter and various measures of credit market imperfections.

Excess sensitivity, durability, and habits

A correlation between changes in consumption and lagged changes in income is readily explained once preferences are modified so as to permit durability or habits. If we make each period's felicity a function of stocks of habits or durable goods, but maintain the assumptions that felicity is quadratic and that the real rate of interest is constant and equal to the rate of time-preference, then it is not consumption that should be a martingale, but whatever appears in the felicity functions. In Chapter 1.3, we saw that if felicity depends on the quantity $\alpha c_t + \beta S_t$ where S_t is a stock of durables or habits that changes according to $S_t = (1-\theta)S_{t-1} + c_t$, then $\alpha c_t + \beta S_t$ is a martingale, so that repeating equation (1.62),

$$(\alpha + \beta)\Delta c_{t+1} = \alpha(1 - \theta)\Delta c_t + u_{t+1} - (1 - \theta)u_t, \qquad (3.32)$$

where u_t is an innovation. Note that the parameter θ measures the depreciation of the stock, so that if durables or habits only wear down slowly, the moving-average term in (32) should be important. Given this equation, consumption changes will no longer be serially uncorrelated, nor will the change in consumption be uncorrelated with the lagged changes in income, since u_t will be determined by the income innovation. The positive correlation between Δc_t and Δy_{t-1} in the data can then readily be interpreted in terms of habit formation. In the Blinder–Deaton data, β in (31) is estimated to be 0.36 with a t-value of 2.2 in an instrumental variables regression using twice-lagged consumption and income changes as instruments. However, if (32) is correct, the lagged consumption change belongs in the regression; if it is included and the equation again estimated using the same twice-lagged instruments, the evidence of excess sensitivity vanishes, largely because the predicted income change and lagged consumption change are highly collinear, and neither parameter can be well estimated.

Consider the case of 'pure' durable goods, where the parameter α is zero so that only the stock S_t appears in the felicity functions. This is the case investigated by Mankiw (1982), and would apply to durable goods if each felicity function were strongly separable between durable goods on the one hand and non-durable goods and services on the other. If so, according to (32), the change in purchases of durable goods ought to display first-order negative autocorrelation. But Mankiw found that purchases of durable goods, like purchases of non-durable goods and services, are themselves close to being a martingale; in the Blinder and Deaton data, the first-order autocorrelation of changes in durable purchases is –0.02. The behavior of durables is even more at odds with the martingale property of durable *stocks* than is the behavior of non-durables and services with the martingale property of consumption flows. However, there are good reasons for supposing that there are other factors at work for durable goods, and recent work by Bertola and Caballero (1990) has shown how non-convex and asymmetric adjustment costs at the individual level will result in a slow and prolonged adjustment in the aggregate. And as Caballero (1990a) has separately argued, the time-series of changes in durable purchases show negative autocorrelation over substantially longer periods than a single quarter, a finding that is consistent with the predictions of the adjustment cost models.

To explain the data on non-durables and services, habit formation is a better candidate than is durability. The first-order autocorrelation coefficient in the Blinder and Deaton consumption series is positive (0.27), which by itself is consistent with habits, with time-aggregation, or with some combination of the two. Heaton (1990) has undertaken the complex task of sorting out the respective roles of these various factors in accounting for the time-series property of the data. He notes, as does Ermini (1989), that *monthly* consumption changes are *negatively* autocorrelated, not positively autocorrelated as are the quarterly changes. Such a finding may arise spuriously from the way in which the data are constructed, see Wilcox (1991), but it is also consistent with the presence of measurement error or transitory consumption, components whose variance is likely to be reduced by aggregation over time. However, it is not consistent with consumption being a martingale with a planning interval shorter than a month, and would thus tend not to support the continuous planning interpretation of Christiano, Eichenbaum, and Marshall (1991). If consumers make decisions more frequently than monthly, and if they conform to the theory, then time-aggregation will induce positive autocorrelation in consumption changes measured at both monthly and quarterly frequencies. Heaton suggests a model in which felicity depends positively on stocks that come from the accumulation of purchases, and negatively on habits, which accumulate, not from purchases, but from the use of the stocks. In such a model, durability dominates over short periods, since purchases that are close in time are close substitutes, but habits become important as the observation period increases.

3.3 Consumption and permanent income: a first summary

This chapter has examined a formal version of the permanent income hypothesis, whereby consumption is postulated to be the annuity value of the sum of expected human and financial resources. Such a model is consistent with the general theory of intertemporal choice developed in Chapter 1, although it is a special case, requiring that felicity functions be quadratic, and that the real rate of interest be both constant and equal to the rate of time preference. Consistency with the theory is a good feature of the model, because it is thereby protected from the internal inconsistencies that are always a possibility in *ad hoc* models, but is less fortunate in the particular assumptions that are required. Not only does the permanent income hypothesis abstract from the incentives for intertemporal substitution that come from real returns on assets, but much more seriously, the certainty equivalence that comes with quadratic preferences limits the applicability of the theory by eliminating any precautionary motive for saving. Nevertheless, for the last thirty years, the model has been the basic tool for the interpretation and understanding of the behavior of aggregate consumption by macroeconomists.

The permanent income hypothesis has also proved a convenient vehicle for exploring the implications for consumption of rational expectations. In particular, the consumption of forward-looking permanent income consumers should follow a martingale, so that future consumption changes should be currently unpredictable. Most of this chapter has been concerned with the empirical work that has established that this proposition does not hold for aggregate time-series data in the US, or indeed elsewhere. There are a host of interesting econometric issues that arise in connection with the tests, but the conclusion is almost certainly not an artefact of statistical technique. The importance of the finding, for macroeconomic policy, and for welfare, is something that is open to dispute. The deviation of the facts from the theoretical predictions is not small. Anticipated changes in income should not affect consumption, and yet actual consumption of non-durables and services changes by perhaps 30–40% of the predictable income change. Of course, much of this is a matter of timing, not of amounts; there is relatively little disagreement about the long-run relationship between consumption and income. However, if macroeconomic policy-makers wish to use taxes to fine-tune the economy, something that political institutions render infeasible in the US, but not in most other countries, then the empirical failures of the theory are certainly large enough to make a big difference to policy prescriptions.

Welfare calculations, by contrast, suggest that there is only a trivial utility cost to the deviations from optimality that are detected by the excess sensitivity tests, at least as long as we stay within the framework of the representative agent. Cochrane (1989) has forcefully made this point, and has supplied the calculations. The basic argument is that the failures of the permanent income hypothesis are timing failures, with consumption changes coming too early or too late, but not being lost altogether. But we know that, in general, fluctuations in consumption do not reduce welfare very much, since the utility loss depends only on second-order effects. For example, the fraction of consumption that someone would forgo for a reduction in its variability is approximated by the reduction in the *squared* coefficient of variation multiplied by a half the coefficient of relative risk-aversion, see for example Newbery (1989). But as we have seen, aggregate consumption is not very variable to start with, so that optimal allocation would improve matters very little. Indeed, Cochrane calculates that, for reasonable measures of risk-aversion, and for a representative agent inhabiting the world defined by Flavin's data, the utility loss to (the crude rule) of setting consumption equal to income is only between $0.10 and $1.00 per quarter. It is worth noting, however, that not everyone is comfortable with the fact that expected utility theory typically attributes so little cost to consumption variability. We see many institutions in the world that appear to be set up to mitigate risk, and many individuals (and indeed countries) complain both frequently and loudly about the variability of their incomes, particularly farmers and the governments of countries whose incomes depend on the prices of primary commodities. While a complaint about income variability is frequently a cover for a request for income subsidy, the cost that is devoted to stabilization seems to be too large relative to the estimates of its costs that come from standard economic theory. It is not impossible that it is the theory that needs to be revised.

The other major problem with the cost estimates is that they are based on the experience of a representative agent, and it is difficult to know what the estimates mean for the individuals whose behavior is being averaged. While it is clear that the variability of individual consumption is larger than the variability of the average, this in itself provides few clues about how to translate Cochrane's estimates to the micro level. Indeed, the aggregation issue is a serious one for all of the material discussed in this chapter, and it is far from clear whether the excess sensitivity problems are problems of individual behavior, or problems in passing from the individual to the aggregate. I shall return to these issues in detail in Chapter 5, where I shall also report evidence that Cochrane's low cost estimates do in fact carry over to the level of individual households.

Before that, I turn to another loose end from this chapter. In Section 1, I devoted a good deal of attention to the derivation of formulas that used rational expectations theory to predict how much consumption ought to change in response to news about income. These formulas, although derived in Flavin's paper, were not used or tested there, and yet they are one of the keys to whether or not consumption behaves as permanent income theory predicts. The next chapter is devoted to an examination of the issue.

CHAPTER 4

The Volatility of Consumption

A central insight of the permanent income hypothesis is that agents look into the future when deciding on how much to consume, and that they use whatever information is available to them when they do so. As we have seen in Chapter 3, such a theory yields powerful predictions about the properties of consumption over time, predictions that are not generally supported by the data. However, the analysis has largely been concerned with the *negative* predictions of the theory, that the change in consumption *not* be correlated with lagged information. Yet the permanent income theory ought to be able to deliver positive predictions about what consumption ought to be. Provided we can say something about how permanent income is formed from measured income, we should be able to predict the behavior of consumption from the behavior of income. Indeed, perhaps the most obvious fact that permanent income theory is called upon to explain, and indeed was designed to explain, is that consumption is less volatile than income.

In Chapter 3, I derived the formula (3.14) which describes how much consumption ought to change for a given innovation in income, but the result was not pursued in the empirical analysis. Although Flavin's paper contains the relevant formulas, her supplementary assumptions prevented her from testing whether actual consumption changes were equal to those warranted by innovations to income, and led her instead to tests of the orthogonality between consumption changes and lagged income. The question of whether the permanent income theory accurately predicts how consumption changes was left unresolved, and is the topic of this chapter. There are three main issues. First, in Section 4.1, we must think more deeply about the behavior of income, and how permanent income and measured income are related. In particular, we must relax the assumption that income is a stationary process. Having done so, we are in a position in Section 4.2 to enquire as to the conditions under which the permanent income theory really does deliver the prediction that consumption should be smoother than income. Sections 4.1 and 4.2 are conducted under the implausible but near-universal assumption that consumers' expectations and econometricians' expectations are the same. In fact, consumers almost certainly know a good deal more about their own futures than can be derived from a mechanical forecasting formula, however sophisticated. Section 4.3 shows how this superior information can be incorporated into empirical tests of the permanent income hypothesis, and allowed for in the assessment of whether the hypothesis is consistent with the fact that consumption is so much smoother than income.

4.1 Measured income and permanent income

Forecasting non-stationary income

The first task is to consider how to make forecasts and how to calculate the consumption change when we allow for the fact that labor income is not stationary. There are two ways of doing so. The first, which essentially requires no adjustment at all, is to follow Flavin, and assume that labor income is stationary around a deterministic trend, or 'trend stationary' for short. In this case we can write

$$y_t = \psi(t) + \tilde{y}_t, \tag{4.1}$$

where $\psi(t)$ is some predetermined, non-stochastic function of time, for example an exponential or linear trend. Since the function is deterministic, it can be predicted perfectly in advance, so that revisions in expectations affect only the detrended part of the series, not the trend. Hence

$$(E_t - E_{t-1})y_t = (E_t - E_{t-1})\tilde{y}_t \tag{4.2}$$

and since $\tilde{y}_t$ is stationary, it can be modelled as an ARMA process, and the consumption formula (3.14) applied without further modification.

Since this is so simple, why consider other, more complex alternatives? The reason is that, in many respects the deterministic trend model is not credible. Although there is no consensus in the profession on the issue, and although it is difficult or impossible to settle the matter statistically, I and many others find it hard to believe that income is tied to any non-stochastic function of time. Perhaps the most telling argument is to ask whether or not the accuracy of forecasts should decrease with time, whether, with even the best information and the best analysis, any forecast of income twenty years from now is not inherently more uncertain than a forecast of income five years ahead. According to the deterministic trend model (1), this is not so. Income is tied to and cannot stray too far from its fixed trend, a trend about which there is no uncertainty whatever. Because such a position is hard to believe, we must consider alternatives that do not have such implications.

One such is the difference-stationary or integrated process that has already been introduced in Chapter 3. According to this, the first difference of income is stationary, so that if, for example we take a moving-average representation, we can write:

$$\Delta y_t = \mu_g + \sum_0^\infty \beta_k \varepsilon_{t-k}, \qquad (4.3)$$

where μ_g is the trend rate of change or drift, and β_0 is taken to be unity. For future reference, note that this is still an autoregressive moving-average process as in (3.8), although the polynomial $\alpha(L)$, which is here $(1-L)$, has a unit root. This difference-stationary specification has a constant non-stochastic drift μ_g, but that does not give it a deterministic trend. Although income will always have a constant rate of increase as *part* of its change, there is no fixed trend to which income has to return. Suppose, for example, that the innovations have happened to be zero for a number of periods, so that income has been moving steadily upwards along a linear trend. There is then a positive innovation, so that income is above its trend line. Subsequent innovations can be positive or negative, but they have expectation zero, so that income is now expected to stay above the previous trend for ever. Of course, subsequent innovations will shift these expectations, but there is never anything that pulls income back to the original trend line. Looking at the data *ex post*, there will be an upward trend, partly determined by μ_g, but that trend is itself stochastic, and could well have been different.

At the individual level, (1) and (3) represent two quite different processes of income determination. Let me give two examples from my own experience. I was once for a (very brief period) chairman of an economics department in a British university. Having visited the US, I was much impressed by the effects on behavior of the chairman's discretion over faculty salaries. So I was pleased to have the opportunity in Britain to submit to the university authorities my own salary recommendations. But I was abruptly stopped in my presentation of the scholarly achievements of one of my junior colleagues, and told that discrepancies from 'the age-wage norm' were the *only* valid reasons for special treatment. Such a process would be well described by (1). In American universities, by contrast, and probably by now in British ones, salaries are set by something that looks much more like (3). Discussions concern increases, and little attention is paid to levels. There is a baseline percentage increase for the year, and individuals negotiate deviations upwards or downwards around it. It is not unusual for professors to be pleased or outraged with their salary increase, even when they have forgotten the level of their salary, see the example in Rosovsky (1990: 40–1). While deans may be more Machiavellian (even) than they appear, there is no general presumption that an above average increase will lead to below average increases in later years, as the administration attempts to claw back its advantage and restore each professor to his or her predetermined trend.

The question of which of the two processes best fits the data is left aside for the moment, although the result can be given in advance: they cannot be told apart with any confidence given the amount of data available. For the moment, however, I need to derive the implications of income innovations for consumption under assumptions that allow income to be difference-stationary. To do so, note that income k periods ahead is current income plus the k changes from now to then. The revision in expectations following the current innovation is therefore

$$(E_t - E_{t-1})y_{t+k} = (E_t - E_{t-1})y_t + \sum_{j=1}^{k} (E_t - E_{t-1})\Delta y_{t+j}. \tag{4.4}$$

We can use the moving-average representation of the first difference in (3) to evaluate this expression; if there are autoregressive terms, we convert to the moving-average representation just as in the stationary case. The first term on the right-hand side is simply the current innovation ε_t, while the terms in the sum can be evaluated from the moving average in exactly the same way as in the stationary case, see (3.12) above. Hence, (4) can be rewritten

$$(E_t - E_{t-1})y_{t+k} = \varepsilon_t + (\beta_1 + \beta_2 + \ldots + \beta_k)\varepsilon_t. \tag{4.5}$$

The warranted change in consumption is therefore given by, see (3.6)

$$\Delta c_t = \left(\frac{r}{1+r}\right)\sum (1+r)^{-k}(E_t - E_{t-k})y_{t+k}$$

$$= \left(\frac{r}{1+r}\right)\left(1 \sum_0^{\infty} (1+r)^{-k} + \frac{\beta_1}{1+r}\sum_0^{\infty} (1+r)^{-k} + \ldots\right)\varepsilon_t, \tag{4.6}$$

so that, substituting for the sums and rearranging,

$$\Delta c_t = \beta\left(\frac{1}{1+r}\right)\varepsilon_t = \frac{r}{1+r}\frac{\beta\left(\dfrac{1}{1+r}\right)}{\alpha\left(\dfrac{1}{1+r}\right)}\varepsilon_t \qquad (4.7)$$

since $\alpha(x) = 1-x$. But this is identical to the formula in the stationary case, (3.14), a result first shown by Hansen and Sargent (1981). This means that we can use the ARMA representation (3.8), together with the formula (3.14) for the warranted change in consumption, *whether or not* there is a unit root in the autoregressive polynomial $\alpha(L)$.

Note the importance of the requirement that the real interest rate be strictly positive; if $r = 0$, and there is a unit root, the autoregressive polynomial evaluated at unity will be zero, and (4.7) is not defined. If we had defined the permanent income hypothesis over a finite lifetime, zero or negative real interest rates would not present any difficulty. The reason for not following this (theoretically superior) route is the increase in the complexity of the algebra, and for the avoidance of which the positive real interest rate is a small price to pay.

A historical digression

A useful application of the forecasting formula for non-stationary income is the stochastic process considered by Muth (1960) in his exploration of the link between rational expectations and the geometrically declining weighted sum of past incomes that was originally used by Friedman and others to measure permanent income. Muth's model is one that will be used several times in the rest of the book.

Suppose that labor income y_t is the sum of a random-walk x_t, and white-noise ε_t. Hence,

$$y_t = x_t + \varepsilon_t, \qquad (4.8)$$

so that, in first differences

$$\Delta y_t = \eta_t + \varepsilon_t - \varepsilon_{t-1}, \qquad (4.9)$$

where the first term is the innovation in x_t. To keep things simple, I am ignoring any drift in income. Muth assumes that the consumer has no way of separating the two sets of shocks in (9), so that the best that can be done is to recognize that the first difference of income is a moving-average process of order one, which can be written

$$\Delta y_t = u_t - \lambda u_{t-1}, \tag{4.10}$$

where λ is a number between one and zero. The value of λ can be derived by equating the variances and autocovariances of (9) and (10); it will be large, approaching unity, if the variance of ε_t, the transitory component, is large relative to the variance of η_t, the permanent shock, and will approach zero as the variance of ε_t approaches zero. The quantity $1 - \lambda$ thus measures the degree to which the compound shock to income is likely to have effects that persist into the future.

From equation (8), we see that the expectation of values of all future values of labor income is simply the random-walk component x_t, so that

$$E_t y_{t+j} = E_t y_{t+1} = x_t = y_t + E_t \Delta y_{t+1}. \tag{4.11}$$

But (10) gives us a formula for the one-period-ahead expectation of the change,

$$E_t \Delta y_{t+1} = -\lambda u_t = -\lambda \sum_0^\infty \lambda^k \Delta y_{t-k}, \tag{4.12}$$

where the last equality comes from 'inverting' (10), so that u_t is expressed in terms of current and lagged values of the change in income. Finally, if (12) is used to substitute into (11), we reach

$$E_t y_{t+j} = x_t = y_t - \lambda \sum_0^\infty \lambda^k \Delta y_{t-k} = (1-\lambda) \sum_0^\infty \lambda^k y_{t-k}, \tag{4.13}$$

so that the permanent component of income, which is also the forecast for future levels of income, is given as a geometrically weighted sum of current and past levels of income. As is easily checked from (13), the permanent component x_t can also be obtained as a weighted average of current income and its own lagged value,

$$x_t = \lambda x_{t-1} + (1-\lambda) y_t = x_{t-1} + (1-\lambda)(y_t - x_{t-1}), \tag{4.14}$$

thus justifying the standard 'adaptive expectations' rule. Hence, provided that the income process is indeed the sum of a random-walk and white-noise, adaptive expectations, or equivalently the geometric weighting of past values, is the correct forecasting rule and not just an *ad hoc* device. Note the link between the persistence of the process, measured by $1-\lambda$, and how much current income is weighted in updating the forecast.

The optimal response of consumption for this model comes from (7), which gives

$$\Delta c_t = (1 - \frac{\lambda}{1+r})u_t = (1 - \frac{\lambda}{1+r})\sum_0^\infty \lambda^k \Delta y_{t-k}, \tag{4.15}$$

so that, apart from the interest rate term, the change in consumption is a weighted average of current and past changes in income, or equivalently, a weighted average of its own past value and the current change in income. The dependence in (15) of the consumption change on past income changes does not, of course, contradict the unpredictability of consumption changes, since, as the first equality makes clear, the geometric weighted sum of current and past income changes is itself unpredictable.

Difference-stationary and trend-stationary income

Although the same formulas link the innovation in income to the change in permanent income (or consumption) whether income is trend stationary or difference stationary, the predictions for warranted consumption changes are likely to depend on which we choose. As we shall see, once we admit the quite reasonable possibility that income is an integrated process, it is possible to generate some very strange results. Indeed, the possibility will threaten the very essence of the permanent income hypothesis, that permanent income is smoother than measured income.

To see the problem, consider the two stochastic processes estimated for labor income in the previous chapter, (3.19) on the detrended data, and (3.23) on the first differences. Both are pure autoregressive processes, so the moving-average polynomials $\beta(L)$ are unity. For the trend-stationary model, (3.19), the autoregressive polynomial is

$$\alpha(L) = 1 - 1.42L + 0.45L^2 \tag{4.16}$$

while for the difference-stationary specification

$$\alpha(L) = (1 - L)(1 - 0.44L) = 1 - 1.44L + 0.44L^2. \tag{4.17}$$

These two equations are remarkably similar, even though the former applies to a series that has already been detrended. Clearly, the detrending has not had a major effect on the time-series properties of income, something that many time-series analysts would regard as prima facie evidence that the series is integrated. Even so, it is hard to believe that much can hinge on the difference between these two specifications. Unfortunately, what is hard to believe may nevertheless be true.

Suppose for the sake of argument that the real interest rate is 1% per quarter. Use this together with the parameter estimates in (16) and (17) to compute the change in permanent income and warranted consumption corresponding to an income innovation. From (16), we get for the trend-stationary model:

$$\Delta c_t = \Delta y_t^p = 0.28\varepsilon_t, \tag{4.18}$$

so that, as is the conventional wisdom, a dollar innovation in income generates only 28 cents of additional permanent income and consumption. Consumption and permanent income are smoother than income. However, if the same formula is used for the difference-stationary model (17), we get

$$\Delta c_t = \Delta y_t^p = 1.77\varepsilon_t, \tag{4.19}$$

which is exactly the *opposite* of the conventional wisdom. Innovations in income generate changes in permanent income that are larger than the innovations, \$1.77 to the dollar, so that permanent income theory actually *magnifies* innovations in actual income. Consumption should be *less* smooth than income, the very opposite of the stylized fact around which the theory was constructed!

The mathematics behind the result are straightforward enough. The quantity that multiplies innovations in income to give changes in permanent income is very sensitive to small deviations from a unit root in the autoregressive process. Suppose, for example, that the income process takes the autoregressive form

$$(1 - \rho L)\big(1 - (1-\delta)L\big)y_t = \varepsilon_t, \tag{4.20}$$

where $\delta > 0$ is small. Then the formula (7) gives

$$\Delta c_t = \Delta y_t^p = \frac{r\varepsilon_t}{(r+\delta)(1+r-\rho)}, \tag{4.21}$$

so that, while the multiplier is large when $\delta = 0$, only small positive values are required to reduce it to more reasonable, or at least more conventional values.

To see the intuition, refer back to the discussion of the difference between trend-stationary and difference-stationary processes. The British academic who gets an unanticipated increase in salary knows that, in the end, he or she will return to the 'age-wage norm,' that the increase is temporary, and so justifies only a modest increase in consumption. The professor in the US, by contrast, has much more grounds for optimism. An unanticipated pay rise means that the base is lifted for ever, so that an extra $1,000 this year is in fact worth, not $1,000, but $1,000 per annum. Indeed, it may be worth even more if academic pay increases, like the aggregate data, are autoregressive. Good fortune this year means that the dean feels good about your work, and since deans' feelings are notably slow to change, you can probably expect an above average pay rise next year too. In such a world, the extra $1,000 now can support more than $1,000 worth of consumption, if not in perpetuity, at least for the rest of your career. The calculations above, using the actual aggregate data, show that the difference between the two schemes can be very large, even when the trend-stationary series reverts only very slowly to its trend.

4.2 Is consumption too smooth?

Our position is now something as follows. If labor income is trend-stationary and detrended income follows the (just) stationary second-order autoregression (16), changes in permanent income are smaller than innovations in income, so that consumption itself does not respond fully to news about income. This appears to be consistent with the data, but for many people is inconsistent with a deeply held belief against the plausibility of deterministic trends. If labor income is difference-stationary, and its first difference follows (17), something that is a good deal more intellectually appealing, permanent income responds more than one for one with innovations in income, and we have considerable difficulty doing what we have always done, which is to use the permanent income theory to explain why consumption is smoother than income.

Of course, intellectual aesthetics are a poor substitute for statistical tests. There exists in the statistical literature a number of tests for the presence of unit roots, for example Dickey and Fuller (1981) or Phillips and Perron

(1988), and these tests are capable, in principle, of separating between trend-stationary and difference-stationary processes. However, the predictions of the two estimated equations (16) and (17) are so close to one another that it should come as no surprise that the tests cannot separate them. Over a sufficiently long run the two processes would look very different, but they are so close that the long run is very long indeed, much longer than the available span of data.

A non-parametric estimate of income persistence

Even so, there is more direct approach to measurement that uses a model that has both trend-stationary and difference-stationary versions as special cases. Rather than attempting to estimate a stochastic process for income, to make a decision about detrending, and then to calculate the innovation multiplier, an ideal procedure would be to estimate the multiplier directly, using the data to provide an estimate of the quantity (7). In fact, this is not possible, but we can come close.

Look again at the moving-average representation of the first difference of income (3). Although this was put forward as a competitor to the trend stationary model, it is in fact consistent with it, at least if the deterministic trend is linear, and if we do not require the moving-average polynomial to be invertible. To take the simplest example, if income is the sum of a linear trend and a white-noise error, the first difference of income satisfies

$$\Delta y_t = \mu_g + \varepsilon_t - \varepsilon_{t-1}, \tag{4.22}$$

which is in the form (3) with $\beta_1 = -1$. In this case, since $\beta_0 = 1$, the moving-average terms sum to zero, which is what guarantees that the income series returns to its (linear) trend. Suppose more realistically that the income process is tied to a trend to which it returns only very slowly. The moving-average representation of the first difference will also have coefficients that add to zero, but there will be a predominance of positive terms early in the series, with the negative 'trend-reverting' terms only appearing later. The simple zero-sum $(1, -1)$ sequence of (22) is now drawn out over a much longer period. Such a series could easily be mistaken for a difference-stationary process, since the positive trend-deviating terms are attached to the first few lags, where time-series analysts tend to look, while the trend-reverting terms are individually small, possibly statistically insignificant, and are attached to higher-order lags, where we are less likely to look. What we need is a procedure that estimates not just the first few moving-average or autoregressive terms, but that somehow estimates a statistic that captures them all.

Suppose then that the first-difference of labor income is a stationary moving average with coefficients $\beta (L)$—see (3)—so that the quantity we want to measure is the change in permanent income Δy_t^p, which, by (7), is given by

$$\Delta y_t^p = \beta \left(\frac{1}{1+r} \right) \varepsilon_t. \tag{4.23}$$

If the real interest rate were zero, the multiplier of the innovation would be $\beta(1)$, the sum of the coefficients in the moving-average representation of the first difference of income. In this case it turns out that the variance of permanent income can be estimated directly from the data without having to fit a parametric time-series model. The following result is helpful in this task:

$$\text{var}(\Delta y_t^p) = \sigma_\varepsilon^2 \beta(1)^2 = \sigma_{\Delta y}^2 \sum_{-\infty}^{+\infty} \gamma_i = \sigma_{\Delta y}^2 V, \quad \text{say} \tag{4.24}$$

where $\sigma_{\Delta y}^2$ is the variance of the income change, and γ_i is its ith order autocorrelation coefficient, the correlation between Δy_t and Δy_{t-i}. The middle equality in (24) can readily be checked either by using (3) to evaluate the autocorrelation coefficients of income change in terms of the β's, or by using the generating function approach of Granger and Newbold (1986, sect. 1.6). Hence, if the interest rate is zero, the square root of V is the ratio of the standard deviation of the change in permanent income to the standard deviation of changes in labor income,

$$\sqrt{V} = \left(1 + 2 \sum_1^\infty \gamma_k \right)^{0.5} = \frac{\text{s.d.}(\Delta y_t^p)}{\text{s.d.}(\Delta y_t)}. \tag{4.25}$$

Hence, if V can be estimated from the data, we have a direct check on whether consumption is too smooth, or not smooth enough.

The need to work with a zero interest rate is troublesome, since for some income processes, discounting is required to make the innovations in permanent income finite, at least if we work with an infinite horizon. Moreover, if r is not very small, the multiplier in (23) depends on the entire pattern of the β coefficients, and not just on their sum. However, there seems to be no way of avoiding the compromise, and the procedure for deriving V that is described below cannot be extended to deal with non-zero interest rates. Even so, for particular cases where we have some idea of the pattern of the moving-average coefficients, for example positive at first followed by a large number of small negatives, the effect of discounting is obvious enough and so can be allowed for informally.

The quantity V is known in the statistical time-series literature as the normalized spectral density at frequency zero—see for example the discussion in Priestley (1981: 432–71)—and it (or closely related measures) has recently been used in the economics literature as a general measure of *persistence* in economic time-series, see in particular Cochrane (1988) and Campbell and Mankiw (1987). The spectral interpretation is a useful one since mass in the spectral density at or near frequency zero is an indication of the presence in the time-series of very long-term components, so that innovations persist for a long time or even indefinitely. This interpretation also highlights the fact that these smoothness issues within the permanent income hypothesis involve the very low-frequency or long-run features of the time-series, features that are typically difficult to measure precisely with finite amounts of data.

Estimating the persistence of labor income

There exist standard procedures for estimating V without having to estimate (typically low-order) parametric time-series models. While it is obviously not possible to calculate the infinite-order autocorrelation coefficients in (24) and (25), consistent estimates of V can be obtained by taking a suitable weighted average of a finite but large number of autocorrelation coefficients. One standard procedure (see again Priestley) uses a weighted average of a finite number of autocorrelations. As is usual in spectral analysis, there is a 'window' that determines how many terms are included, and a set of weights that determines the way that they are included. The Bartlett window uses a triangular pattern of weights, so that, for window width k, define $\hat{V}^k$, by

$$\hat{V}^k = 1 + 2\sum_{j=1}^{k}\left[1 - j/(k+1)\right]\hat{\gamma}_j, \tag{4.26}$$

where $\hat{\gamma}_j$ is the estimate of the jth order autocorrelation coefficient and I have used the fact that $\gamma_i = \gamma_{-i}$. This estimate is asymptotically normally distributed with a t-value that depends only on the sample size T and the window width k,

Table 4.1: Autocorrelation coefficients for labor income

i	γ_i	i	γ_i	i	γ_i	i	γ_i
1	0.45	6	−0.04	11	0.05	16	−0.07
2	0.20	7	−0.01	12	−0.01	17	−0.07
3	0.18	8	−0.09	13	0.05	18	−0.06
4	0.08	9	−0.02	14	−0.12	19	−0.05
5	−0.17	10	0.08	15	−0.22	20	0.08

Note: The coefficient γ_i is the ith order autocorrelation coefficient

$$t(\hat{V}^k) = \sqrt{0.75 T / (k+1)} . \tag{4.27}$$

Table 4.1 lists the first twenty autocorrelation coefficients for the labor income series. The positive autocorrelation coefficients for the first four lags decline at an approximately geometric rate accounting for the fact that an AR(1) is a good fit to the first differences. However, the next coefficient is negative, and at higher lags still, there is a preponderance of (mostly small) negative coefficients, as might be expected if the series were indeed subject to slow trend-reversion. Whether or not these would be sufficient to outweigh the initial positive effects is best judged by looking at the estimates of the persistence measure V. These are listed in Table 4.2 for a range of window widths, together with their estimated asymptotic standard errors.

The choice of window width matters in practice; ideally, it should be infinite but as k approaches the sample size, the estimate becomes zero in a purely mechanical way that tells us nothing about the properties of the series. Too small a window may obscure trend-reversion, if it exists, since the larger the window, the more autocorrelations are included, and slow trend-reversion may not be apparent in the low-order autocorrelations. While the figures in the table decline for the largest window sizes, they are above unity throughout, and are above two for window sizes of 40 or less. Indeed, the square roots of the first four estimates are quite close to the values that come directly from the first-order autoregressive model for income differences. The standard errors are large, and become larger with the window widths, but this is to be expected from a non-parametric procedure. Furthermore, Monte Carlo experiments reported in Campbell and Deaton (1989) show that if the true model is an AR(1) in differences, the

Table 4.2: Estimates of income persistence at different window widths

Window width	Persistence	Standard error
10	2.23	0.76
20	2.06	0.97
30	2.19	1.26
40	2.12	1.39
50	1.67	1.22
60	1.18	1.95

persistence estimates look very like those in the table, whereas if the true process is a just stationary AR(2) around a linear trend, the estimates would be much lower.

Nevertheless, Hall (1989) has argued that these persistence estimates are biased upwards, presumably because the triangular window places more weight on low-order autocorrelations. However, such an argument is not supported by the Monte Carlo evidence, and indeed, the use of rectangular instead of triangular windows generates similarly high results. Nor can the absence of discounting explain the high estimates. If there is truly trend-reversion, the negative moving-average coefficients are certainly at long lags, and so will be given *less* weight if discount factors are applied. Of course, it is possible that, with more data, we could find more negative autocorrelations at yet longer lags, which would reverse the findings; in-finite series cannot be evaluated with a finite number of observations.

Although the precision of none of these estimates is sufficient to force a determined skeptic to change position, the point estimates are in favor of the contention that labor income in the US is highly persistent. Evidence from Canada in Cogley (1989) uses a much longer time-series and finds similar or even stronger results. If these results are accepted at their face value, the representative agent version of the permanent income theory has a very hard time explaining why consumption is so smooth.

Measuring the persistence of consumption

It is also possible to calculate measures of persistence for the consumption series, and neither they nor their standard errors are very different from the figures given for labor income in Table 4.2, although at all window widths between 10 and 60 the persistence measures are between 2 and 2.26. Such numbers are too large to be consistent with the permanent income hypothesis, since if consumption is a random-walk, its first difference is white-noise, there are no autocorrelations at any order, and the persistence measure ought to be unity. Galí (1991*a*) has argued that we can go beyond this simple point, and use the measure of consumption persistence to estimate the extent to which consumption changes are smoother than changes in permanent income.

Start from equation (25) above, substitute consumption for income, and rewrite the equation as

$$\frac{1}{\sqrt{V_c}} = \frac{\text{s.d.}(\Delta c_t)}{\text{s.d.}(\Delta c_t^p)}, \tag{4.28}$$

where Δc_t^p is the limit as r goes to zero of

$$\Delta c_t^p = \frac{r}{1+r} \sum_0^\infty (1+r)^{-k}(E_t - E_{t-1})c_{t+k}. \tag{4.29}$$

But if the intertemporal budget constraint is to hold, Δc_t^p must equal the change in permanent income Δy_t^p. (This is obvious enough, but to check it multiply (3.2) by $r/(1+r)$, take expectations at t and expectations at $t-1$, then subtract one from the other.) Hence the reciprocal of the square root of consumption persistence can be interpreted as a measure of the ratio of the standard deviation of consumption change to the standard deviation of the change in permanent income. As Galí emphasizes, this calculation requires only that the budget constraint hold, not that the permanent income theory be true. The technique also makes no use of the income forecasting formulas, because it requires no assumptions about the way in which consumers forecast the future.

Galí's estimates of V_c are a little higher than those for the Blinder and Deaton data, but the statement that consumption changes are only about 70% as variable as permanent income changes would fit both findings. Galí (1991*b*) has extended the analysis to handle durable and non-durable goods and services separately, and repeated the calculations for the US, Canada, the UK, Japan, Italy, and France. He finds that non-durables expenditures are smoother than permanent income in the US and in Italy, but somewhat less smooth than permanent income in Japan and France. Durables expenditures are too smooth in all six countries.

Excess smoothness: a summary

The point of this section has been to demonstrate, not that permanent income is less smooth than measured income, but that the smoothness of permanent income is something that has to be demonstrated and that is neither obviously true nor true by definition. There is a standard textbook treatment that presents Figure 3.1, or a similar graph of consumption and income, that takes the income series as typical of a representative agent, and that points to the proportionality of consumption to a smoothed version of income. If permanent income is the annuity value of the sum of financial wealth and expected human capital, and if labor income is as shown in Figure 3.1, then the results of this section show that there is no empirical evidence that decisively supports either the contention that permanent income is smoother than permanent income, or that the transition from measured to permanent income can account for the smoothness of consumption.

I have illustrated the story with two contrasting time-series processes that look very similar, that fit the data equally well, but that have very different implications for the behavior of consumption. It is worth returning again briefly to the question of why such an important difference is so hard to detect in the data. Once again, the spectral representation is helpful. The solid line in Figure 4.1 shows for frequencies from 0 to π the normalized spectral density of the income differences, when the first difference is the AR(1) given by (3.23). For the trend-stationary model, suppose that the autoregressive parameters in (16) apply to a linearly detrended series, so that the first difference can be represented by

$$(1 + 1.42L - 0.45L^2)\Delta y_t = a + \varepsilon_t - \varepsilon_{t-1}, \qquad (4.30)$$

where a is the coefficient on the time-trend. The spectral density for (30), as well as that for the differenced model, can be calculated using the transfer functions corresponding to the lag polynomials—see for example Granger and Newbold (1986: 55–6)—and is shown in the figure as the broken line. The normalized spectral density is the standard spectrum multiplied by 2π divided by the variance, so that at frequency zero, the graphs show the theoretical persistence measures V.

I think that this diagram provides the clearest illustration of why the permanent income theory draws such a distinction between these two

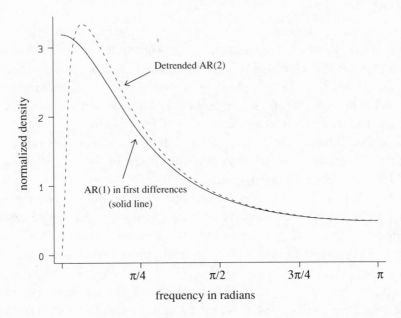

Figure 4.1: Normalized spectral densities for two models of the first differences of labor income

models, and why they are so hard to tell apart on the data. The two densities are almost coincident at high frequencies, but deviate at low frequencies. As we approach zero frequency, where the long-run features of the series are determined, the two densities diverge markedly, with the difference-stationary model continuing to increase as the frequency declines, while the density of the trend-stationary model dips sharply downwards to zero at zero frequency. That this spectrum goes through the origin is characteristic of the first difference of a trend stationary series. Because it has to come back to the deterministic trend in the end, innovations are always ultimately reversed, so that the sum of the moving-average coefficients and thus the spectrum at zero frequency are both zero. The volatility of permanent income depends on the long-run properties of measured income, especially if interest rates are low, and so it is the low frequencies, where the spectra diverge, that matter for the theory. The data, however, are informative about the other end of the frequency range. Think of the effective number of observations at each frequency as proportional to the frequency. Hence, at high frequencies, the spectra are very close, as they must be, given that the models must match the data. At low frequencies there is little or, in the limit at zero frequency, no information, the data are not informative, and the two spectra are free to diverge.

In practice, the estimates of the persistence parameters in Table 4.2 yield answers because, as in all non-parametric procedures, estimates are constructed using information near the point of interest, as well as at it. Note too that the effect of a positive real rate of interest would be to discount most heavily the long-delayed effects of innovations, so that the effects of income innovations on permanent income will depend, not on the spectrum at zero, but at some frequency larger than zero. Unfortunately, a more precise statement requires knowledge, not only of the interest rate, but also of the shape of the response function.

It should also be emphasized that there is nothing special about the two time-series processes with which I have been working, and whose spectra are illustrated in Figure 4.1. They are useful to illustrate the argument, but there are many other possibilities, some of which are illustrated in diagrams similar to Figure 4.1 in Christiano and Eichenbaum (1990). There are also processes in the literature that generate spectra similar to that of the trend-stationary model, also mimicking the behavior of an AR(1) in first differences at high frequencies, but which at low frequencies go not to zero, but to some number between one and zero. Watson (1986) shows that GDP can be modelled as the sum of a random-walk and a stationary AR(2), so that the deterministic trend is replaced by a stochastic one. Watson's process is difference-stationary, but the addition of the stationary process to the random-walk generates a persistence measure that cannot be larger than unity. Such a model also fits the labor income data, and would, by assumption, guarantee that permanent income responds by less than unity to a unit innovation in measured income. The recent literature also discusses 'fractionally' differenced processes; these are also persistent, but not sufficiently so as to generate permanent income paradoxes (see Diebold and Nerlove (1990) and Diebold and Rudebusch (1991) for further details). These models are attractive because they have stochastic rather than deterministic trends, while not generating enough persistence to contradict the permanent income hypothesis.

Given this large menu from which to choose, it is clearly possible to select a model for labor income that allows one to continue to believe that the representative agent version of the permanent income hypothesis can explain why consumption is smoother than income. It is no part of my argument to deny this. My point is different. Since the development of modern consumption theories in the 1950s, it has been taken as obvious that permanent income should be smoother than measured income. My argument is that it is not obvious, and that the length and structure of the data on income are such that it is essentially impossible to infer whether the permanent income theory does or does not offer an explanation for the smoothness of consumption. One can select explanations according to one's preferences, but it is hard to cite evidence that would convince others that any given explanation is correct.

4.3 *Superior information, smoothness, and sensitivity*

The tests of this chapter, which examine the sensitivity of consumption to innovations in income, suffer from a major difficulty that does not afflict the orthogonality tests in Chapter 3. Past incomes, and only past incomes, appear in the forecasting formulas that are used to calculate the changes in consumption that are warranted by income innovations. While it is quite reasonable to suppose that consumers use this information when thinking about their future incomes, it is *not* at all reasonable to suppose that they use nothing else. Individuals have an enormous amount of personal information about their future. Farmers know the state of their crops, salesmen and manufacturers know the state of their order books, and salaried employees have bosses and deans who can tell them something about what the future holds for them. Econometric analysis cannot hope to match this information, although even an econometrician would certainly try more variables than just lags of income.

That agents have superior information poses no problem for the orthogonality tests. The change in consumption ought to be unpredictable by *any* information possessed by the agent, so that, in order to reject the hypothesis, it is only necessary to find some variable that is known to the agent but is not orthogonal to the change in consumption. However, when we come to make positive predictions, the problem of superior information must be faced. At first glance, it seems insoluble, although note that the Galí's (1991*a*) test discussed above makes no assumptions about what consumers know. Even so, it would seem that almost any behavior could be justified with reference to private information. What may look like a one-period windfall to the analyst may be known to the agent to be the first instalment of a multiperiod gain, with quite different implications for consumption. What look like positive innovations may in fact be bad news if the agent was actually expecting more.

Remarkably, it is possible to finesse these problems without losing the essential predictions of the permanent income hypothesis, essentially by using the fact that, if the permanent income hypothesis is true, consumers' own behavior will reveal to us enough of what they know to allow us to control for their superior information in constructing a test of the hypothesis. There are various versions of such tests in the literature. Hansen, Roberds, and Sargent (1991) construct a test that uses data only on consumption and labor income, while Campbell (1987), West (1988), and Campbell and Deaton (1989) use tests that rely on the information contained in saving. Because saving is the excess over consumption of *total* income, including capital income, it brings new information to the analysis, essentially information about assets, and this information can be used to good effect. Campbell's and West's tests are closely related; here I follow Campbell (1987), because his procedures allow me to develop the links between the tests of orthogonality on the one hand and the tests of excess smoothness on the other.

Saving, consumption, and income

Campbell's analysis begins by rewriting the standard permanent income hypothesis (3.3) so as to make more explicit the predictions of the model for the behavior of saving. This turns out to yield interpretative insights of its own, although its main point is its usefulness for further analysis. Start from the basic permanent income hypothesis (3.3) reprinted here:

$$c_t = \frac{r}{1+r} A_t + \frac{r}{1+r} \sum_{k=0}^{\infty} (1+r)^{-k} E_t y_{t+k} \qquad (4.31)$$

and define saving s_t by

$$s_t = \frac{rA_t}{1+r} + y_t - c_t. \qquad (4.32)$$

If we define disposable income y_t^d as the sum of the first two terms on the right-hand side of (32), we have a standard definition of saving as the difference between consumption and total income, including capital income. (Note that capital income is not rA_t, but $rA_t/(1+r)$, the difference coming from our assumptions about the time at which it is received.)

Equate the two expressions for consumption in (31) and (32), and note that the asset terms cancel to leave

$$-s_t = -\frac{y_t}{1+r} + \frac{r}{1+r}\sum_1^\infty (1+r)^{-k} y_{t+k}.$$ (4.33)

If the term in $E_t y_{t+1}$ is taken out of the sum, (33) can be rewritten as

$$-s_t = \frac{E_t \Delta y_{t+1}}{1+r} - \frac{E_t y_{t+1}}{(1+r)^2} + \frac{r}{1+r}\sum_2^\infty (1+r)^{-k} y_{t+k}.$$ (4.34)

If we repeat the operation for $E_t y_{t+2}$, and so on, we can follow Campbell and obtain the following equation for saving:

$$s_t = -\sum_{k=1}^\infty (1+r)^{-k} E_t \Delta y_{t+k}.$$ (4.35)

This makes very clear the role of expected income *falls* in generating saving. If income is expected to rise, and the permanent income hypothesis is true, consumption should rise now, financed by borrowing or running down assets, so that in either case net assets should fall. If there is indication that income will be lower in the future, for example because the consumer sees a higher chance of unemployment, or because income will be low in retirement, assets should be accumulated in the present to accommodate the future shortfall.

The saving equation (35) is also useful from a statistical and econometric point of view. Suppose that income is growing and that the first difference of income is a stationary process. Then by (35), if the permanent income hypothesis is true, saving is also stationary. A version of the permanent income hypothesis that relates saving and the change in labor income therefore avoids the problems of trends and integrated regressors that bedeviled the standard version of the theory linking consumption change to the level of labor income. The definition of saving (32) also implies that consumption and disposable income y_t^d are co-integrated. Each is integrated of order one, consumption follows a random-walk, and there is a linear combination of consumption and income, in this case $y_t^d - c_t$ or saving, that is stationary. By a theorem of Engle and Granger (1987), there is therefore an 'error correction mechanism' operating between consumption and disposable income, and lagged deviations from the equilibrium relationship alter the current values of the variables so as to bring them back into line. Since consumption follows a random-walk, so that consumption changes are orthogonal to lagged income and lagged consumption, the error correction mechanism cannot take the form of consumption adjusting to the lagged difference between consumption and income. Instead, it is disposable income that adjusts, with saving and income playing the equilibriating role. If consumption in period t is low relative to income, then under the permanent income hypothesis, we know that the consumer expects income to decline in the future, and is saving to protect consumption during the shortfall. Hence, in subsequent periods, we will observe the fall in income, bringing income and consumption back into line over the long term. As we shall see, it is the observation of this mechanism that enables us to allow for the possibility that agents base their decisions on more information than we can hope to possess.

Superior information

We can now use the saving version of the permanent income hypothesis, (35), to examine the implications of the fact that the consumer knows more about future income than does the econometrician. To emphasize the role of information, denote the information set of the consumer at time t by I_t and rewrite the saving equation making this explicit:

$$s_t = -\sum_{k=1}^{\infty} (1+r)^{-k} E(\Delta y_{t+k} | I_t). \tag{4.36}$$

The information set of the observer is written H_t and we have to decide what is the relationship between this set and the agent's information set I_t. It is possible that the econometrician has *more* information about some variables than does the agent, for example about aggregate macroeconomic variables, but we can make progress only if we rule this out. We assume that everything that is known to the econometrician is also known to the agent, with a general presumption that there will be many things that are known only to the latter. Hence we assume that

$$H_t \subseteq I_t. \tag{4.37}$$

We need one further assumption, that the econometrician observes the current saving decision of the consumer, so that s_t is contained in H_t. Given these two assumptions, we take expectations of (36) conditional on H_t, or we 'project' (36) on to H_t:

$$E(s_t | H_t) = -\sum_{k=1}^{\infty} (1+r)^{-k} E\big(E(\Delta y_{t+k} | I_t) | H_t \big). \tag{4.38}$$

Under our two assumptions, this expression simplifies. On the left-hand side, the assumption that saving belongs to the economist's information set H_t means that its expectation conditional on H_t is saving itself; if we know H_t we know saving. On the right-hand side, we can use the 'law of iterated expectations', a simple but powerful result from probability theory that says that if $A \subseteq B$, and x is a random variable, then $E\big(E(x|B)|A\big)$ is simply $E(x|A)$; if you know more than I know, and I have to guess your expectation of a random variable, my best guess is what your expectation would have been, given my information. If we apply this result to the right-hand side of (38), we obtain

$$s_t = -\sum_{k=1}^{\infty} (1+r)^{-k} E(\Delta y_{t+k} | H_t). \tag{4.39}$$

This equation essentially re-establishes the original version of the model, (36), but with the information set of the observer replacing that of the agent.

Given the arguments at the beginning of this section, that superior information poses apparently insuperable problems for testing, how can equation (39) be true? How do the very simple arguments used to derive it finesse the problem that there may be little or no relation between the agent's and the observer's expectations? The answer lies in the crucial role played by the assumption that saving is observed by the economist. If the permanent income hypothesis is true, the agent's saving behavior reveals to us what we need to know about the agent's expectations to control for the fact that the agent knows more than we do. Saving does not reveal everything, and we certainly cannot infer from it what the agent expects income to be next period or the period after. However, we can tell what is the agent's expectation of the discounted present value of future income falls, and this information allows us to control for the agent's superior information when we predict income.

The high degree of similarity between the model (39) and the original equation (36) tends to give a misleading impression of the operational importance of the difference between them. After all, any model with expectations contains unobservable variables that have to be proxied somehow, so that in practice, it is inevitable that econometricians should simply replace agents' expectations by their own. Indeed, this was the way we proceeded in Chapter 3 when trying to implement a rational expectations approach to the consumption function. The derivation of (39) may be a nice exercise, but surely it is no more than a justification for what we should have done in any case, and thus cannot have any operational content. In fact, there is a good deal more to it than that. Once again, recall that the derivation assumed that saving is observed by the econometrician, so that the result is not valid unless expectations of future income are conditioned on current saving. Operationally, this is quite different from predicting income using a univariate time-series model as we have done so far. The recognition that consumers have superior information means that the econometrics have to be done differently, and raises at least the possibility that the results might come out differently.

A bivariate model of saving and income

Suppose that we take the lesson to heart, then the minimum valid extension of our previous procedure is to add lagged values of saving to the equation predicting future income. At the same time, we want to follow in the excess sensitivity tradition, and allow consumption, and therefore saving, to depend on lagged income in a general way, testing the restrictions implied by the theory. The natural vehicle for the analysis is therefore a vector autoregression in saving and the change of income. As always, I illustrate with the simplest possible case with one lag of each, so that

$$\begin{pmatrix} \Delta y_t - \mu \\ s_t \end{pmatrix} = \begin{pmatrix} a_{11} & a_{12} \\ a_{21} & a_{22} \end{pmatrix} \begin{pmatrix} \Delta y_{t-1} - \mu \\ s_{t-1} \end{pmatrix} + \begin{pmatrix} u_{1t} \\ u_{2t} \end{pmatrix} \tag{4.40}$$

or in an obvious notation,

$$x_t = A x_{t-1} + u_t. \tag{4.41}$$

These equations provide the extension that we require. Income changes depend on lagged saving, and we can test the relationship between consumption and lagged income.

Given the vector autoregression, we can follow the same procedure as before, deriving forecasting formulas for income, and substituting the result into the permanent income hypothesis, in this case in the saving form (39), and deriving restrictions on the *A* matrix that will guarantee that the hypothesis is satisfied, so that the level of saving should be exactly the amount predicted by the permanent income theory. While this looks different from testing whether the change in consumption is the amount warranted by the innovation in income, the difference is in form only. Campbell's saving equation simply rewrites the permanent income hypothesis (3.3), and there is no change of content.

Instead of dealing with the general case, I work with the first-order vector autoregression (41). Forecasts of the vector x are formed using

$$E_t x_{t+i} = A^i x_t, \qquad (4.42)$$

which delivers a forecast of both saving and income change. In order to pick out the income change and saving elements from the vector x, we need the two vectors

$$e_1 = \begin{pmatrix} 1 \\ 0 \end{pmatrix} \quad e_2 = \begin{pmatrix} 0 \\ 1 \end{pmatrix} \qquad (4.43)$$

so that the expectation of future income change can be written

$$E_t \Delta y_{t+i} = e_1' A^i x_{t+i}. \qquad (4.44)$$

Saving is $e_2' x_t$, so that the saving equation (39) can be written in the form

$$-s_t = -e_2' x_t = \sum_{k=1}^{\infty} \rho^i E_t \Delta y_{t+k} = \sum_{k=1}^{\infty} e_1' A^k \rho^k x_t, \qquad (4.45)$$

where $\rho = (1+r)^{-1}$ is the discount factor. Since (45) has to be true for all values of the vector x, we must have

$$e_2' = -e_1' \sum_{k=1}^{\infty} A^k \rho^k = -e_1' [(I - \rho A)^{-1} - I], \qquad (4.46)$$

which on rearrangement gives the two linear restrictions

$$e_2' = \rho(e_2' - e_1') A. \qquad (4.47)$$

Here then is a straightforward procedure for testing for excess smoothness; estimate the vector autoregression (41) and test the two linear cross-equation restrictions on the estimated matrix A. Exactly how this works can best be seen by looking at the effect of the restrictions on the two equations of the vector autoregression. Write the change in labor income as:

$$\Delta y_t - \mu = \alpha(\Delta y_{t-1} - \mu) + \beta s_{t-1} + u_{1t}, \qquad (4.48)$$

so that α and β are the elements in the first row of A. Then the restrictions imply that the saving equation should take the form:

$$s_t = \alpha(\Delta y_{t-1} - \mu) + (\beta + 1 + r)s_{t-1} + u_{2t}. \qquad (4.49)$$

As usual, the form of the income process implies restrictions on saving behavior, although the inclusion of lagged saving alters the form of the tests from those used to test excess sensitivity in Section 1. But these formulas were derived, not to test orthogonality, but to test excess smoothness; they are derived from the saving equation (39), a formula that explicitly guarantees that the change in consumption is exactly the amount that is warranted by the innovation in income. Even so, the resemblance between these tests on saving and the earlier ones for consumption orthogonality are close enough to require further examination.

We require an equation that expresses the change in consumption in terms of saving and the change in labor income. Start from the definition of saving, (32), lag it one period, and multiply by $(1+r)$ so that

$$(1+r)s_{t-1} = rA_{t-1} + (1+r)(y_{t-1} - c_{t-1}). \qquad (4.50)$$

But the evolution of assets is governed by

$$A_t - (1+r)A_{t-1} = (1+r)(y_{t-1} - c_{t-1}). \qquad (4.51)$$

so that, substituting (51) in (50) and rearranging gives the link between saving and assets

$$(1+r)s_{t-1} = \Delta A_t. \qquad (4.52)$$

This equation is useful in a number of contexts, for example in linking assets and expected income change using the saving equation (35). For the moment, however, use it to substitute for the change in assets in the first difference of the definition of saving (32) so as to yield

$$\Delta c_t = \Delta y_t + (1+r)s_{t-1} - s_t, \qquad (4.53)$$

which allows us to derive from the vector autoregression its implications for the change in consumption, and thus to see the relationship between the excess sensitivity tests and the bivariate tests for excess smoothness.

If we use the two equations (48) and (49) to substitute into (53) and so calculate the change in consumption, we can see immediately that, if the restrictions on the vector autoregression hold good, then

$$\Delta c_t = u_{1t} - u_{2t}, \tag{4.54}$$

so that consumption is a random-walk, and the change in consumption is an innovation that is predictable by neither lagged saving nor the lagged income change. As must be the case, the change in consumption is also the change in permanent income, which can be confirmed directly from

$$\Delta y_t^p = \Sigma \rho^k (E_t - E_{t-1}) \Delta y_{t+k} = e_1'(I - \rho A)^{-1} u_t$$

$$= (e_1 - e_2)' u_t = u_{1t} - u_{2t}, \tag{4.55}$$

The first equality in (55) is from (7), the second from applying the forecasting formula (44), and the third from the restriction (46) or (47). Not only do (54) and (55) provide an explicit check that consumption changes and permanent income changes are indeed equal, but (55) shows very clearly how saving behavior reveals the private new information received by the consumer. The change in permanent income is the innovation in labor income minus the innovation in saving, and the latter reveals what the consumer has just learnt about permanent income.

If the restrictions on the vector autoregression hold good, then the change in consumption is an innovation, but it is not just any innovation, it is precisely the change in permanent income. In this context, excess smoothness and excess sensitivity are not different, but two aspects of the same phenomenon. If consumption changes are orthogonal to lagged information, then they must be equal to changes in permanent income, and they cannot be too smooth. Correspondingly, if the change in permanent income and the change in consumption are equal, then consumption is a random-walk, and there is no excess sensitivity. There is therefore no need to test for excess smoothness allowing for the fact that consumers have superior information, because we already know what we shall find. Excess sensitivity is well established, and so there must be excess smoothness. It is indeed possible that consumers are better informed about their incomes than are econometricians, or that, as argued by Quah (1990), they can distinguish long-run from short-run innovations. But this cannot resolve the excess smoothness puzzle, since their superior information would show up in their saving behavior, and the restrictions on the vector autoregression would not be rejected. But the excess sensitivity literature, as reviewed in Chapter 3, tells us that consumption is not a random-walk, and that the restrictions are indeed rejected.

Excess smoothness and excess sensitivity originated in different branches of the literature; each is motivated by different considerations, excess sensitivity requiring that consumption change be unpredictable and excess smoothness that the consumption change be exactly the right amount. What is more, the assessment of excess smoothness seems to require more information than the assessment of excess sensitivity, requiring that superior information be recognized and accounted for. It is therefore surprising to find that the two phenomena are the same, and it is important to understand exactly what this means and how it comes about. The key to reconciliation is the intertemporal budget constraint.

If consumption is not to be excessively sensitive within the permanent income hypothesis, then it is necessary and sufficient that it follow a random-walk, and that the change in consumption be an innovation. For consumption not to be excessively smooth, this innovation has to be further restricted, and must equal the change in permanent income, itself an innovation. This is why the tests for excess smoothness seem to be stronger than the tests for excess sensitivity. That this is not so is because the budget constraint is in the background enforcing the required restriction. Given that, *ex post*, the discounted present value of consumption must equal the value of assets plus the discounted present value of labor incomes, changes in consumption, if they are innovations, must be tied to innovations in income in exactly the right way. Indeed, this was exactly how I derived the permanent income hypothesis in Chapter 3.1. Starting from the random-walk for consumption, equation (3.1), the *ex post* budget constraint (3.2) implied the permanent income hypothesis (3.3), which in turn implied the formula for the warranted change in consumption (3.6). If consumption is a random-walk, and if there is intertemporal budget balance, then the change in consumption is the change in permanent income, and there is no excess smoothness.

What about the reverse argument, that 'correct' smoothness rules out excess sensitivity? The change in permanent income, the right-hand side of

(3.6), is certainly an innovation, so that if consumption changes are equal to permanent income changes, consumption is itself a martingale, and there is no excess sensitivity. In this sense, if the volatility comparisons are right, so must be the tests of orthogonality. However, it is important to note that this definition of excess smoothness, or of the lack of it, is a good deal stronger than that used in Section 2 above. The typical volatility comparison is between the *variance* of consumption changes and the *variance* of changes in permanent income, and while the equality of random variables implies the equality of their variances, the reverse is far from true. With this wider definition of excess smoothness, it is possible, for example, that there be excess sensitivity even though the variances of consumption change and permanent income are perfectly matched. Indeed, we have already seen one such example. When labor income is trend-stationary, as assumed by Flavin when she first found excess sensitivity, there is no volatility problem, see equation (18) above.

Other insights from the bivariate approach

Although the bivariate model accounts for superior information by conditioning on saving and by using the additional information contained in assets, it is nevertheless incapable in principle of yielding different results from the excess sensitivity tests of Chapter 3. This is a disappointment in only the narrowest of senses, since the link between smoothness and sensitivity was hardly obvious in advance. Indeed, if it had been, the confusion inherent in the terms could have been avoided! Moreover, there are a number of other useful insights that come from the bivariate regressions. First, the linear restrictions on the vector autoregression treat income and saving (and thus consumption) symmetrically instead of treating the parameters of the income process as if they were known when investigating the behavior of consumption. As a result, the statistical inference is easier, and there is no need to pretend that parameter estimates are certain, or to make special allowances for the fact that they are not. Second, the recognition that consumers have superior information tells us that it is important to include lagged saving when testing for orthogonality. In the data, this turns out to make little difference; it is the lack of orthogonality between consumption change and lagged income change that, as always, is the problem. There is no similar difficulty between consumption change and lagged saving.

There is a third important insight from the superior information approach. As Campbell emphasizes, the analysis shows that when consumers know more than the econometrician, lagged saving ought to be a useful predictor of future income change, even controlling for lagged values of income. In other words, saving should Granger-cause income. In the simplest case, one might expect this effect to be negative; positive saving indicates that the agent is expecting an income *fall* in the future. However, the restrictions (47) on the vector autoregression exhaust the implications of the model, so that there is no general presumption on the sign of the coefficient. Nevertheless, Campbell's own empirical results, replicated in a slightly different model in Campbell and Deaton (1989), do show a significant negative effect in the aggregate data; for US quarterly data, and controlling for lagged income change, income grows more rapidly immediately after quarters in which the saving ratio has been low. This finding has been replicated for Britain by Attfield, Demery, and Duck (1990), and by Campbell and Mankiw (1991) for Britain, Canada, more doubtfully for France and Sweden, but not for Japan. That this implication of the permanent income hypothesis is (at least mostly) verified is a result worth having. Although other aspects of the model fail, we might still hope for such a result; that consumers look ahead, that they save against anticipated declines, and that they have superior information about their own incomes, are all aspects of behavior that might be expected to be true, even if consumption is not a random-walk. Flavin (1990) has constructed a model in which consumption responds to both permanent and actual income, and shows that this too implies that saving predicts income falls, and the result should also hold even outside the permanent income framework. Even so, the test would be a good deal more convincing on micro than on macro data. In the aggregate economy, it is easy to think of other mechanisms—simple Keynesian feedbacks being the obvious example—that generate a correlation between saving and future income change, for example if positive consumption shocks are propagated into income increases in subsequent periods.

4.4 The volatility of consumption: a summary

Consumption is less volatile than income, it fluctuates less about its trend, the amplitude of its business cycle variation is less, and the variance of its growth rate is less than the variance of the growth rate of income. To the extent that permanent income is thought of as a weighted average of incomes, we should expect the same to be true of the comparison between permanent and measured income. If so, then the permanent income theory provides an explanation of why consumption is smoother than income.

None of this is obvious once we adopt the formal version of the permanent income hypothesis. If consumption is equal to the annuity value of wealth together with the discounted expected value of future labor incomes, then whether permanent income is or is not smoother than measured income depends on how expectations are formed. If expectations are rational, and thus based on the mathematical expectations of future income, then the relationship between future incomes and past incomes depends on the way in which current incomes evolve and are perceived to evolve. Any presumption that permanent income is smoother than measured income is just that; there is nothing in the general theory that implies that it must be so. As we have seen in this chapter, there are simple, well-fitting models of income for which permanent income is smoother than measured income, and there are simple, equally well-fitting models for which permanent income is less smooth than income. The properties of permanent income depend on the very long-run properties of income, and on the extent to which innovations have effects that persist into the future. With a finite amount of data, it will always be difficult to measure such persistence with any satisfactory degree of accuracy. The result is that something that has often been treated as obvious, the proposition that permanent income must be smoother than measured income, is neither obvious nor obviously true.

This chapter has also shown how to deal with the fact that agents, and perhaps the representative agent, has more information about future income than does an observer. If the permanent income hypothesis is true—and in some cases even if it is not—saving behavior contains information about what people expect to happen to their incomes, so that, by making forecasts conditional on saving, we can use consumers' private information in our own forecasts. This allows us to rule out the possibility that consumption is smooth because apparent surprises in income have been long known and long discounted by the recipients. We also saw that the excess smoothness of consumption is a direct consequence of the failures of the orthogonality conditions that were documented in Chapter 3. If consumption is a random-walk, and if the intertemporal budget constraint is satisfied, then the innovations in consumption have to be exactly those warranted by the innovation in income. In this sense, this chapter is simply a different way of looking at (and thinking about) the evidence already discussed in Chapter 3.

When the permanent income theory is presented in textbooks, and the arguments are put for the smoothness of permanent income, the examples are always microeconomic ones, of individuals who experience transitory income, or who are temporarily out of work. Of course, the empirical illustrations are typically macroeconomic, and typically involve data like those in Figure 3.1. None of the evidence in this chapter (nor in the previous one) can be interpreted as showing that permanent income is not smoother than measured income for individual households. The case has to be made, but the macroeconomic evidence is essentially irrelevant, except in so far as we must respect the constraint that individual incomes aggregate to total income. It is to the microeconomic evidence that I now turn.

CHAPTER 5

Macroeconomics and Microeconomics

Much of Chapters 3 and 4, arguably too much, was concerned with the interpretation of the aggregate data directly in terms of the permanent income hypothesis as derived for a single individual or household. It is now time to adopt a different viewpoint, to go back to the microeconomic data, and to see whether the theory fares better there, and whether we might not be able to make progress in understanding the macroeconomics of consumption and saving by working from the bottom up. In Section 5.1 through 5.3, I follow the earlier survey of Hayashi (1987) and look at a range of studies that have used microeconomic data on consumption and income to look at various aspects of the theory of intertemporal allocation. I have found it difficult to find any good taxonomy for these studies. Some clearly belong together, but several studies use very different models to explore what are clearly the same empirical regularities. Somewhat arbitrarily, I have chosen to devote Section 5.1 to tests of the permanent income hypothesis on micro data, where the permanent income hypothesis is defined in the same way as in Chapters 3 and 4, that consumption equals the annuity value of total resources. The studies in Section 5.2 are more disparate, and although many are concerned with the same issues as the permanent income model, for example with excess sensitivity, others work with models of intertemporal choice that are not consistent with the permanent income hypothesis, and so focus on very different questions. Section 5.3 is the shortest of the three empirical reviews, and looks at the relationship between consumption patterns of different households, whether the consumption of different households moves together, whether there is a consumption link between the households of parents and those of their grown-up children, and whether people manage to pool risks so as to protect their living standards.

Apart from the last topic, these studies have not produced the sort of widely agreed stylized facts that have come out of the macroeconomic literature. Some authors find no conflict with the theory, while others have interpreted their findings as reinforcing at the household level the rejections of the theory in the aggregate data. At least as far as short-run behavior is concerned, the econometric analysis of the micro data does not appear to generate the obvious inconsistencies with the theory that have been documented in Chapter 3. Even so, there is a good deal of less formal evidence that liquidity constraints are important, including, for example, the evidence documented in Chapter 2 that consumption tracks income over the life cycle. But given the greater ambiguity of the micro data, it is worth exploring whether the macroeconomic problems are not generated in the aggregation, by a failure of one of the assumptions required for the micro results to go through to the macro level. As I discussed in Chapter 1.3, the main assumptions are that people (or at least households) live for ever, and that aggregate variables are known to the individual agents. Relaxing either one of these assumptions generates macro models that differ in interesting ways from their micro parents, and that go at least some way towards explaining the aggregate findings, even if the theory holds good at the individual or household level. The two aggregation issues, finite lives and heterogenous information, are discussed in Section 5.4 within the context of the permanent income hypothesis. Section 5.5 is a brief summary.

5.1 The permanent income hypothesis and the micro data

So as to ease the transition from the aggregate time-series, I start with a general discussion of some of the problems that confront any attempt to use microeconomic household-level data on consumption and income. While we lose many of the technical difficulties that took up so much space in the last two chapters, new difficulties spring up to take their place. The most important substantive study of this section is that by Hall and Mishkin (1982), who examine food expenditures from the Panel Study of Income Dynamics (PSID). This paper occupies much the same position in the micro literature as does Flavin's paper in macroeconomics; it was written at about the same time, it uses similar basic concepts, and it set the agenda for much of the subsequent research. I follow the same outline here as in Section 3.1, with the results of the original research followed by the various revisionist interpretations from later work.

General problems of data and methodology

Microeconomic studies have the immediate attraction that they use the data that are appropriate for the theory. The theoretical framework of Chapter 1 applies to an individual or a household and not to an aggregate or average of all individuals or households in the US or elsewhere. Nevertheless, there are immediate practical problems, problems that are different from those encountered with the time-series data, but real none the less. One of the virtues of a representative agent is that the process of aggregation destroys all individual personality. The representative agent is neither young nor old, is neither male nor female, and has a uniform and more or less constant number of perpetually youthful children, all of which characteristics can be ignored in the estimation. In the micro data, by contrast, the econometrician is immediately confronted with the differences between the individuals in the sample, and with the need to control for them if any progress is to be made in understanding their consumption. The convenient fiction of an invariant felicity function, with age doing no more than adding a discount factor, may be convenient for aggregate data, but it is nonsense at the micro level. Age and family composition matter, as do a host of other possible variables such as race, education, place of residence, and occupation. Indeed, diversity is so obviously important that it is hard to justify models that do not allow for the presence of unobservable individual fixed effects, effects that are certainly correlated with the income and consumption variables that concern us, and whose introduction generates sometimes intractable problems of statistical inference.

Aggregation not only smooths away individual idiosyncracies, it also eliminates or much reduces the effects of measurement error. No one who has looked at the year-to-year variation in reported consumption and income in a microeconomic data set comes away without being convinced that much of the variation is measurement error (see for example Altonji and Siow's (1987) description and analysis of the income and food consumption data from the PSID). Income changes in the microeconomic data typically display negative autocorrelation, both over years (MaCurdy 1982 and Abowd and Card 1989), and over quarters (Pischke 1991). This could reflect the importance of transitory incomes, or it could reflect the importance of random measurement error; they are not easily told apart. Furthermore, as we have seen in Chapter 3, the aggregate quarterly income changes are *positively* autocorrelated over time, and the difference needs to be part of any complete story of micro and macro consumption and income.

It is also the case that many household surveys of income and expenditure do not generate plausible figures for saving. Most likely, the problems are again to do with measurement error; small percentage errors in either or both of the two large magnitudes, income or consumption, will cause much larger proportionate errors in measures of the small difference between them. Moreover, survey data often show households, particularly poor households, spending more than they earn. For many LDCs, household surveys record the bottom 50–80% of the income distribution apparently dissaving, and the phenomenon is so widespread that it is hard to attribute it to the surveys having been collected only in years of abnormally low income—see for example Visaria (1980). Such an effect is predicted by random measurement error; the slope of the regression function of consumption on mismeasured income is biased towards zero, generating apparent dissaving at low incomes, and apparent saving at high incomes. This is of course exactly the same effect that Friedman's (1957) permanent income theory used to explain the positive intercept and slope less than unity in the cross-section 'Keynesian' regression of consumption on income. Even so, there is also a suspicion that there is systematic under-reporting of income, particularly among the self-employed, and for whom it is extremely difficult even to define income, let alone to measure it.

Finally, and perhaps most seriously, there is a real lack of household survey data that are suitable for testing the predictions of consumption theory. The ideal would be long time-series data that track individual households. The Panel Study of Income Dynamics (PSID) has been recording income data for a panel of households since 1967, but it collects data neither on saving nor on total consumption. Data are available for consumption of food, currently some 17% of total consumption in the National Accounts, and, as we shall see, several authors have used these data to model aggregate consumption, typically under the assumption that the elasticity of food consumption (or the marginal propensity to spend on food) is a constant. The Consumer Expenditure Survey (CEX) conducted by the US Bureau of Labor Statistics is not a panel, but households are visited on five occasions over a fifteen-month period, are asked about income on two of the visits, and about consumption on all but the first. This type of situation is perhaps the most common, with either a single cross-section containing some element of panel data, or a short panel, but in either case there will be few observations per household, where in most cases few means two. In such cases, the time-series variation that would ideally identify the model has to be replaced by cross-sectional variation, and this cannot be done without additional and (as we shall see) dangerous assumptions.

One other possibility should be noted. In some cases, there are household income and expenditure surveys that have been in the field for many years, so that, although individual households cannot be tracked, we have a time-series of independent cross-sections. The Family Expenditure Survey in the UK is perhaps the most notable example, and has been collecting annual data on some 7,000 households a year since 1954. With such data, it is possible to construct synthetic cohorts following the method introduced in Browning, Deaton, and Irish (1985) and Deaton (1985). Although no household or group of households is observed more than once, we can think of a constant population of households, from which the successive surveys are drawing different samples. For example, think of the cohort of men born in 1945. In the 1975 sample, there is a subsample of all male 30-year-olds, and averages can be calculated of their income, consumption, hours worked, or whatever is the variable of interest. In the 1976 survey, the procedure is repeated for 31-year-olds, in 1977 for 32-year-olds, and so on. In this way, we can track a cohort through their sample averages. For some purposes, and if the subsamples are large, the sample averages may be precise enough to be analyzed as if they were panel data. Otherwise, the sampling errors can be explicitly taken into account using an appropriate errors-in-variables estimator. Although this procedure uses (semi-) aggregated data, we do not face the usual functional form problems associated with aggregation, because averages can be computed for whatever function of the data is desired, for logarithms as well as for levels, or whatever the functional form may be. But note again that, as with short-panel data, we are embroiled in econometric complexities because we do not have the data, long-panel data, that would be ideal for testing the theory of consumption.

Hall and Mishkin's study

One of the most frequently cited and influential of the papers on the microeconomic data is a study of food expenditure in the PSID by Hall and Mishkin (1982). The general approach is closely related to that used by Flavin (1981), with due adaptation for the nature of the data. In Flavin's study, consumption and income are detrended prior to estimation on the assumption that income possesses a deterministic trend. In Hall and Mishkin's paper, the individual components in income and consumption are allowed for by running preliminary regressions on household characteristics, and then working with the residuals from the two regressions. The change in income is assumed to have a deterministic component that is a function of age, age squared, time, and the changes in the numbers of adults and children in the household. The corresponding equation for the change in consumption includes these variables plus a relative price term. The income regression is designed to identify the part of permanent income that can be calculated by the household in advance, so that the change in the consumption residual should be determined only by innovations in the income residual. These issues dealt with, it is possible to focus on the topic of interest, which is the short-run dynamic response of consumption to income.

Let $\tilde{y}_t$ and $\tilde{c}_t$ denote labor income and consumption with the individual effects swept out. Hall and Mishkin propose the following time-series model for income:

$$\tilde{y}_t = y_t^L + y_t^S, \tag{5.1}$$

where the superscripts denote long run and short run, or permanent and transitory, respectively. Each of these follows its own stochastic process; y_t^L a random-walk:

$$y_t^L = y_{t-1}^L + \varepsilon_t, \tag{5.2}$$

and the transitory component a stationary moving average process:

$$y_t^S = \sum_{m=0}^{M} \phi_m \eta_{t-m} \tag{5.3}$$

with $\phi_0 = 1$. It is assumed that the household is able to separately identify the short and long run components, so that consumption can respond to each. Although the assumption can be criticized, it is not completely implausible. Innovations in y_t^L are immediately consolidated into the income base, while innovations to y_t^S are (at least eventually) transitory, and it is possible that the agent can recognize which is which; salary increases versus consulting income is an obvious possibility, changes in wage scales versus overtime payments is another.

If the permanent income hypothesis is correct, consumption will respond one for one to the change in the long run component, and by an amount β_t to innovations in the transitory component, where β_t is the finite life equivalent of equation (3.14) or (4.7),

$$\beta_t = \frac{\sum_{\tau=0}^{T-t} (1+r)^{-\tau} \phi_\tau}{\sum_{\tau=0}^{T-t} (1+r)^{-\tau}}. \tag{5.4}$$

Hence if f_t is food expenditure, and if the marginal propensity to spend on food is a constant α, then the null hypothesis is that

$$\Delta f_t = \alpha \varepsilon_t + \alpha \beta_t \eta_t. \tag{5.5}$$

Hall and Mishkin also allow for the presence of transitory consumption, or equivalently for the presence of measurement error in consumption, modelled as a second-order stationary MA with coefficients λ_1 and λ_2. Hence, if the transitory component of income is taken to be a third-order moving average, we have two equations for the change in income and the change in consumption. For the former,

$$\Delta \bar{y}_t = \varepsilon_t + \eta_t - (1-\phi_1)\eta_{t-1} - (\phi_1-\phi_2)\eta_{t-2} - \phi_3\eta_{t-3}, \tag{5.6}$$

while for the consumption change, and allowing for changes in transitory consumption and consumption measurement error, we have

$$\Delta f_t = \alpha \varepsilon_t + \alpha \beta \eta_t + v_t - (1-\lambda_1)v_{t-1} - (\lambda_1-\lambda_2)v_{t-2} - \lambda_2 v_{t-3}, \tag{5.7}$$

where v_t is the innovation in transitory food consumption and β is treated as a constant. The three innovations are assumed to be independent, and to have constant variances, the last being taken as parameters to be estimated along with α, β, the ϕ's, and λ's. (These equations are in fact simplified versions of those estimated by Hall and Mishkin, who also allow for the fact that, by the design of the survey, about a quarter of the year has already passed when consumption is measured, so that agents already know something about 'future' income.)

Estimation of these two equations on panel data is straightforward, at least in principle. The data for each of the six years 1969–70 through 1974–5 are used to calculate the cross-sectional sample variances and covariances for the changes in income and the changes in consumption. Theoretical moments are calculated from (6) and (7), and the parameters estimated by a maximum-likelihood technique that can be thought of as matching theoretical and sample moments as closely as possible. All the parameters in the two equations are identified. Both moving averages have positive parameters, 0.294 and 0.114 for transitory income, and 0.215 and 0.101 for transitory consumption. The marginal propensity to spend on food is estimated to be 10%, and the variance of the innovation in transitory income is more than twice as large as the variance in the innovation of the long run random-walk component. The β parameter, which is the response of consumption to innovations in transitory income, is estimated to be 0.292, which can be reconciled with the moving-average parameters for transitory income only if the real interest rate is very high, greater than 30%. Hence, according to these estimates from the microeconomic data, consumption is not too smooth, but not smooth enough. The high subjective discount rate that would reconcile such an estimate with the permanent income hypothesis implies that people have limited horizons exactly as proposed by Friedman (1963); they look forward, not over an infinite horizon or over the whole life cycle, but about three to four years into the future. Such a finding is also consistent with the evidence in Chapter 2 that consumption tracks income over periods longer than a few years. As we shall see in Chapter 6, it can also be interpreted in quite different terms.

There is one major feature of the data that cannot be matched by Hall and Mishkin's model. There is a significant *negative* covariance between changes in consumption and the change in income in the previous period, a covariance that should be zero according to equations (6) and (7). As always, lagged variables should not be able to predict the change in consumption if the permanent income hypothesis is correct, and the hypothesis founders in much the same way with micro data as it does with macro data: the change in consumption is not orthogonal to the lagged change in income. Hall and Mishkin estimate a second model in which consumers are divided in fixed proportions between permanent income consumers who follow (6) and (7), and liquidity-constrained or 'rule-of- thumb' consumers who simply consume their incomes; this model was later adopted by De-Long and Summers (1986) and Campbell and Mankiw (1991) who use it to interpret their excess sensitivity findings on aggregate data. Hall and Mishkin estimate that the proportion of such 'rule-of-thumb' consumers in the PSID is 20%. Their part of the change in consumption is equal to the change in their income, which is negatively correlated with their lagged income change, so that allowing for such consumers can account for the negative correlation. The findings can also be interpreted in terms of borrowing restrictions, or liquidity constraints. Although it is not true that consumers who cannot borrow will typically consume their incomes, it is true that such consumers who anticipate an income increase will sometimes have to wait to increase their consumption, so that the presence of liquidity constraints can be expected to introduce a correlation between consumption change and predictable changes in income. In the micro data, lagged income change (negatively) predicts income change, and so the presence of consumers who cannot borrow will induce a (negative) correlation between consumption changes and the lagged income changes.

As we saw in Chapter 3, aggregate consumption changes are *positively* correlated with lagged income changes, and lagged income changes *positively* predict income changes, so while the interpretation in terms of liquidity constraints works for both individual and aggregate data, it is hardly possible to claim that these microeconomic results provide any sort of coherent explanation for the macroeconomic findings. Even so, Hall and Mishkin's results certainly suggest that liquidity constraints might play a useful part in a more complete account of the behavior of consumption.

Reinterpretations: measurement error

Hall and Mishkin allow for the possibility that food consumption is mismeasured in the PSID by including terms for transitory consumption that can also be thought of as reporting error. However, within their econometric framework, and as they note, measurement error in income would destroy the identification of their parameters. For example, even if measurement error in income is orthogonal to everything else, it is impossible to separate innovations in income from measurement error, so that no inferences are possible about whether or not consumption is too smooth. The more fundamental question then arises whether all or part of the failure of the permanent income hypothesis in their data can be attributed to this source. The topic is addressed by Altonji and Siow (1987).

The presence of measurement error in income can hardly be doubted. Altonji and Siow report that the regression coefficient of the change in food expenditure on the change in income is tripled when ordinary least squares is replaced by instrumental variables estimation, using information on lagged income, wages, and other employment information as instruments. The question is what effect this mismeasurement of income can be expected to have on tests of the permanent income hypothesis.

Consider a typical excess sensitivity or liquidity constraints test in which the change in consumption is regressed on the previous period's expectation of the change in income,

$$\Delta c_t = \alpha + \beta E_{t-1} \Delta y_t + u_t. \tag{5.8}$$

If the permanent income hypothesis is true, then $\beta = 0$, while the presence of some liquidity-constrained consumers should show up as $\beta > 0$. Provided there is no measurement error, and provided the change in income is correlated with its lag, we can use a standard instrumental variables procedure estimating β by

$$\tilde{\beta} = \frac{\text{cov}(\Delta y_{t-1} \Delta c_t)}{\text{cov}(\Delta y_{t-1} \Delta y_t)} \tag{5.9}$$

and test whether $\tilde{\beta}$ is zero or positive. However, suppose that the level of income is subject to a white-noise error of measurement, so that we observe, not the true change in income, but an error-ridden income change, which is the true income change plus the first-difference of the measurement error,

$$\Delta y_t^* = \Delta y_t + e_t - e_{t-1}. \tag{5.10}$$

Substituting into (8), we have

$$\Delta c_t = \alpha + \beta E_{t-1} \Delta y_t^* + \beta e_{t-1} + u_t, \tag{5.11}$$

so that, although the lagged change in true income is orthogonal to the innovation in consumption, the mismeasured lagged change in income, which contains e_{t-1}, is not orthogonal to the compound error in (11) and so is not valid as an instrument for the consistent estimation of β. It appears as if the mismeasurement of income will cause a rejection of the permanent income hypothesis by biasing the estimate of β away from zero. However, this is not the case. If the permanent income hypothesis is true, $\beta = 0$, and there is no bias because the lagged error in (11) no longer appears. Provided the lagged change in income is still correlated with the current change in income, mismeasurement of income cannot explain a non-zero instrumental variable estimate of β if the permanent income hypothesis is true.

Nevertheless, when Altonji and Siow estimate a (more complicated) version of (8), they find that the permanent income hypothesis is rejected in favor of liquidity constraints when lagged income is used as an instrument, but cannot be rejected if the lagged employment determinants of income are used as instruments. But as we shall see, there are reasons other than measurement error why these results might differ from Hall and Mishkin's.

Reinterpretations: time-series versus cross-sections

Other doubts about Hall and Mishkin's results have been forcefully put in a recent paper by Mariger and Shaw (1990). One issue is whether the original results can be reproduced using other years of data from the PSID. More fundamentally, Mariger and Shaw follow up a remark from Chamberlain's survey on panel data econometrics, Chamberlain (1984: 1311), that cross-section moments cannot be treated as if they were time-series moments, and argue that it is incorrect to test excess sensitivity by looking at the correlation in the cross-section between changes in consumption and lagged variables. I take up each of the points in turn.

Mariger and Shaw use the individual years of the PSID data from 1970 through 1981 (excluding 1972–3 where there are no consumption data) to regress the change in consumption on the change in income lagged once and twice. The coefficients on the second lags are typically small, and typically smaller than their standard errors, and can be ignored for the moment. The coefficient on the first lag, which corresponds to Hall and Mishkin's excess sensitivity test, is negative in 1971, 1974, 1975, 1976, and 1980, the first three of which are used by Hall and Mishkin, but is positive in 1970, 1977, 1978, 1979, and 1981, only the first of which appears in the Hall and Mishkin sample. None of the positive estimates is larger than its standard error, and all of the negative ones are, except for 1980. On balance, one might conclude with Hall and Mishkin that there is more evidence of a negative covariance than of a zero one. Indeed, the pooled estimate for the whole period shows a negative coefficient of −0.0057, but the standard error is 0.0053, compared with an estimate of −0.0181 (0.0101) over the three years 1971, 1974, and 1975, all of which are in Hall and Mishkin's sample. The result that seemed to indicate liquidity constraints does not seem to be a feature of every year's data from the PSID, and it does not seem to be present at all in the more recent data.

Mariger and Shaw suggest an interpretation of this evidence that explains the year-to-year variability in the PSID covariances, as well as why estimation over a short period might lead to incorrect inferences. The point can be made most clearly using a very simple model of individual income processes. Suppose that aggregate income is a random-walk, that everyone gets a share of this aggregate, together with an idiosyncratic and transitory income shock. Household i therefore experiences an income change that can be written as

$$\Delta y_{it} = \varepsilon_t + u_{it} - u_{it-1}, \tag{5.12}$$

where ε_t is the innovation to the random-walk and is common to all, and u_{it} is idiosyncratic transitory income. I assume that these individual components of income are uncorrelated across individuals, and that, in keeping with the aggregation assumptions of Chapter 1.4, that the aggregate shock ε_t is known to everyone. Suppose too for simplicity that horizons are infinite so that the change in consumption for each household is given by

$$\Delta c_{it} = \varepsilon_t + \frac{r}{1+r} u_{it}. \tag{5.13}$$

We are now in a position to calculate the regression coefficient of the change in consumption on the lagged change in income. Suppose we do this for a single year t. Elementary calculation gives:

$$\operatorname*{plim}_{n\to\infty} \tilde{\beta}_t = \operatorname*{plim}_{n\to\infty} \frac{\sum_{i=1}^{n} \Delta c_{it}\Delta y_{it-1}}{\sum_{i=1}^{n} \Delta y_{it-1}^2} = \frac{\varepsilon_t \varepsilon_{t-1}}{\varepsilon_t^2 + 2\sigma_u^2}, \tag{5.14}$$

where the sums are taken over the n households in the cross-section. Although the time-average of the $\tilde{\beta}_t$ estimates will converge to zero as the number of time-periods goes to infinity, that is not the situation that we are in. For single years, or for short panels, the coefficients will vary randomly from year to year, depending on the aggregate shock for each year. Indeed Mariger and Shaw, using a random coefficients model, argue that the pattern of coefficients in the data are consistent with this interpretation, and that there is therefore no evidence for liquidity constraints. They also attribute Altonji and Siow's positive findings to the fact that they use a longer data period than do Hall and Mishkin, so that there is less scope for the average coefficient to deviate from zero.

In the particular example given above, where the aggregate shocks are simply added to the idiosyncratic components of income, the result depends on the fact that we computed the regression without an intercept. The means of the consumption change and lagged income change are ε_t and ε_{t-1} respectively, so that regressions that allow dummies for each period would not be expected to show excess sensitivity, even with few time-periods. It should also be noted that Altonji and Siow, unlike Hall and Mishkin, use time-dummies in their preliminary regressions, so that their income and consumption changes have cross-household means of zero by construction. However, there are plausible specifications for individual incomes where time-dummies will not remove the effects of the aggregate shocks. For example, add an interactive term to (12) to give

$$\Delta y_{ti} = \varepsilon_t + \eta_i \varepsilon_t + u_{it} - u_{it-1},$$ (5.15)

so that the effect of the aggregate shock varies over individuals according to a time-invariant parameter η_i which I assume to have mean zero over the population. According to (15), although everyone's income has a component that goes up or down with the aggregate economy, each person's total income is affected differently, some benefiting more than average when the economy is booming, some less, and some losing out. The change in consumption will be as in (13) except that the common shock ε_t must now be multiplied by the idiosyncratic factor $1 + \eta_i$.

We then follow Altonji and Siow and remove time-effects in preliminary regressions before running the excess sensitivity tests in the cross-section. This amounts to subtracting from the consumption and income changes the cross-sectional means for each year $\Delta c_{.t}$ and $\Delta y_{.t}$. The probability limit in (14) is now replaced by:

$$\operatorname*{plim}_{n \to \infty} \frac{\sum_{i=1}^{n} (\Delta c_{it} - \Delta c_{.t})(\Delta y_{it-1} - \Delta y_{.t-1})}{\sum_{i=1}^{n} (\Delta y_{it-1} - \Delta y_{.t-1})^2} = \frac{\varepsilon_t \varepsilon_{t-1} \sigma_\eta^2}{\varepsilon_t^2 \sigma_\eta^2 + 2\sigma_u^2}.$$ (5.16)

so that the removal of the time-means has not solved the problem. Of course, if we knew in advance how the aggregate shock affected each individual, we could design an estimator that was consistent in the cross-section, but it is not obvious how such knowledge could be obtained, so that it is hard to see how we can believe that the aggregate shocks have been eliminated. If so, it would appear that excess sensitivity tests on panel data require at least enough time-periods to allow some assessment of the variability over time of the excess sensitivity parameter.

5.2 More microeconomic studies of intertemporal choice

In the last few years, there have been a large number of studies using household data to estimate various models of intertemporal choice. The papers of Zeldes (1989*a*) and Runkle (1991), which are reviewed first, follow the lead of Hall and Mishkin in examining food expenditures in the PSID, and testing for excess sensitivity. However, I have placed them in a new section, because both authors use an isoelastic felicity formulation which is not consistent with the formal version of the permanent income hypothesis. As we shall see later, the distinction is deeper than simply the choice of functional form. Other studies address much the same questions as Zeldes and Runkle, but instead of the food data in the PSID use the much fuller data in the Consumer Expenditure Survey (CEX), a survey that has been in the field since 1980, and which has by now generated enough data to permit useful analysis. I also review a number of even less easily classified studies, using a variety of data sets, from a variety of countries. A final subsection draws together some (very) tentative conclusions.

Further evidence from the PSID

Zeldes (1989*a*) and Runkle (1991) do not work with the permanent income hypothesis, but use the Euler equation approach, particularly equation (2.11) which links the rate of growth of consumption to the expected real interest rate, and which is derived as an approximation to the Euler equation that applies when the felicity functions are isoelastic and there is constant relative risk-aversion. If we expand (2.11) to include household-specific variables, and write for household i at time t:

$$\Delta \ln c_{it+1} = \alpha + \eta_i + \zeta_t + \beta_1 E_t r_{it+1} + \beta_2 age_{it+1}$$
$$+ \beta_3 \Delta \ln FS_{it+1} + z_{it} + \varepsilon_{it+1}. \tag{5.17}$$

where η_i and ζ_t are individual and year effects respectively, *age* is the age of the household head, *FS* is a measure of family size, and z_{it} is a positive number if liquidity constraints are binding, and is zero otherwise. Equation (17) is Zeldes' specification, but it is also useful for describing Runkle's results.

Family size, age, and age squared can be expected to appear in the felicity functions, and so their first differences are included contemporaneously with the change in consumption. The family fixed effects capture other household-specific determinants of consumption change, and the time effects any additive aggregate shocks in individual household innovations. The liquidity constraints variable is derived by Zeldes from the Euler equation when borrowing is not allowed and is interpreted as follows. For a household that is not constrained *in the current period*, the Euler equation will hold, even if liquidity constraints can be expected to bind at some point in the future. For a household that wishes to borrow but cannot, consumption today is too low relative to tomorrow's consumption, so that one period ahead consumption growth will be too high, which is represented in the equation by a positive z_{it}. Liquidity constraints cannot generate too low a growth rate, because the household, even if it cannot consume more, can always save more, and thus increase its growth rate of consumption. Zeldes' methodology explicitly recognizes this behavioral asymmetry induced by borrowing constraints, and represents a marked improvement over assuming that liquidity constraints cause consumers simply to spend their incomes. On the other hand, and as we shall see in Chapter 6.2, liquidity constraints can have a dramatic effect on consumption with only occasional violations of the Euler equation, so that tests based on the Euler equations may be neither very powerful nor very informative.

Zeldes uses data from the PSID for years from 1968 through 1982, so that, deleting years without food expenditure, he has up to ten observations for each household; in practice the average is between three and four, depending on the experiment. Each household is allocated in each year to a high-asset or low-asset regime, depending on its ratio of assets to income, and variants of (17) are estimated for each subsample separately. The interest rate variable is instrumented by each household's marginal tax rate in period t; without variations in tax rates the interest rate effects would not be distinguishable from the year effects ζ_t. In the regressions, the year effects are modelled using dummy variables, and the household fixed effects are eliminated by sweeping out the individual household means. This differencing introduces a time-average into the error term, which therefore can no longer be guaranteed to be orthogonal to variables dated t and earlier. Nevertheless, if fixed effects are not taken into account, but are in fact present, they will generally be correlated with assets, so that splitting the sample by asset levels will cause selection bias. For example, especially cautious households will have both high assets and high rates of consumption growth. If (17) is estimated on the high-asset sample, where z_{it} should be zero, and the parameters used to calculate predicted growth rates of consumption for the low-asset sample, the average underestimation is 1.7% a year, with a *t*-value of 1.63. Supporting evidence comes from estimating (17) for each sample without the liquidity constraint variable, but including

$\ln y_{it}$. This excess sensitivity test generates a significant negative coefficient for the low-asset group; the lower is income, the greater the effects of not being able to borrow, and the higher the growth rate of consumption. For the high-asset group, the coefficient is also negative, but half the size and statistically insignificant. Note that, although both these coefficients may be biased downwards by the treatment of the fixed effects, there is no reason to suppose that the bias is any worse for the low- than for the high-asset group, and there is no reason to challenge Zeldes' conclusion.

Although Runkle also uses the PSID, with data from 1973 to 1982, his results are quite different. His version of (17) includes only the interest rate and age terms, although he also investigates whether time and individual effects should be included. He detects neither of these in the data, although there is evidence of substantial measurement error in consumption, which is allowed for by adding a moving average measurement error term to (17), and making appropriate corrections to standard errors and test statistics. Again the technique is instrumental variables, but now using generalized methods of moments estimation, with the over-identification test statistic as a measure both of model adequacy and of orthogonality between the instruments and the innovation. If the test fails, at least some of the instruments, all of which are dated t or earlier, cannot be orthogonal to the supposed innovation, so that we have the equivalent of excess sensitivity. The instruments are a constant, age, the marginal tax rate, hours worked, disposable income, asset income, and liquid assets in period $t-1$ and period $t-2$. Runkle accepts the hypothesis for the sample as a whole, as well as for subsamples according to asset-to-income ratios, evidence that he takes to be strongly supportive of the theory. Unlike Zeldes, he also finds strongly significant interest rate effects, although the estimated coefficient is around 0.45 in both studies.

I find it difficult to reconcile Runkle's results with Zeldes' findings, or indeed with those of the other studies of the PSID that I have already discussed. For example, in one experiment Runkle includes time-dummies as instruments, but still obtains an over-identification test statistic that is insignificant, and interprets the result as demonstrating that aggregate shocks are not important. If so, the rate of growth of consumption in the aggregate data should be constant, something that we know is not true. Similarly, it is surprising that none of hours, income, or liquid assets affect the test statistic, given the results of Hall and Mishkin, Zeldes, and even Mariger and Shaw on the lagged income change, and those of Hotz, Kyd-

land, and Sedlacek (1988) that lagged hours strongly influence food consumption. The change in consumption in Runkle's subsample appears to be
orthogonal to everything except age and the marginal tax rate!

I suspect that, as noted by Runkle, a major source of discrepancies is
the way the sample is selected. Zeldes has almost *six times* as many observations as does Runkle, who has an average of little more than one change
per household, 2,830 observations on 1,144 households. There is also an
econometric issue; as noted above, the differencing used by Zeldes to eliminate the fixed effects can potentially invalidate the instruments. This
point has been taken up by Keane and Runkle (1992), who show how to
avoid the problem, and who re-estimate (17), excluding the family-size
term, using a yet different sample from the PSID, this time of 3,762
households between 1975 and 1982. On these data, Keane and Runkle use
Zeldes' estimation method to replicate his 'excess sensitivity' finding that
low income in t predicts high consumption growth into $t+1$, and argue
that the effect does not appear when more appropriate techniques are used.

A further twist in this tale has been provided by Carroll (1991). He
argues that, if the intertemporal Euler equation holds in the micro data, the
lagged income term *ought* to help predict consumption growth! The point
can be seen by referring back to (2.11), which shows that the rate of
growth of consumption should depend, not only on interest rate and preference variables, but also on a variance term. If next period's consumption
growth is risky, consumption now should be lower, and consumption growth higher, because there is a greater precautionary motive for saving. But
it is precisely those consumers who have low income and/or low assets
who are the least protected from consumption variability, and who must
therefore hold back on consumption now. In consequence low income and
low assets ought to predict high consumption growth, just as Zeldes finds.
Of course, these precautionary saving effects are removed by the quadratic
felicity assumptions that underlie the permanent income hypothesis, and
their presence is an important reason why empirical work using isoelastic
felicity should separated from work on the permanent income hypothesis.
We need further work on this issue to decide whether Carroll's effect is
large enough to be important. If it is, we would have the irony that Zeldes'
results, which he interpreted as rejecting the theory, would in fact be
consistent with it, while the results of Runkle and of Keane and Runkle,
which dismiss an effect predicted by the theory, cannot be interpreted as
evidence its favor.

We also need more work to sort out the data issues. Given the difficulties of working with data sets such as the PSID, which after all was designed for quite different purposes, it is not surprising that authors cannot always replicate previous work when proposing their own models. However, it is clear from other work using the PSID, particularly studies of labor supply, that results can be sensitive to the construction of the subsample, and the issue needs more investigation. Ideally, we need a study like that of Mroz (1987) on labor supply, where the contribution of sample selection, econometric technique, and model choice are carefully disentangled.

Evidence from the Consumer Expenditure Survey

The US Consumer Expenditure Survey (CEX) is a rotating panel of households that has been in operation since 1980 and has by now provided enough data to make it a serious alternative data base to the PSID. The main advantage of the CEX is that there is a relatively complete accounting of consumption, not just of food. The compensating disadvantage is that households do not remain in the sample for more than fifteen months, and so cannot be tracked over long periods as is the case with households in the PSID. Nevertheless, it is possible to derive for each household a single matched income and consumption change, and to test for excess sensitivity by regressing changes in consumption on any component of income change that can be previously predicted. This experiment is undertaken by Lusardi (1992). Her main difficulty is that income changes at the level of the individual household are extremely variable, and extremely hard to predict using the CEX data. Lusardi deals with this by using data from the PSID to estimate income prediction equations, and then applies the coefficients to the same covariates in the CEX data to derive predictions of short-period income change. It turns out that these predicted income changes have a significant effect in predicting consumption change, and have magnitudes comparable to the excess sensitivity effects found in the macro literature reviewed in Chapter 3.

The effects documented by Lusardi are *short-term* effects. Longer-term effects have been examined in Carroll (1992), who uses data from both the CEX and the PSID to estimate income profiles by age and occupation and thus to compute estimates of expected lifetime resources for households in the CEX. These numbers have little predictive power for consumption over and above that of current income. In effect, a college student and a motor mechanic with the same current income have the same consumption, even though the former is much better off over the life cycle. Once again, such evidence is not consistent with the permanent income hypothesis, except over very short horizons, nor with simple constant-consumption versions of the life-cycle model.

Attanasio and Weber (1992) also use the CEX data to construct average cohort data for the ten years 1980 through 1990. This is done along the same lines as their earlier study using the British Family Expenditure Survey, work which I discussed in Chapter 2.2 above. For the CEX, they compute average quarterly data for nine 5-year age-cohorts, the oldest born in 1915–9 and the youngest born in 1955–9. The use of the cohort technique to produce quarterly data largely circumvents Chamberlain's problem discussed in the previous section, that the orthogonality restrictions of the theory have implications only for time-averages, and not for cross-section averages. Attanasio and Weber estimate a cohort version of (17), using the same isoelastic model as Zeldes and Runkle. However, their excess sensitivity tests work by including the change in current income in the regression, and then estimating using (two-period) lagged instrumental variables, compare (3.31). In a regression including only the real interest rate and the anticipated rate of growth of income, the former is poorly determined, but the latter attracts a coefficient of 0.25 with a standard error of 0.12, indicating significant excess sensitivity. However, Attanasio and Weber argue that the finding is largely spurious, and comes from a failure to condition adequately on other variables. For example, if the regression is augmented, not only by the standard demographic variables, but also by a number of indicators of earning and educational status, the excess sensitivity result disappears.

These results raise an important issue on which it is possible to hold different views. Attanasio and Weber argue against the assumption that leisure and consumption are separable in preferences; for example, households with more workers are likely to spend more on travel to work, more on clothes, meals eaten away from home, and such like. If so, consumption needs to be conditioned on variables such as hours worked and numbers of earners, with instrumental variables techniques used to deal with the likely endogeneity. If they do so, there is no evidence in their data for excess sensitivity, while if they do not, there is. While the logic of the argument is unchallengeable, there remains a concern that once labor supply variables are allowed as right-hand-side variables, excess sensitivity becomes essentially untestable, or equivalently, that any degree of excess sensitivity can be explained away as non-separability. Nevertheless, Attanasio and Weber's empirical work for both the US and Britain documents their belief that 'the excess sensitivity evidence can be explained to a large extent by aggregation and non-separability issues.'

Other tests: the US, Italy, Japan, Norway, and Ivory Coast

The PSID and the CEX are not the only source of data that can be used to test the theory of consumption. Hayashi (1985*a*, 1985*b*) has pioneered the use of imaginative tests on quite different data. In Hayashi (1985*a*), use is made of a single cross-sectional household survey, the Survey of Financial Characteristics of Consumers, collected in the US in 1963–4 by the Board of Governors of the Federal Reserve System. Although the data do not contain consumption, estimates can be made from income and from asset transactions; given likely under-reporting of both income and assets, such a technique is not to be recommended in general, but in this case there is little choice. Hayashi's basic idea is again to split the sample into those who are possibly liquidity-constrained and those who are almost certainly not, to estimate a consumption function for the latter, and see how it predicts the former. Hayashi selects the unconstrained group according to its saving rate; households who are saving positive amounts are assumed not to face a borrowing constraint. Consumption is regressed on assets, income, age, and interaction terms, and a Tobit procedure used to correct for the bias that would otherwise result from selecting the sample on the endogenous variable. The estimated parameters can then be compared, using a Hausman test, with the estimates obtained from the whole sample, which if the theory is correct, should have the same probability limit, but be more efficient. As it turns out, the parameters are not the same, and the consumption predictions for the low-asset group using the parameters obtained from the high-asset sample tend to overpredict consumption of the former, especially for younger households, who are those whom we might expect to be most likely to be subject to borrowing constraints. These (earlier) results are, of course, very similar to those obtained by Zeldes. They have also been replicated in a matching study by Jappelli and Pagano (1988), who use an Italian cross-section from 1984. Once again the results indicate that the largest shortfall in desired consumption is for households

headed by people under 30. The magnitudes of the shortfalls are propor-
tionally larger than in Hayashi's estimates, which Jappelli and Pagano
interpret as reflecting the relatively more developed system of consumer
credit in the US compared with Italy, even given the twenty-year difference
between the surveys.

Hayashi (1985*b*) has also looked at consumption behavior in a short
panel of Japanese households. In this survey, collected in 1981–2, households were visited four times each at quarterly intervals, and asked, not
only about their consumption and incomes, but also about their expectations of consumption and income in the following quarter. The availability
of this direct information on expectations means that Hayashi is also able
to avoid the time-series cross-section problem, and use estimation techniques that allow for the presence of quite arbitrary aggregate shocks. He
works with a sevenfold disaggregation of consumers' expenditure, and
permits each to have some degree of durability. The model is the one
originally proposed by Mankiw (1982), and discussed in Chapter 1.2,
whereby felicity depends, not on purchases, but on the accumulated stock
of the good, see equations (1.51) and (1.52) with $\alpha = 0$. Marginal utility is
therefore also a function of the stock, so that if we adopt the permanent income assumptions of certainty equivalence, and a constant real rate equal
to the rate of time-preference, it is the stock, not the purchases, that
follows a random-walk. Hence if the change in stock is an innovation
ε_{t+1}, and purchases in $t+1$ are the difference between the stock at $t+1$
and $(1-\theta)$ times the stock at t, we have at once that, compare (1.62),

$$\Delta c_{t+1} = u_{t+1} - (1-\theta)u_t. \tag{5.18}$$

Hayashi adds additional stochastic terms to (18) to allow for preference
shocks in the two periods, and to incorporate measurement error in the
reported expenditures. He also follows Hall and Mishkin in adding a fixed
proportion of rule-of-thumb consumers who consume their incomes. These
equations can then be used to derive theoretical covariances between the
expected and unexpected changes in consumption and the expected and unexpected changes in disposable income. If there is no measurement error in
income, knowledge of these covariances is sufficient to identify the parameters of the model without having to assume that the individual innovations have zero mean, or are uncorrelated in the cross-section with lagged
variables like income. Instead these covariances are estimated in each

period along with the other parameters of the model. In order to minimize mismeasurement of income, Hayashi excludes all but wage-earners from his sample.

Except for food, Hayashi finds some durability for all the commodity groups. He also finds evidence of excess sensitivity, with the proportion of rule-of-thumb consumers estimated to be 15%. Hayashi also runs standard excess sensitivity tests for food, where there is no complication from durability, by regressing for each quarter in the cross-section the change in food against the anticipated and unanticipated changes in disposable income. These coefficients are 0.014 (0.004), 0.015 (0.005), and 0.025 (0.006) for the three quarterly differences, all small, but all significantly positive. Of course, these results, unlike the earlier ones, could be explained by an appropriate pattern of aggregate shocks, but they are also in accord with the evidence for liquidity constraints from the PSID and the CEX, and they come from data where the presence of excess sensitivity has been established by tests that are robust against the aggregate shock problem.

As we have already seen in Chapter 3.2, durability can explain a negative correlation between the change in consumption and the lagged income change. The result can also be seen from equation (18) where Δc_{t+1} is affected by the lagged innovation, which is itself typically correlated with lagged income. When felicity functions depend on stocks, so that the stocks follow a random-walk, an innovation in income in t will increase stocks in t, implemented by making purchases in t, but since the stock in $t+1$ is expected to be the same, expected consumption next period will be confined to making good the physical deterioration. Consumption can therefore be expected to fall in the period after a positive income innovation. Of course, this is not an issue for food, where stocks and purchases will usually be very similar. However, it is notable that Hayashi finds evidence of excess sensitivity even after allowing for the effects of durability, an allowance that would typically reduce the role of excess sensitivity in explaining the negative correlation in the micro data.

Flavin (1991) uses a previously unexploited data set, a subset of 1,600 households from the 1967 Survey of Consumer Finances who were reinterviewed in the two succeeding years. Once again, these data do not measure consumption directly, but there is information on income and on a detailed menu of assets. Flavin regresses the change in savings on the change in income, using an instrument constructed from the reported future income expectations of the households in the panel. She finds that only 20–30% of anticipated income changes are saved, as opposed to the 100% predicted by the permanent income hypothesis. However, when households are split by wealth status, there is no suggestion that the excess sensitivity is any less severe for rich households than poor ones, so that it is far from clear that the findings can be attributed to the operation of liquidity constraints.

Mork and Smith (1989) have used panel data from Norway to test a model similar to that developed by Hall and Mishkin. The data come from two separate two-year panels in 1975–6 and 1976–7, and respondents also reported consumption and income in the year prior to the surveys, so that there are three successive observations for each of the households. However, as with the PSID, there are problems matching the timing of reported consumption and reported income, so that changes in consumption will generally be correlated with the lagged income changes, even if the permanent income hypothesis is correct. Mork and Smith therefore base their orthogonality test on the independence of the change in consumption and the *level* of income two periods previously. Since income in $t-2$ is certainly known at t, it can be argued that it should be orthogonal to consumption change in period t. In the data, the correlation is negative, but it is not significantly different from zero, and Mork and Smith conclude in favor of the hypothesis. However, it is not clear that such a test is likely to be very powerful in detecting the effects of liquidity constraints, if indeed they are present. Liquidity constraints will induce a relationship between the change in consumption and the anticipated change in income, but there seems little to reason to suppose that the latter will be strongly related to the previous *level* of income.

In my own work, Deaton (1992*a*), I have looked at very different data, from households in Ivory Coast. There are two separate panels, 1985–6, and 1987–8, but there are only two annual observations for each household. In such circumstances, it is difficult to say much about consumption unless strong assumptions are made. However, Ivory Coast is a country where, at least in the rural areas, there has been very little real economic growth over the last twenty years, so it makes some sense to analyze behavior under the assumption that individual income processes are stationary, so that trend issues do not arise. One can then visualize these predominantly agricultural households, many of whom are tree-crop farmers, trying to smooth their consumption in the face of the quite large income fluctuations generated by year-to-year variations in weather, pests, and fires.

The basic econometric problem in working with these data is how to estimate any sort of dynamic model, while allowing for at least minimal individual heterogeneity in income processes. The trick is to use the implications for saving of the assumption that incomes are stationary. In particular, consider Campbell's saving equation, (4.35), which shows that, under the permanent income hypothesis, saving is the discounted present value of expected future declines in income. Hence, if income is stationary, the *unconditional* mean of saving is zero for each household, no matter what its average income level. I have assumed away any life-cycle motives so that saving by these households is only to smooth out their income fluctuations and there is no reason for them to accumulate assets over the long term. Suppose too that each household's income y_{it} is stationary around its own individual mean f_i. Then consumption must also be stationary around the same individual mean because the mean of saving is zero for everyone. An appropriate excess sensitivity test, accounting for fixed effects, would be to run the regression

$$c_{it} - f_i = \gamma + \alpha(c_{it-1} - f_i) + \beta(y_{it-1} - f_i) + \varepsilon_{it} \tag{5.19}$$

and test that $\alpha = 1$ and $\beta = 0$. Unfortunately, there is no way to eliminate the unobservable fixed effects from this regression without at least three observations, so that, at the least, I could difference one more time. *Faute de mieux*, I can simply run the regression of consumption against lagged consumption and lagged income, absorbing the fixed effects into the error term, so that

$$c_{it} = \gamma + \alpha c_{it-1} + \beta y_{it-1} + \varepsilon_{it} + ((1-\alpha) - \beta)f_i, \tag{5.20}$$

a regression which, in general, will deliver inconsistent estimates of both parameters. However, if the permanent income hypothesis is true, the coefficient multiplying the fixed effect in the regression is zero, so that there is no inconsistency. If α is not unity, and β is not zero, the permanent income hypothesis cannot be true, fixed effects or no fixed effects. The argument is the same as that for testing the hypothesis with mismeasurement of income—see the discussion surrounding (11) above.

As with all the other studies, it is necessary to make some attempt to allow for measurement error. I do this by using the various correlates of income as instruments; areas of various crops, hours worked, and weather conditions, none of which is used directly in the calculation of income and consumption. It is easily checked that moving from OLS to IVE does not affect the unimportance of the fixed effects if the permanent income hypothesis is true. However, my estimates do not support the model, at least in this form. Although the data are consistent with the hypothesis that β is zero, they are not consistent with α being unity. Habits or slow adjustment are an obvious possibility, but so must be the suspicion that the effects of measurement error have not been completely eliminated by the instrumentation. However, there is no evidence here for the standard excess sensitivity story, although in view of the extreme difficulty of estimating income for self-employed farmers, the results should be treated with a great deal of caution.

A tentative summary

It is difficult to distil any very firm conclusions from all of this evidence, which I have presented in some detail so that it is possible to see the diversity of the results, as well as the difficulties that have to be overcome in using the microeconomic data on consumption. Perhaps it is unreasonable to expect uniform results from different data sets, but as we have seen for the PSID, widely divergent results can be obtained even from the same data. Nevertheless, it would be safe to conclude that the evidence against the theory in the micro data is weaker and less transparent than in the aggregate data. There is less evidence against the permanent income hypothesis for individual agents than there is against the permanent income hypothesis for the representative agent, a conclusion that extends from the permanent income hypothesis to the Euler equation predictions of the isoelastic model. Even so, my own judgement is that the micro data provide *some* evidence against the hypothesis, and that the problems are those that would be expected if there are restrictions on borrowing for at least some of the consumers some of the time. While I have no doubt that all of the contrary evidence can be explained if we try hard enough, I find the evidence for some form of liquidity constraints both plausible and convincing. Hayashi's two studies offer good evidence for such effects for both the US and Japan, as does Jappelli and Pagano's replication for Italy. As far as the PSID is concerned, although it must be recognized that the negative correlation between the change in food consumption and the previous change in income is neither constant over time, nor free of contamination by possible aggregate shocks, it is present in most years, and it is in the direction predicted by the presence of liquidity constraints. Furthermore, it is consistent with the evidence from the CEX, at least if we disallow the non-separability effects advocated by Attanasio and Weber.

It should also be emphasized that the standard tests on panel data, whether for violation of the Euler equations, or for excess sensitivity, may not be very good at detecting the operation of liquidity constraints. In Chapter 6.2 below, I construct an example of an impatient consumer, who would ideally like to borrow for high consumption early in life, but whose consumption plan is forced to be a stationary process by a prohibition on borrowing. Nevertheless, the Euler condition for optimal intertemporal allocation is satisfied in most periods of life. As we shall see, liquidity constraints have the effect of reducing the effective planning horizon, so that it is also worth recalling Hall and Mishkin's finding that the horizon is only a few years ahead even for their permanent income consumers, as well as Hayashi's (1982) result that much of the time-series evidence can be reconciled with the theory if labor income is discounted at a much higher than market rate. In Chapter 6, I shall also discuss cases where the Euler equation holds in every period, but where income uncertainty and the precautionary saving motive interact to generate behavior that is much more like that under liquidity constraints than that predicted by the permanent income model. Once again, it should be emphasized that the existence of the precautionary motive is a major difference between isoelastic and quadratic utility models of intertemporal choice.

To the results of the econometric tests from the panel data must be added other, less formal evidence. In particular, we should take account of the finding that consumption tracks income closely over the life cycle, over occupations, and over countries. Since we know that the occupational and national profiles of consumption and income are reasonably stable over time, it is possible to use future income profiles to predict that the consumption of someone aged 30 will grow by less over the next two decades if the person is a motor mechanic rather than a trainee physician or lawyer, or if the person is an Ivorian as opposed to a Korean or a Thai. Consumption change is related to predictable income change, as it should not be if the theory is correct. That such tracking does not appear in the tests on the PSID or other data sets may be more a reflection of the short-term nature of these tests rather than the absence of the phenomenon.

There is also some direct time-series evidence that is not subject to the ambiguities of the excess sensitivity tests in Chapter 3. From the end of post-war rationing until the late 1960s, the British government controlled the terms on which consumers could borrow for the acquisition of durable goods. The controls were specific by type of durable good, with distinctions between cars, radio and electrical goods, and furniture and floor coverings. The regulations, which applied only to 'hire-purchase finance companies' and not to banks or other financial institutions, defined the minimum down payment required as well as the maximum number of months over which the loan had to be repaid. As with all such controls, the market eventually found ways to undermine their effectiveness, but for many years, changes in the percentage down-payment exerted a strong influence on total consumers' expenditure, and was used by the Treasury as a fine-tuning instrument of macroeconomic control. See Dow (1964: 246–8, 278–82) for an institutional description, and Stone (1966, 1973) for the (very convincing) evidence of the effects on consumption. Credit restrictions, even over a small segment of the market, can clearly have a large effect on consumer behavior. Consumers regularly report that one of the reasons for their saving is to enable them to buy something, again an indication of restrictions on borrowing, or at least of an unwillingness to borrow. In the US, Wilcox (1989) has found overwhelming evidence that payments of social security benefits, even when announced many weeks in advance, are accompanied by increases in expenditure when the checks arrive, and not when the increase in benefits is announced. Of course, in this case, people may not believe what they read, or they may not choose to keep themselves informed, an issue to which I shall return below. The 'knowledge' interpretation is given some further support by Wilcox's (1987) other finding, that income tax refunds are typically *not* associated with synchronous increases in consumption.

Finally, I see no reason to neglect the informal evidence that we see in the environment around us that tells us (or at least me) that I do not have access to unlimited borrowing, and that people who are poorer than I am have even less. A young, temporarily poor, but impatient consumer, who expects income to grow in the future, might want to have a very large negative net worth early in life. I see no reason to not to believe that there are many such people, and I do not believe that in the absence of collateral they can borrow as much as they would wish. Indeed, Jappelli (1990) reports that in the US Survey of Consumer Finances 12.5% of households reported in 1982 that a financial institution had turned down their request for credit in the last few years, with a further 6.5% reporting that they had been discouraged from applying by the belief that their request would be denied.

It is important not to misinterpret the seriousness of this evidence against the theory. If it is true that some people would like to borrow and cannot, that does not mean that there are many other households, perhaps most, who either can borrow, or who are capable of detaching their consumption streams from their incomes with no or only very limited access to credit. That the permanent income story is not *all* that is going on does not mean that it is not a great deal of it. There is nothing in the evidence of this section that suggests that everyone spends all of his or her income, that the dynamics of income and consumption are identical, or that denies the basic insights of the theory of intertemporal allocation.

5.3 Consumption interactions between households

In Chapter 1.3 I discussed what would happen if there existed complete markets in contingent claims, and I showed how, in such a world, where all idiosyncratic risk can be pooled, the marginal utilities of consumption of different households would move in lock step. With identical tastes, and isoelastic preferences, the rate of growth of consumption would be the same for all households with access to these markets, and more generally, consumption growth rates would differ only because of changes over time in the individual felicity functions, not because of changes in resources, whether anticipated or not. That there is no idiosyncratic variation in the growth of individual consumption levels seems like a proposition that is hardly worth testing, although there is perhaps more interest in the weaker prediction that, conditional on aggregate resources, individual consumption change should be orthogonal to changes in individual resources. More interesting still is the possibility that limited groups of people are insured in this way, extended families, clans, or even unrelated individuals whose occupations or living conditions bring them into close and intimate contact with one another. It is also plausible that formal or informal arrangements can effectively insure consumption against certain types of shock, but not others; for some risks, moral hazard is a problem, while for others it is not. All of these various propositions have been tested in the recent literature.

The simplest tests are in Mace (1991), who is brave enough to test the strongest of all these propositions, that complete markets exist (presumably behind some impenetrable veil), and that for the US economy as a whole, individual consumption changes in the CEX are insensitive to individual income changes once we condition on the aggregate consumption change. This test is closely analogous to the excess sensitivity tests of the permanent income hypothesis. In the latter, there is excess sensitivity if consumption responds to any *previously predictable* component of income change. In the complete markets tests, there is 'excess sensitivity' if individual consumption responds to the *idiosyncratic* component of income change. The dimension that was occupied by time in the tests of the permanent income theory is now occupied by other households. Mace runs regressions using both the change of consumption and the rate of growth of consumption. For the latter, there are some cases where idiosyncratic income growth matters, but in the majority of her tests, she fails to reject the prediction of the complete markets model. However, as we have seen several times previously, measurement error is likely to be a problem in these survey data, and even if markets are far from complete, measurement error in income changes will bias the regression coefficient towards zero, apparently in favor of the complete markets model. Indeed, Attanasio and Weber (1991) repeat Mace's experiments using their cohort version of the CEX data. In this context, cohort averaging can be regarded as an instrumental variables technique that reduces the component of measurement error in variance of income growth, and the results are what would be expected if markets are not complete but measurement error is important. Conditional on the aggregate quarterly growth rate of consumption, the growth rate of cohort consumption responds to the growth rate of cohort income with a coefficient of 0.23 with a standard error of 0.03.

Townsend (1991) examines risk-sharing on a somewhat smaller scale than does Mace, using data for households in three poor villages in south India. The argument here is that such villages are often stable over time, that the agricultural and weather-based sources of risk are both stationary and well understood, and that the inhabitants' extensive common knowledge about one another can control the problems of moral hazard. The data consist of observations from 1975–84 on samples of 33, 34, and 36 households in each of three villages. Townsend finds that the co-movement of individual consumptions with each village's average consumption is much stronger than the similar co-movements of income, something that is certainly consistent with risk-sharing, but perhaps also with autarkic consumption smoothing by each household separately. Like Mace, he finds few rejections of the insensitivity of consumption change to idiosyncratic income shocks, but as with Mace measurement error in income is almost certainly important. Ravallion and Chaudhuri (1992) argue the mismeasurement case in some detail, and obtain a rejection of the risk-pooling model on their version of the same data.

Cochrane (1991) uses PSID data on the growth rate of individual food consumption over the period 1980 to 1983, and tests whether the cross-sectional variation is or is not independent of various reported exogenous 'shocks' to the households. Since there is only one time-span here, the growth in aggregate consumption is absorbed into the intercept term. Cochrane finds that consumption changes are strongly related to income changes, contrary to Mace's results, but in accordance with those of Attanasio and Weber, but he attributes the result to the non-exogeneity of income, an argument that mirrors the attribution of excess sensitivity in the permanent income hypothesis to non-separability of consumption and leisure. Consumption also falls in response to long illnesses and to involuntary job losses, though not to unemployment spells, strike-related work loss, or involuntary moves. Once again, it seems appropriate to worry about measurement error attenuating correlations, although the problem is perhaps less severe using data on discrete events like illness.

The implications of risk-sharing within extended families have been examined in a series of papers by Abel and Kotlikoff (1988), Altonji, Hayashi, and Kotlikoff (1989), and Hayashi, Altonji, and Kotlikoff (1991), and these papers also explore the links between complete markets and altruism. That individual consumption levels should move together within a family or an extended family is a good deal more plausible than that they should do so for the economy as a whole, and there are various models of behavior that produce the result. Altruism between parents and children is one possibility; as Becker (1974) showed, if the 'clan head' is concerned about the welfare of other members of the clan, and makes transfers from his or her own resources to maximize his or her altruistic utility function, then even if the other members of the family are not altruistic, the behavior of each clan member is that which maximizes the head's utility. In particular, provided there are positive transfers from the head, individual resources do not affect individual consumption, since they are offset by adjustments in transfers. This situation provides the strongest prediction that *levels* of consumption within the clan are independent of individual resources. Such an outcome would also imply the weaker result that changes in consumption or rates of growth of consumption would be independent of changes in individual resources. This version allows individual resources to affect individual consumption levels, perhaps through a process of intra-clan bargaining, but there is complete risk-sharing within the clan.

None of these models survives empirical testing. Abel and Kotlikoff provide the weakest test, noting that if the age structure of each clan is the same, equalization of consumption growth within each clan implies that consumption growth should be the same for all age cohorts in the aggregate economy. While this proposition is not true, since there is a pronounced age profile of consumption, both in the cross-section and over time, much of the age variation can be explained by demographics, so that Abel and Kotlikoff find that they cannot reject the prediction. Nevertheless, Attanasio and Weber's cohort evidence from the CEX that refutes economy-wide complete markets also refutes the Abel and Kotlikoff prediction, since the growth rate of cohort consumption depends on factors (like cohort income growth) that vary from cohort to cohort.

The papers by Altonji, Hayashi, and Kotlikoff and by Hayashi, Altonji, and Kotlikoff use data on the separate households of parents and children, where we might expect to have the best chance of finding altruism or family risk-sharing. The PSID has been running since 1967, and keeps track not only of the original panel households, but also of 'splits,' new households that are formed by members of the original households, through divorce, or through children forming their own households. It is possible by 1985 to assemble data on over 2,000 independent child households, and their more than 1,000 parent households. However, the results strongly reject the propositions of the altruism model; 'the distribution of resources across households within the extended family is a highly significant (statistically and economically) determinant of the distribution of consumption within the extended family.' Even the weaker proposition of family risk-sharing, that consumption growth rates are independent of household income growth, can be rejected on these data. Nor is there much evidence even of partial risk-sharing; once individual household incomes have been controlled for, the combined resources of the linked households have little predictive power for the consumption of each one separately.

From the perspective of household behavior, these studies provide a useful beginning to research on interactions between the consumption levels of different households. That these particular models are rejected is a good deal less important than the impetus that has been given to the study of how households share risk through formal or informal mechanisms. However, from the macroeconomic perspective, the negative results are of considerable importance, since they show that there is no empirical support for the argument that a representative agent can be formally justified by a combination of intergenerational altruism and complete markets. Such assumptions are (absurdly?) strong, and their implications are just as strongly rejected by the data.

5.4 The reconciliation of micro and macro evidence

If we were to take the view that the household data are basically supportive of the permanent income theory, or at least of intertemporal choice theory more generally, then there is a puzzle about why the theory is rejected in the aggregate. Alternatively, if we accept the arguments in favor of the (at least occasional) importance of liquidity constraints, there is no surprise that the theory should be rejected in aggregate, but there is still a problem in reconciling the precise nature of the macroeconomic and microeconomic evidence. The time-series properties of aggregate income and consumption appear to be quite different from their macroeconomic counterparts, and the predictability of consumption changes in the two environments seems to coincide mainly by chance. The household data usually show negative autocorrelation for both income and consumption changes, so that a negative correlation between consumption and lagged income changes can be interpreted as predictable income changes being positively correlated with changes in consumption. In the aggregate data, both consumption changes and income changes are *positively* autocorrelated, so that the *positive* correlation between consumption change and lagged income change can be interpreted, as before, as showing that consumption change can be predicted by predictable income growth. Given the differences in all but the final conclusion, such results can hardly be regarded as a triumph for a representative agent interpretation of the data.

The last section of Chapter 1 contained a preliminary discussion of aggregation, and provides a useful starting-point for trying to reconcile the micro with the aggregate evidence. Following Grossman and Shiller (1982) and others, we know that, if tastes are the same, the Euler conditions will aggregate perfectly if three conditions hold : (*a*) people live for ever, (*b*) felicity functions are quadratic (or the time interval is very short), and (*c*) individuals know all the aggregate information. Of these (*b*) is perhaps the least serious, and as shown in Chapter 1, even when it fails, it may be possible to define a consumption aggregate that behaves very much as does micro consumption. It is the failure of conditions (*a*) and (*c*), infinite lives and private possession of aggregate information, that we have to explore as possible sources of the differences between the micro and macro findings, and I shall consider each in turn.

In this section, I work under the basic assumption that the theory is true for individual data and explore the consequences of failure of the aggregation assumptions. The analysis of aggregation when people are liquidity-constrained is a good deal more difficult, although I shall report some evidence in Chapter 6.2 below. Note also that what I am concerned with here is the aggregation of the martingale property, that there exists some function of consumption whose future change is unpredictable given current information. I shall not be concerned with the prediction that relates consumption growth to the rates of return and risk properties of financial assets because I do not believe that this supposition is well based even at the microeconomic level. Perhaps a fifth of consumption in the US is attributable to consumers who do not even have a checking account, let alone interest-bearing assets, so that it stretches credulity to model their consumption decisions on the assumption that they can borrow on the same terms as the US federal government. Even if this chimera were mistaken for reality, there is no reason to suppose that it would aggregate to the macro level unless, against all available evidence, people are immortal (see again the discussion at the end of Chapter 3).

Aggregation with finite lives

A world populated by finitely lived life-cycle consumers will generate aggregate consumption that exhibits both excess sensitivity to current income and excess smoothness to innovations in current income. This result is due to Clarida (1991) and to Galí (1990), and my discussion is based on their work. I take the simplest possible case of Clarida's model. Each worker lives for three periods, working in the first two periods of life, and retiring in the third. In year t, each worker receives an identical amount of labor income y_t while they are working, and zero in retirement. The common quantity y_t follows a random-walk with drift g, so that average labor income, which is two-thirds of what each worker receives (the third generation is retired), also follows a random-walk with drift two thirds of g. Suppose that the interest rate is zero, and that everyone is a pure permanent income life-cycler. Now compare the situation in t with that in $t-1$ and look at the consumption of each group. Those who are now retired but were old workers in the last period receive no income, which is what they expected, so their consumption does not change. The old workers now receive y_t, and as young workers were previously receiving y_{t-1}. They have thus had an innovation ε_t, half of which they will consume now, so that their consumption change is $\varepsilon_t/2$. The new-born workers receive y_t, they expect $y_t + g$ next period, and so will consume $(2y_t + g)/3$ in period t. The picture is completed by looking at the consumption of the newly dead group, previously retired. In the first period of their lives, which was $t-3$, they consumed $(2y_{t-3} + g)/3$, in middle age, period $t-2$, this plus $\varepsilon_{t-2}/2$, and the same in the last period of their lives, $t-1$, since there are no surprises after retirement. But

$$y_{t-3} = y_t - 3g - \varepsilon_t - \varepsilon_{t-1} - \varepsilon_{t-2}, \tag{5.21}$$

so that, if all the changes in consumption are added up, we get

$$\Delta C_t = 2g + \frac{7}{6}\varepsilon_t + \frac{2}{3}\varepsilon_{t-1} + \frac{1}{6}\varepsilon_{t-2}. \tag{5.22}$$

Recall that average income is two-thirds of total income, with corresponding drift $\tilde{g} = \frac{2}{3}g$ and innovation $\tilde{\varepsilon}_t = \frac{2}{3}\varepsilon_t$, so that if (22) is rewritten in terms of the change in average consumption, and the drift $\tilde{g}$ and innovation $\tilde{\varepsilon}_t$ in average income, we obtain finally

$$\Delta c_t = \tilde{g} + \frac{7}{12}\tilde{\varepsilon}_t + \frac{1}{3}\tilde{\varepsilon}_{t-1} + \frac{1}{12}\tilde{\varepsilon}_{t-2}. \tag{5.23}$$

The change in average consumption has a drift term equal to the drift in average income, and is a distributed lag of the innovations in average income with weights adding to one. Consumption is not orthogonal to lagged innovations, nor does it respond one for one to innovations in current income, even though the latter is a random-walk. Aggregation generates both excess smoothness and excess sensitivity although there is none for any individual consumer. Clarida's paper works out the more general case with arbitrary lengths of working and retirement periods, and with a positive real rate of interest, and shows that the result still holds, although the numerical values of the coefficients will be different. There are two factors driving the result. First, since people receive income only when they are working, and have to make provision for retirement, they will consume only a fraction of an innovation to income, even when they know that the innovation will persist through the rest of their working lives. At the aggregate level, the response of consumption to aggregate innovations is essentially the average of these fractional responses, and will be a good deal less than unity. Second, because people die and are replaced by those newly born, who do not share their history, the income experience of the now dead generation affects the change in consumption. In addition, because incomes are growing, the prospects for the new generations are better than those of their defunct forebears, so that there is an upward drift in consumption. It might be thought that these generational effects would be small over short time-periods such as a quarter or a year, but working through the arithmetic shows that this is not so. Indeed, the model can be reworked in continuous time with very similar results.

Another feature of these results has been emphasized in Galí's work. The aggregate equation (23) implies that average consumption and aggregate *labor* income are co-integrated, and are tied together in the long run. This can be seen in the example either by subtracting the average income change from the consumption change in (23) and noting that the resulting moving average on the right-hand side involves only the first differences of the innovations, or by aggregating the model explicitly to recover average consumption, and showing that it differs from average income by a quantity that is stationary.

Recall from Chapter 4.3 that the permanent income hypothesis implies that, for individual agents, consumption and *total* income, including property income, are co-integrated, but that there is no long-run relationship between consumption and labor income at the microeconomic level. Indeed, the absence of such a relationship is at the core of the theory of intertemporal allocation without borrowing restrictions. In the aggregate, the turnover of generations transmits income growth to consumption growth. The difference between consumption and income is stationary and we avoid the absurdity of having to believe that in aggregate, desired consumption could be many times larger than actual income, as well as the implication of equation (4.35) that saving will be large and negative when labor incomes are expected to grow.

There remains the empirical question of whether an aggregate model, modified to take these considerations into account, can account for the features of the aggregate data that in Chapter 3 were interpreted as casting doubt on the theory. Both Clarida and Galí conclude not. Clearly, the direction of the effects is right, and they go some way to explaining both excess smoothness and excess sensitivity. Clarida calculates that for reasonable values of the interest rate and of the length of life and retirement, but still on the assumption that income processes are the same, the warranted change in aggregate consumption to an innovation in random-walk income should be around two-thirds, still too large to account for the actual smoothness of the aggregate series. Similarly, it is clear from Galí's work that the co-integration between aggregate consumption and aggregate labor income, although real enough, is a long-run phenomenon, and cannot account for the short-run tracking of consumption and income that generates the excess sensitivity results. Note that if this position is accepted, as I believe it ought to be, then we must find another explanation for Attanasio and Weber's (1991) findings (see Chapter 2.2) on British data that excess sensitivity vanishes once exits and entrances are removed by using the means of cohorts with fixed membership.

Individual households and aggregate information

The leading candidate left to account for aggregation problems is the failure of individuals to be aware of aggregate information. The issue here is partly accessibility, since consumers may find out about aggregate income or other macroeconomic variables only with a substantial lag, and partly relevance, whether aggregate information is sufficiently valuable to individual agents so that they will bother to obtain it, even when it is available. Large corporations buy economic forecasts, but private individuals rarely do so. Even if the information is readily available in newspapers or government publications, many people would require training and experience to interpret it and to infer from it the implications for their own futures. Indeed, many graduate students in economics do not know the gross national product of the US to within an order of magnitude. While it is somewhat easier to understand and remember rates of growth, it is still implausible to suppose that those with no training in economics can monitor, let alone interpret the latest macroeconomic shock. The consequences of aggregate information with lags, and of no aggregate information, have been worked out in papers by Goodfriend (1992) and Pischke (1991). Here I follow the simplest example in Pischke, which neatly highlights the issues.

Suppose that average income follows a random-walk with drift, and that each consumer's income is the average plus an idiosyncratic component that is purely transitory, represented by white-noise. This is the process analyzed by Muth (1960), and discussed in Chapter 4.1. The first difference of individual income is the first difference of the random-walk, including drift, plus the first difference of white-noise. Hence:

$$\Delta y_{it} = g + \varepsilon_t + u_{it} - u_{it-1}, \tag{5.24}$$

where the suffices t and i differentiate the aggregate, common components from those that are specific to the individual households. Pischke's assumption is that the household does not choose to acquire the aggregate information about the macro shock that would allow the separation of the two components in (24). Instead, each person observes only their sum, which is the moving-average process:

$$\Delta y_{it} = g + \eta_{it} - \lambda \eta_{it-1}. \tag{5.25}$$

The parameter λ can be calculated by solving the quadratic that results from equating the autocorrelation coefficients of the original and derived processes, (24) and (25). However, we know from studies of the PSID and elsewhere that aggregate shocks account for very little of the variation in individual incomes, so that the parameter λ must be close to unity. If all we have to choose is a combination of the two, actual individual incomes are much closer to white-noise than to random-walks.

It is now straightforward to calculate individual and aggregate consumption change. Again, suppose that each household satisfies the infinite-life permanent income model of Chapter 3, so that we abstract from the finite-life aggregation phenomena of the previous subsection. By equation (4.7), individual consumption obeys

$$\Delta c_{it} = (1 - \frac{\lambda}{1+r}) \eta_{it}, \tag{5.26}$$

so that, since λ is close to unity, individual consumption changes are much smoother than the individual income changes. Although the consumer knows that there is an aggregate persistent shock in his or her own innovation, there is no way of knowing exactly what it is, so the response of consumption is only a little more than it would be if the income shock were purely transitory. The change in aggregate consumption is obtained by averaging (26) over the population, so that, dropping the individual suffices so as to denote means,

$$\Delta c_t = (1 - \frac{\lambda}{1+r})\eta_t. \tag{5.27}$$

However, if we compare the population means of (24) and (25), and use the fact that the idiosyncratic components have zero mean over the population, we have

$$\varepsilon_t = \eta_t - \lambda\eta_{t-1}. \tag{5.28}$$

Hence, from (27), the change in aggregate consumption follows the autoregressive process

$$\Delta c_t = \lambda\Delta c_{t-1} + (1 - \frac{\lambda}{1+r})\varepsilon_t. \tag{5.29}$$

Finite-life effects would add an intercept term to (29), as well as some additional terms in lagged innovations, although they will not be as important as in Clarida's example where all incomes were identical.

Far from being white-noise, the change in aggregate consumption is strongly autoregressive, with only a small response to the innovation in aggregate income. If (29) really holds in the data, aggregate consumption will indeed be very smooth, responding only with long lags to innovations in aggregate income. Although this is no more than an illustrative example, it captures a number of features of reality. Data from the PSID, MaCurdy (1982) and Abowd and Card (1989), as well as from the Survey of Income and Program Participation, Pischke (1991), suggest that the income changes of individual households follow an MA(2) rather than an MA(1), although the latter is a relatively good approximation. Presumably, the idiosyncratic elements of individual incomes also have some persistence over time, which would tend to decrease the λ parameter in the example. Nevertheless, the model can readily be reworked using more general processes for both micro and macro components, but the basic point remains unchanged; indeed, Pischke estimates both micro and macro income processes that are mutually consistent, and attempts to reconcile the implications with the behavior of aggregate consumption. He finds that individuals have in fact very little incentive to obtain aggregate data. The amount that they would pay for it, calculated as the cash equivalent of the increased welfare from better planning, is less than 50 cents per quarter, a figure that is within the range of estimates obtained by Cochrane (1989) from the aggregate data using a representative agent. Given that people never do learn the aggregate shock, Pischke's best-fitting model, like the simple example, tends to predict too much smoothness for consumption, rather than too little.

Note the importance of the fact that people *never* learn the aggregate shock. In Goodfriend's model, the shock becomes known with a one-period lag, so that changes in aggregate consumption, although not orthogonal to variables dated one period ago, which are effectively 'news' this period, will be orthogonal to variables dated two periods back or earlier. In consequence, lagged learning cannot explain Campbell and Mankiw's (1991) findings that changes in consumption are correlated with changes in income that were predictable on information available two periods earlier. But given the trivial benefits of learning about the aggregate, and the non-trivial costs, it seems quite plausible that individuals choose to remain in ignorance indefinitely. Note too that if Pischke's model is correct, it should in principle be possible to reject the Euler equation on the micro data, because the consumption change is not orthogonal to previously known information, namely last period's aggregate shock, even though it is orthogonal to what the agent actually knew. However, such a failure would not be detected using the sort of cross-sectional tests discussed in Section 1. Only long time-series data on individuals would reveal whether individual consumption changes are orthogonal to common aggregate shocks. Nor is it possible to test for excess sensitivity using cohort data as in Attanasio and Weber (1991, 1992); cohort-level shocks are as unlikely to be known to individuals as are aggregate shocks.

Aggregation under imperfect information has an effect that is close to the effect of habit formation. Aggregate shocks are more persistent than micro shocks, but are only imperfectly perceived, so that aggregate consumption responds only slowly to aggregate income. Habits exert a direct drag on consumption change at the individual level; consumption variability is much more painful than it is in the absence of habits, and an over-enthusiastic response to good luck will only give a hostage to future misfortune. The effects at the aggregate level are very similar; indeed equation (29), generated here by the simple aggregation story, is identical to equation (1.63) which represents the behavior of an individual agent whose current utility is decreased by the previous period's consumption.

5.5 Macroeconomics and microeconomics: a summary

I have already attempted to summarize the empirical studies reviewed in the first two sections of this chapter. The econometric problems associated with testing the theory on the microeconomic data are if anything more formidable than those associated with macroeconomic time-series. As a result, there is less agreement about what the empirical results mean, and few people have been persuaded away from their original positions. Even so, I argued for my own interpretation, that the data do not support the formal version of the permanent income hypothesis, nor conventional versions of life-cycle models. (Just what 'conventional' means in this context, and what exactly are the unconventional life-cycle models are topics that must wait until the next chapter.) As we have known since the 1950s, consumers engage in high-frequency smoothing, and consumption is not tied to income over very short intervals of time. Friday's consumption is not tied to Friday's income, and although 1990s consumption is more closely tied to 1990s income, there is still some room for divergence, although there will be little over periods of a few years. Consumption tracks income over the life-cycle, and predictable life-cycle changes in income help predict consumption changes, in both the short and long run.

All of this sounds very much like the macroeconomic evidence that was reviewed in Chapter 3. Qualitatively it is indeed similar, but the details simply do not correspond. Microeconomic income processes are very different from macroeconomic income processes, and autocorrelation patterns in first differences typically have different signs in the household level and aggregate data. So even if predictable income is correlated with consumption in both types of data, predictable income in household data is a very different thing from predictable income in the aggregate. It may be comforting to have the same qualitative results at the two levels of aggregation, but it would be more comforting if the two levels were two countries, or two planets, where there was no need to reconcile the details of one with the other.

I reviewed in Section 3 above recent studies that have looked for traces of complete markets and altruism. This is a promising and under-researched area, but the results of the tests are as conclusively negative as anything reported in this book. As Hayashi, Altonji, and Kotlikoff (1991) emphasize, one route to the existence of a representative agent is the combination of complete markets and intergenerational altruism. The former pools information and co-ordinates marginal utilities, while the latter immortalizes people through their families. But the PSID data on parents and children provide no evidence in favor of the prediction of either one. This is not exactly a surprise, but it is often surprisingly difficult to reject even the most (apparently) absurd models, only occasionally because they are true, but more often because tests are not very powerful. (For a contrary view, see Cochrane's (1991) equating of the resistance to the risk-pooling hypothesis with the earlier resistance to permanent income and similar models in the 1950s.)

If the representative agent does not exist, then aggregation becomes, not a nuisance, but a fruitful source of possible explanations for the data. The work of Clarida and Galí has shown how, in a world without intergenerational altruism, births and deaths cause consumption and labor income to move together over long periods, transferring the rate of growth of productivity from the latter to the former, and causing a weak form of excess sensitivity. These are important insights, although they hardly explain the short-run excess sensitivity that exists in the aggregate data. A more promising route to reconciliation is through imperfect information, as discussed in the work of Goodfriend and of Pischke. If consumers are unable to sort out idiosyncratic from aggregate shocks, they will make small individual mistakes in their consumption choices. If the correct part of their response is largely idiosyncratic, aggregation can leave us with a representative agent who makes very large mistakes, and who responds only very sluggishly to innovations in aggregate income. This topic deserves further research, not on the macroeconomic data, whose information is surely exhausted, but on micro data, and the way it aggregates. A promising tool for this work is the analysis of cohort data, which are partially aggregated, and which have some of the features of both household and aggregate data. The work by Attanasio and Weber (1991, 1992) on data from both the US and the UK is particularly promising in this regard.

CHAPTER 6

New Directions: Beyond Permanent Income

In this chapter I return to two important issues that were raised in Chapter 1 but have since made only brief appearances: precautionary saving and liquidity constraints. Both topics have been at the center of a good deal of recent research, so that this chapter is inevitably more speculative than the earlier ones. It is also more technically demanding, although it should be possible to skim the material without much loss of continuity.

The precautionary motive for saving is entirely consistent with the basic theory of intertemporal allocation, but is ruled out by the certainty equivalence assumptions that generate the permanent income model. Certainty equivalence provides great analytical convenience, and abandoning it greatly increases the analytical and practical difficulties. Nevertheless, the effort is almost certainly worth while; there is a good argument that the permanent income assumptions emasculate the life-cycle theory, and that no amount of mathematical convenience can compensate for the loss of substance. Liquidity constraints, by contrast, are ruled out by assumption in the life-cycle model, and as we have seen, they have often been seen as likely culprits for the empirical failures of the model. Indeed, even as matter of theory, there are problems with the permanent income hypothesis if liquidity constraints are *not* imposed. As we shall see, there are perfectly reasonable specifications for labor income, such as a constant plus an independent and identically distributed shock, where the theory predicts that assets will follow a random-walk, so that if the consumer lives long enough, liabilities will exceed *any* predetermined limit. It is far from obvious how such an eventuality could occur. The second section of the chapter builds a model where consumers cannot borrow at all. Although this is admittedly an extreme case, it generates useful insights, and perhaps surprisingly preserves many of the useful features of the permanent income theory while helping to explain at least some of the difficulties with the data.

6.1 Precautionary saving

That saving provides insurance for future contingencies has long been recognized in the literature, but formal treatments of the precautionary motive have played a relatively minor role in the debate, at least until recently. As we saw in Chapter 1.3, if the marginal utility of consumption function is convex, increases in the uncertainty of future consumption will prompt a reduction in current consumption and an increase in saving. Convex marginal utility means not only that the marginal value of consumption is higher when consumption is low, but also that the rate at which the marginal valuation rises with shortfalls in consumption should be greater when consumption is low than when it is high. If so, increases in uncertainty raise the valuation of future consumption, because of the inclusion of more possible states when the valuation of consumption is very high, and the incentive to save is increased. In permanent income models, where the felicity functions are quadratic and marginal utility is linear, the expectation of marginal utility is the marginal utility of the expectation, so that increases in future uncertainty do not by themselves affect saving.

It is difficult to judge the plausibility of the convexity a priori, although prices of basic commodities often rise to very sharp peaks at times of real or perceived shortage, a phenomenon that is consistent with increasingly steep demand functions at low levels of consumption. Constant elasticity demand functions are also convex, as is the marginal utility of consumption $c^{-\rho}$ when felicity takes the standard isoelastic form ($\rho > 0$ is required for concavity). In the case of isoelastic utility, risk-aversion and precautionary saving are controlled by the same parameter ρ; the higher is risk-aversion, the greater will be the curvature of the marginal utility function. The example suggests that the degree of precaution and risk-aversion are much the same thing, but this is not true in general. Risk-aversion is controlled by the degree of concavity of the utility function (here the felicity function), but the degree of precaution is the degree of convexity of the *marginal* utility function. Risk-aversion depends on the second derivative of the utility function, and precaution on the third derivative, and it is only for very special functions that one can be inferred from the other. In an elegant paper, Kimball (1990) has explored the parallels and contrasts between risk-aversion and what he labels *prudence*, and proposes the elasticity of the slope of the marginal utility function as a measure of the latter just as the elasticity of the marginal utility function is a measure of the former.

Although some economists would doubt whether introspection can reveal very much about the third derivative of utility, many find the precautionary motive intuitively appealing. The quadratic felicity functions that support the permanent income hypothesis may be analytically convenient, but they rule out precautionary motives, as well as having other unattractive implications, such as the existence of a 'bliss' utility level, beyond which the marginal utility of consumption is negative. Models that rely upon tests of Euler equations, such as Hansen and Singleton's (1982) study of aggregate data (Chapter 2.3), or Zeldes' (1989*a*) paper using the PSID (Chapter 5.2) use isoelastic felicity functions, and these models implicitly allow for precautionary saving. Nevertheless, Euler equations by themselves cannot provide the insights into behavior that are yielded by the explicit solutions that are obtained under certainty equivalence, and that are not obtainable for the more interesting models.

An approximation and a special case

Although models with precautionary saving are hard to solve, there are a number of special cases and approximations that give useful insights. In Chapter 2.2, I used the Euler equation for isoelastic felicity together with a first-order Taylor expansion to derive (2.11), repeated here,

$$E_t \Delta \ln c_{t+1} = \rho^{-1}(E_t r_{t+1} - \delta) + \frac{1}{2}\rho\,\omega_t^2, \qquad (6.1)$$

where ω_t^2 is a variance term, indexed on t, that depends on the one-period-ahead anticipated variability of the rate of growth of consumption and real returns, see (2.12). Although (1) is only approximate, it shows how the degree of prudence, represented in the isoelastic utility formulation by the risk-aversion coefficient ρ, controls the extent to which people should postpone consumption in response to uncertain prospects. Equation (1) also demonstrates an important insight due to Carroll (1991). Any variable that helps predict the future variability of consumption, for example current assets, will have a role in predicting the rate of growth of consumption. This is a feature that is specific to models with precautionary saving, and it shows how misleading it is to think of (1) as a sort of logarithmic version of the random-walk prediction of the permanent income hypothesis. Models with isoelastic felicity incorporate a precautionary motive for saving, and are fundamentally different from the permanent income hypothesis, which rests on certainty equivalence.

A useful special case is where felicity functions are negative exponential, so that there is constant absolute risk-aversion. Blanchard and Fischer (1989: ch. 6.3,) and Caballero (1990*b*), assume that the felicity functions are $-\alpha^{-1}\exp(-\alpha c_t)$, and show that if the real interest rate is zero, then for a consumer with a finite life ending at calendar date T, and whose labor income follows a random-walk whose innovations are normally distributed with variance σ^2, consumption at t is given by

$$c_t = \frac{A_t}{T+1-t} + y_t - \frac{\alpha(T-t)\sigma^2}{4}. \tag{6.2}$$

Given the random-walk and zero interest rate assumptions, the first two terms are what would be predicted by the permanent income hypothesis, while the third is the contribution of the precautionary motive. Variance in the income process tilts the consumption trajectory downward early in life, so that, as before, uncertainty generates additional consumption growth, because it induces consumers to postpone their consumption. Equation (2) also implies that consumption follows a random-walk, but with a drift term $\alpha\sigma^2/2$. Since the drift is constant, negative exponential felicity does not have the property shown in (1) that consumption change may be predictable (except for the constant) by previously known variables that condition variance.

While the exponential case provides a nice example, it cannot be more than suggestive; negative exponential utility does nothing to rule out negative consumption, especially early in life if assets are low and income innovations are variable, see (2).

To make further progress, we need to find some other way of investigating the properties of consumption where precautionary saving is important. Recent progress has depended on numerical solutions, and the next subsection contains a relatively informal discussion of how these solutions can be obtained. My discussion draws on the work of Skinner (1988), Zeldes (1989b), Carroll (1991), and Deaton (1991). Readers who are not interested in these matters can skip to the subsection on implications, where I try to summarize what we have learned from the calculations that have been done, and to draw out the implications for the way we should think about consumption.

Computing consumption without certainty equivalence

We wish to find a procedure for obtaining the solution of the consumer's intertemporal allocation problem. The problem is the basic one of Chapter 1, and we can start from the Euler equation (1.50), restated as:

$$\lambda(c_t) = E_t\left(\frac{1+r}{1+\delta}\lambda(c_{t+1})\right), \tag{6.3}$$

where I am working with a constant real interest rate, and with the case where felicity functions differ only by discounting at the rate of time-pre-ference δ. As before, $\lambda(c)$ is the marginal felicity function $\upsilon'(c)$. The dif-ficulty of this problem is almost entirely due to the presence of uncertainty, and to the resulting expectation operator in (3). The problems would vanish if we could pass the operator through the function, but this is only valid when the marginal felicity functions are linear, which rules out the precau-tionary motive, which is our main focus of interest. Jensen's inequality tells us that for convex marginal felicity, the expectation of the function is greater than the function of the expectation, and, if we are to understand precautionary saving, we must take the inequality seriously.

The budget constraint implies that the evolution of assets is governed by

$$A_{t+1} = (1+r)(A_t + y_t - c_t). \tag{6.4}$$

There is an initial level of assets A_0, and we need an assumption about what happens to assets at the end of the period. I shall take the simplest (and safest) case where life is finite, and the consumer dies for sure in period T, so that A_{T+1} is zero. I shall consider the infinite-horizon case at several points below, but there is nothing to stop us looking at people for whom T is very far away. The allocation problem as stated here is quite general, in that there is no assumption about the convexity or otherwise of the marginal utility function. Precautionary saving behavior is permitted, but so is certainty equivalence and the permanent income hypothesis, as well as other cases covered by the general requirement that $\lambda(c)$ be mono-tone-decreasing. Indeed, it is useful to keep the certainty equivalence case in mind as a limiting case, since its analytical solution, the permanent in-come hypothesis, can be used as a check for the more cumbersome met-hods that I am about to discuss.

Our aim is to derive a function that delivers consumption given assets and income. The first point to note is that the form of this function, and indeed its list of arguments, cannot be independent of the form of the income process. For example, in the certainty equivalence case, the perma-nent income solution (3.3) holds no matter what the income process. How-ever, as soon as we make the equation operational by replacing the expec-ted income terms by observable magnitudes, consumption becomes a func-tion of assets and past and present incomes, with the number and form of the latter depending on the income process. If income is first-order autoregressive, and if the consumer knows it to be so, then consumption is a function of assets, income, and lagged income. If it is second-order autoregressive, there are two lags of income, and so on. Exactly the same sort of thing happens in the more general case, although the details are somewhat more complex. In particular, it is necessary to commit to a particular income process at an earlier stage, and to solve the problem conditional on that choice. I start from the most obvious and simplest case, where incomes are independent and identically distributed (i.i.d.) over time. Given this, it is reasonable to suppose that consumption in each period should be a function only of assets and of current income. Indeed, since money is fungible between assets and income, consumption will be a function of only their sum, a magnitude that I shall refer to as 'cash in hand' and which I denote by x,

$$x_t = A_t + y_t. \tag{6.5}$$

We are looking for a solution to the Euler equation (3) of the form $f_t(x_t)$. The function will typically vary with t because consumers of different ages will wish to spend different amounts out of the same amount of cash in hand. We therefore have to find a sequence of functions $f_1, \ldots, f_t, \ldots, f_T$; these are known as *policy* functions because they define for each age the optimal policy that the consumer should follow conditional on the value of the state variable, here cash in hand x_t. From the definition of x_t, and from the budget constraint (4),

$$x_{t+1} = (1+r)(x_t - f_t(x_t)) + y_{t+1}. \tag{6.6}$$

Since the income process is i.i.d., this is a first-order Markov process; except in the special case where the function $f_t(.)$ is linear (as it turns out to be in the permanent income model), (6) will not be a linear autoregression. Now note that $c_{t+1} = f_{t+1}(x_{t+1})$, and substitute (6) into the Euler equation (3), to obtain

$$\lambda(f_t(x)) = \int \frac{1+r}{1+\delta} \lambda \big(f_{t+1}((1+r)(x - f_t(x)) + y \big) dF(y). \tag{6.7}$$

where $F(y)$ is the distribution function of income and I have dropped the subscript on x since it is the same wherever it appears, and because x is the (dummy) argument of the functions for which we are trying to solve.

The way to think about (7) is as a difference equation, not in a single quantity, but in a sequence of *functions*. Given a function $f_{t+1}(x)$, then for any x, equation (7) defines the function $f_t(x)$, so that provided the solution exists and is unique, (7) establishes a rule for transforming one function into the next, for getting from f_{t+1} to f_t. In spite of the apparent complexity of (7), the calculations are not very difficult. Given the function f_{t+1}, and any number x, we have to solve (7) for the single number $f_t(x) = z$, say. But the left-hand side of (7) is monotone-decreasing in z, while the right-hand side is monotone-increasing in z provided that f_{t+1} is monotone-increasing, so there is a single solution which can be found by standard bisection or secant methods. It is also easy to show that the fact that λ is monotone-decreasing implies that f_t is monotone-increasing provided that f_{t+1} is monotone-increasing. Hence, if we can find a last period function to start the procedure, and provided it is monotone-increasing, then we have a method for solving backwards for the sequence of functions, each of which defines the consumer's optimal consumption level at the various periods of life. But the last period function is easy to derive. In period T, everything is spent, so that consumption is the sum of assets and income. Hence, we have at once that

$$f_T(x) = x_T. \tag{6.8}$$

which is certainly monotone-increasing, and we have all that we need.

In some cases, it is possible to start from (8) and to follow (7) back, and to see a pattern emerging. Indeed it is an instructive exercise to apply the method to the certainty equivalent case, where the λ functions are linear, and under the assumption that $r = \delta$. As is easily seen, the linearity of the rule is passed from function to function, although the coefficients will change as we move further from the terminal date. In this case too, the process converges, so that as we recede from T back towards the beginning of time, we eventually obtain

$$c_t = f(x_t) = \frac{r}{1+r}(\mu + x_t) = \frac{r}{1+r}\left(A_t + y_t + \sum_{i=0}^{\infty}(1+r)^{-i}\mu\right), \tag{6.7}$$

which is indeed the permanent income hypothesis in the case where labor income is i.i.d. with mean μ. For more general cases, it is usually impossible to solve analytically, even one step back from T. It is therefore necessary to turn to the computer.

There are many different ways of calculating the sequence of policy functions for this sort of problem; I confine myself to one of the simplest. Start from a 'grid' of values for the state variable x. This will typically be a vector of equally spaced values

$$m = (x_1, x_2, \ldots, x_N) \tag{6.10}$$

such that x_1 is smaller than, and x_N is larger than any value of the state variable that will be generated by the problem. Of course, until we have solved the problem, it is hard to know what this range should be, but it is usually possible to start with a good guess, and to refine it later if necessary. The object of the calculation is to calculate values for the policy functions for each point on the grid, relying on some sort of interpolation when we need values between grid points; we are calculating a set of 'tables' for the functions that are then available to be consulted as required.

The first function is given by (8); f_T is just the grid itself, m. The next, f_{T-1} is given by solving, see (7),

$$\lambda(z) = \int \frac{1+r}{1+\delta} \lambda\big((1+r)(x-z) + y\big) dF(y) \tag{6.9}$$

for z corresponding to each of the x values on the grid; the z values are then the values of f_{T-1} at each of the points on the grid. Depending on the marginal utility function and on the density function of y, it may be possible to solve (11) analytically (for example, if $\lambda(z) = e^{-az}$, the constant absolute risk-aversion or negative exponential case, and if income is normally distributed), but in general it will have to be solved by an iterative procedure of trial and error, using numerical integration to evaluate the integral. From period $T-2$ and back, the equation that has to be solved is

$$\lambda(z) = \int \frac{1+r}{1+\delta} \lambda\big(f_t\big((1+r)(x-z) + y\big)\big) dF(y), \tag{6.12}$$

which presents only one additional numerical difficulty, that the previously evaluated function appears inside the integral, so that to do the numerical integration, we must be able to evaluate the function at points between the grid points. One method is simply to interpolate between the values at each grid point. This works well provided there are a large number of grid points, and we are not concerned with the fact that the approximating function so calculated is non-differentiable, with a kink at each grid point. It is possible to economize on grid points and to remove the non-differentiabilities by using a more elaborate interpolation procedure, cubic splines being perhaps the natural choice.

Once the functions have been calculated as far back as desired, they can be used to simulate possible consumption paths. A particular life-time profile of income is drawn at random from the distribution of *y*, and initial assets are set. Cash in hand is the sum of first-period assets and income, and consumption is calculated from the first-period policy function. First period consumption also determines first-period saving and thus assets in the second period, and so on. Expected consumption trajectories can be calculated by repeating the experiments and averaging over the trajectories. Using these simulations, and the computed paths of assets, we can check that the asset trajectories lie within the grid. If not, the calculations have to be done with a larger grid. Similarly, if large parts of the grid are unused, the calculations can be repeated with greater precision using a finer grid over a smaller range.

There are (at least) three practical problems that are worthy of note. First, the single most expensive part of the calculations is the numerical integration. In many cases, it is assumed that income (or at least its innovation process) is normally distributed, not for realism, but out of custom and convenience. But normality is extremely *inconvenient* in this case, particularly as compared with a discrete distribution, which would allow the integral to be replaced by a sum. For example, if a random variable takes on the ten values (± 1.28, ± 0.84, ± 0.52, ± 0.25, 0), each with probability 0.1, the resulting distribution will provide a reasonable approximation to an $N(0,1)$ variable, and the cost of the integration is avoided. The second problem is harder to circumvent. It is clear from what we know already that there are many configurations of parameters under which there will be a pronounced life-cycle pattern of assets. Those who are impatient may borrow early in life, and repay debts later. Others will save early, accumulating assets, and running them down as they age. Taking the whole life cycle together, there will be a wide range of assets, and therefore of the amounts of cash in hand *x* over which we need to evaluate the policy functions. Furthermore, the longer the planning horizon, the wider the range of possible *x*-values, and the more complex becomes the problem. In general, the finer the grid, the better the numerical accuracy, so that the smaller the range of *x*, the better the accuracy at fixed computational cost.

If the grid has to cover a large range, it is difficult to obtain good accuracy at reasonable cost, especially for long lives.

The third issue is the fact that the transformation of each policy function from the previous one itself requires an iterative process of solution, so that, if the calculations are being done for many ages, the total computational burden can become very heavy. One way to reduce the burden is to work not with the policy functions, but with the value function for each period. The value functions are frequently of interest in their own right, for example for welfare calculations, so that the alternative procedure is worth consideration, even when computation is not an issue.

For the model as written, the value functions are linked recursively by the equation

$$V_{t-1}(x) = \max_{c}\left(\upsilon(c) + (1+\delta)^{-1}EV_t\big((1+r)(x-c)+y\big)\right), \qquad (6.13)$$

while the value function in the last period is given by

$$V_T(x) = \upsilon(x). \qquad (6.14)$$

Starting from this last period function, and working with a grid m as before, we can solve (13) recursively backwards to evaluate the value functions for as many periods as we wish. A simple way to do so is to have an n_c element grid for consumption c, and to evaluate the expression in brackets on the right-hand side of (13) for all cells of the $n_c \times n$ matrix formed from the product of the two grids. The value of the new value function for each point of m is read off as the largest element in each column, and the policy function as the values of consumption that correspond to these maxima.

A useful question about the sequence of functions $f_T, f_{T-1}, \ldots, f_t, \ldots$ is whether, if we go back far enough, there is convergence to some function f that does not change further. If so, we have a stationary policy, and it is a natural candidate for the solution of the infinite-horizon problem, if such a solution exists. Of course, there will be cases where convergence is not to be expected, and this will be so for most formulations of the life-cycle consumption problem, since age will usually be important in determining the relationship between consumption and resources. Even so, we shall see examples where the stationary policy exists and is informative.

For thinking about the question, it is useful to recognize that (7) is a functional difference equation, in which the function f_t is transformed into the function f_{t-1}, and to write the transformation in the form

$$f_{t-1} = Tf_t. \tag{6.15}$$

The existence of a limiting function comes down to the question of whether there is a fixed point of the mapping T, a function f satisfying

$$f = Tf = \lim_{n \to \infty} T^n f_T. \tag{6.16}$$

There is no reason to suppose that this will happen in general, although we have already seen one such case, when $r = \delta$ and preferences are quadratic so that the limiting policy is the permanent income hypothesis. In general, a sufficient condition for an invariant solution is that T be a contraction mapping, so that the distance between any two policy functions g_1 and g_2 is decreased by applying the transform (7) or (13) to both. In the current case, it appears that the condition $\delta > r$ will usually be sufficient for T to be a contraction mapping. If so, not only does a limiting policy exist, but it is the unique time- (or age-) invariant function that satisfies (7). Provided the convergence is relatively rapid, such a limiting function is useful because it gives a rule that characterizes behavior through much of the life cycle, and saves us from having to calculate different rules for each age.

Note that the existence of a stationary policy does not mean that consumption itself is constant, since the argument of the policy function, cash in hand, will evolve over time. The assumption that $\delta > r$, that impatience is stronger than the reward for waiting, means that the consumer would typically want consumption to be falling in the absence of uncertainty. It is a simple but instructive exercise to prove that with isoelastic utility, and constant real income, the optimal (declining) consumption path can be described by a linear (and invariant) relation between consumption and cash in hand.

Complications: autocorrelation and growth

The analysis of the previous subsection was conducted under the simplest possible assumption, that income is independently and identically distributed over time. As a practical matter, this is not very useful. There is growth in the economy, and although the individual incomes are much less autocorrelated than is average income, even the former are serially correlated. Both issues can be dealt with, although at the price of additional assumptions.

When income is serially correlated, consumption is no longer a function only of cash in hand, but will depend on assets and income separately. For example, if income follows a stationary first-order autoregressive process with positive autocorrelation, then high income today not only means that cash in hand is high, but also that it makes sense to spend more from a given amount of cash in hand because high income today is a signal of higher incomes tomorrow and beyond. Similarly, if labor income follows an MA(1), the state variables will be cash in hand and the current innovation in income, which again carries information about tomorrow's income. Once the point is made, it is easy enough to see how (7) must be adapted. To take the first-order autoregressive case as an example, suppose that $z_t = (y_t - \mu)$ follows the AR(1), $z_t = \phi z_{t-1} + \varepsilon_t$. Then optimal consumption at time t is given by the function $f_t(x_t, z_t)$ with (7) replaced by:

$$\lambda \big(f_{t-1}(x,y) \big) = \frac{1+r}{1+\delta} E \lambda \big(f_t((1+r)(x - f_{t-1}(x,y)) + \mu + a, a \big), \quad (6.17)$$

where $a = \phi(y - \mu) + \varepsilon$, and the expectation is taken with respect to ε. The MA(1) case can be treated similarly and is left as an exercise. The difficulty with these extensions is not in writing down the recursions for the policy functions or the value functions, but in calculating the solutions. In the i.i.d. case, where there is only one argument, the function is calculated for each point on a grid. If there are two arguments, the grid becomes a matrix because we need grids for both x and y, so that the number of calculations is effectively squared. It would be cubed for the three arguments required for second-order autocorrelation, and so on. These calculations are not impossible, but the discretization of income that was recommended for the i.i.d. case is essentially compulsory here. Indeed, there exist techniques for constructing discrete approximations to autoregressive processes that were developed for these sorts of problems, see Tauchen (1986) and Tauchen and Hussey (1991).

Allowing income to grow also requires substantial modifications to the procedures, and seems to be possible only in special circumstances, notably when felicity functions are isoelastic. In this case, it is possible to work with ratios of variables, of income to previous income, and of cash in hand to income, and to derive a policy function for the ratio of consumption to income. Define z_{t+1} by

$$z_{t+1} = y_{t+1}/y_t. \tag{6.18}$$

z_t is assumed to be a stationary process; if income follows a logarithmic random-walk with or without drift, z_t will be i.i.d., but it will be serially correlated if income growth is autocorrelated, as suggested (in different ways) by both macro and micro evidence. Denote the ratios of cash in hand and consumption to income by w_t and θ_t respectively. The budget constraint implies that w_t evolves according to

$$w_{t+1} = 1 + z_{t+1}^{-1}(1+r)(w_t - \theta_t) \tag{6.19}$$

and the Euler equation takes the form

$$\theta_t^{-\rho} = \frac{1+r}{1+\delta} E_t(z_{t+1}^{-\rho} \theta_{t+1}^{-\rho}), \tag{6.20}$$

where, as before, ρ is the coefficient of relative risk-aversion. We can now proceed as in the previous subsection, solving for the consumption *ratio* as a function of the cash in hand to income *ratio*, with as many additional terms in income growth or growth innovations as are needed to handle the serial correlation in the growth process.

The evolution of consumption with precautionary saving

Figure 6.1 shows examples of consumption evolution calculated according to the principles outlined above. Income is taken to be a logarithmic random-walk with no drift; this means that income in the future is expected to be higher than current income, since, if the growth shocks are normally distributed

$$E_t y_{t+k} = y_t \exp(k\sigma^2/2), \tag{6.21}$$

where σ^2 is the variance of the innovations in log income. Note that equation (17) has the implication that the ratio of expected future income to current income is rising into the future, even though there is no drift; the expectation of a convex function, in this case the exponential, is larger than the function of the expectation. The coefficient of relative risk-aversion is taken to be 3, the rates of interest and time-preference are equal at 5%, and the standard deviation of the innovation in log income is 0.15. In all cases,

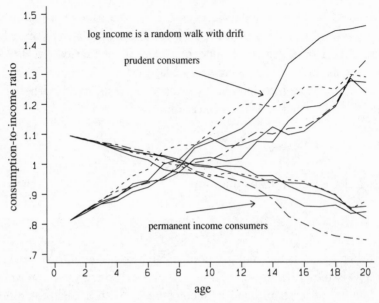

Figure 6.1: Five simulated 20-year lives for permanent income and prudent
consumers

consumers start with no assets, and calculations are for a twenty-year 'life'
and I have made no attempt to incorporate retirement behavior.

Permanent income consumers, with quadratic preferences, would expect
their consumption to be constant, so that their consumption values can be
calculated by setting the discounted present value of a constant consumption stream equal to the discounted present value of current assets and
expected future incomes given by (21). The five falling trajectories are five
random twenty-year simulations for these permanent income consumers.
The ratios fall over time because, given (21), expected income is rising
over time. The prudent consumers, who have to protect themselves against
uncertainty, have the rising consumption to income trajectories. I have used
the same random values of income for each of the two sets, so each prudent individual has a permanent income counterpart with the same income
experience. With these parameter values, precautionary saving is twenty
per cent of income twenty years before death, and the resulting assets
permit consumption to be a good deal higher than income late in the plan.
Clearly, it is possible to generate cases where precautionary saving is

quantitatively important. Longer time-horizons would generate even more saving, as would a higher innovation variance for income, as suggested by the micro data. However, the assumption that all innovations are permanent will tend to exaggerate the amount of precautionary saving; the one-period changes in the micro data most likely have higher variance than here, but lifetime income is probably less at risk than in the example, see Skinner (1988) for further discussion.

Although all of the ten individuals in Figure 6.1 start out with the same level of resources, and have the same stochastic futures, even twenty years of non-stationary income behavior has a dramatic effect on consumption and wealth inequality. Tastes also play a part, and the permanent income consumers never become as wealthy as do the middle-aged precautionary savers. Taste differences and luck are powerful agents for generating and magnifying inequality over time.

Why is precautionary saving important?

The examples in Figure 6.1 illustrate one of the major effects of the precautionary motive, that households will tend to save more earlier in life than would be the case under the permanent income hypothesis. This helps explain why consumption and income often rise together in the early part of the life cycle. Although young people know that their incomes are likely to rise, they do not wish to borrow heavily for consumption because they might be unlucky, and not do as well as they expect. Utility gains from additional consumption now are more than offset by the value of having assets if bad luck strikes in the future. (Note that this does not apply to mortgages for house purchase, which are typically secured by the real estate itself.) Note that if the standard life-cycle picture of Figure 2.1 were correct, with saving throughout youth and middle age, the resulting accumulations of wealth can serve both as a retirement fund, and as a precautionary buffer for shorter-run misfortunes. This argument has been cited by Modigliani (1986, 1990) as a reason for not having to pay separate attention to the precautionary motive, although he also points out that the demand for precautionary saving is likely to be increased by the replacement of personal wealth by pension funds and social security, assets which are not liquid and which cannot be pledged as collateral for loans.

As has long been recognized, precautionary motives can also help explain why older households dissave less than would be explained by permanent income versions of the life-cycle model. Uncertainty about the life-span, about health and health costs, and the extreme unpleasantness of poverty in old age, combine to make older people extremely cautious about running down their assets. Such behavior also explains, at least partially, the important role of accidental bequests in the transmission of wealth.

The recent literature has also considered a number of other consequences of precautionary saving. A number of authors, Zeldes (1989*b*), Skinner (1988), and especially Carroll (1991) have emphasized that, in some circumstances, individuals will never borrow. In particular suppose that there is no positive floor to income, and that there is a positive probability that income will be zero. Suppose too that the coefficient of relative risk-aversion is greater than unity and that the felicity functions are isoelastic, although we can use any other function that has the property that utility tends to minus infinity as consumption tends to zero. Clearly, the consumer will never voluntarily choose a plan in which there is a finite probability of having zero consumption in the last period. Since at the end of this period assets must be zero, and since income may possibly be zero, assets must be positive at the end of the second to last period. By a similar argument, assets must be positive at the end of the previous period, and so on back to the beginning of life. In this sense, the precautionary motive can act like a prohibition on borrowing, although it is a self-inflicted prohibition. Note too that, although borrowing never takes place, the intertemporal Euler equation always holds, something that is not true with formal liquidity constraints, as we shall see in the next section.

It is unclear that the result should be taken very seriously. In practice, there is usually some minimal consumption level that is available from family, friends, or public welfare, although it is hard (or illegal) to borrow against such funds. Such guarantees might allow consumers to borrow large amounts early in life, with the intention of defaulting later and living off the guaranteed minimum later.

There are other ways in which precautionary savers behave very differently from permanent income or (conventional) life-cycle consumers. They may exhibit almost Keynesian responses to changes in income. If consumption depends on the discounted present value of income, as it does under the permanent income hypothesis, cuts in current taxes, which must be financed later, will generally not affect consumption. But as pointed out by Barsky, Mankiw, and Zeldes (1986) and Kimball and Mankiw (1989), if consumers have a precautionary savings motive, and if taxes are an increasing function of incomes, then a substitution of lower current taxes for higher taxes later will reduce the uncertainty of future income, and will reduce the need for current precautionary saving. Even if consumers are making optimal intertemporal choices, and even if the tax cuts have to be repaid in their lifetimes, it makes sense for them to increase their consumption. Precautionary saving motives are thus one (of many) reason(s) why the Ricardian equivalence proposition might fail.

Engen and Gale (1991) have shown how a model of precautionary saving can help explain why households hold Individual Retirement Accounts (IRAs) as well as other forms of saving, given that the former have both higher yields and penalties for early withdrawal. Hubbard, Skinner, and Zeldes (1992) have looked at the effects on wealth accumulation of the existence of social security programs (such as AFDC) that incorporate asset limitations. For poor people, who are never going to accumulate much wealth, and who face health and earnings uncertainty, it can be optimal to make no attempt to accumulate. Only above some critical wealth level does it make sense to try to accumulate savings for retirement or for health expenditures. As a result, consumption can *fall* with wealth over the range where it becomes worth while to save. The simulations in Hubbard, Skinner, and Zeldes suggest that such behavior can help account for at least some of the observed characteristics of the wealth distribution in the US.

The strongest claims on behalf of the precautionary motive come from the work of Carroll (1991), who argues that models with the precautionary motive can explain the tracking of consumption and income over the life cycle, the findings of excess sensitivity, as well as the traditional evidence in favor of permanent income over measured income. Carroll works with standard isoelastic felicity functions, and achieves his results by an appropriate selection of preferences and of the stochastic process for labor income. He argues from the PSID that zero incomes are a real possibility, and thus guarantees the (voluntary) no-borrowing result. He also assumes that consumers are relatively impatient, at least to the extent of having $\delta > r$. Without the uncertainty, such consumers would like to borrow early in life, and let consumption fall over time. In fact they face a great deal of uncertainty, and their prudence is at war with their impatience. They need assets to protect themselves against low income and unemployment, but they basically dislike assets, viewing them as wasted consumption opportunities. Under Carroll's choice of parameters, a compromise is struck in which a few assets are held, but never very many, just enough to act as a buffer against income shocks. The result is that consumption tracks income.

Such an outcome seems to violate everything that we have always known about optimal intertemporal allocation in the absence of borrowing constraints. It also denies the basic insight of all life-cycle models, that the evolution of consumption is independent of the evolution of resources. The key, of course, is the combination of uncertainty and convex marginal utility. The Taylor approximation (1) is useful in seeing how it is possible for Carroll's results to be correct. Consumers who have low incomes and low assets early in the life cycle face greater consumption uncertainty in the future than do those with high incomes or high assets, simply because they have fewer resources, and are less well insured, and so should plan to postpone consumption. As we have seen, such a result can in principle account for excess sensitivity. But it also means that if the life-time profile of income is changed, the life-time profile of consumption will change with it. Of course, the presence of some assets means that consumption can be decoupled from income at high frequencies, but the absence of long-term accumulation means that, at lower frequencies, consumption tracks income.

Carroll's work is undoubtedly important, and must surely change the way that we think about intertemporal allocation. It once again points to the previously underestimated importance of separating permanent income models with their certainty equivalence from models, such as isoelastic felicity, that incorporate precautionary motives. Even so, and although Carroll argues that all his parameters are plausible, his work has so far only scratched the surface of the research that needs to be done to establish that this sort of account is consistent with everything else that we know about consumption and saving.

6.2 Liquidity constraints

Throughout this book, an inability to borrow has been occasionally cited as a possible reason for doubting the general applicability of the life-cycle model. The empirical failings of the theory have also frequently been attributed to liquidity constraints. Even so, there have been very few attempts to model the precise effects of liquidity constraints on consumption. Hall and Mishkin's (1982) assumption that there is a fraction of consumers who simply spend their incomes is certainly useful as a device to test for deviations from the theory in the direction predicted by borrowing restrictions, but it can hardly be taken seriously as a model of consumers who cannot borrow. The inability to borrow does not imply any symmetrical inability to save, and, as we shall see below, there are good reasons why liquidity-constrained consumers will generally want to hold assets. Zeldes' (1989*a*) tests for liquidity constraints use the appropriate modification of the Euler equations for a consumer who cannot borrow, and these permit him, more precisely than Hall and Mishkin, to look for the sort of failure of the model that can be attributed specifically to an inability to borrow. However, as is usually the case, the Euler equations are not very informative about what behavior will look like for those who are liquidity-constrained. Indeed, as we shall see, borrowing restrictions cause only occasional violations of the equations. In this final section, I look in more detail as to exactly what effects liquidity constraints might have, and try to link the results back to the empirical evidence in the earlier chapters.

Theoretical arguments for credit constraints

No one supposes that everyone will always want to borrow more than others will lend to them. As we have already seen, people may have preferences that will make them unwilling to borrow in any circumstances, and there will be many others who, like the standard life-cycle consumers, want to accumulate first and run down assets later, so that the question of borrowing never arises. For those who want to borrow, limited credit is likely to be available, if only through credit cards or bank lines of credit, although the total is likely to be strictly limited. It is those who are impatient, whose preferences make them want to consume more heavily early in life, and whose incomes are rising over time, that are most likely to be unable to find the unsecured loans that would enable them to carry out the consumption plans that they would like.

There are good theoretical reasons why the credit market does not clear. Stiglitz and Weiss (1981) argue that the interest rate on loans cannot be expected to rise to clear the market as would be the case if it were a price like any other price. Borrowers may default on their loans, and it is those who are most likely to repay who are most affected by an increase in the interest rate, and who therefore are less likely to want loans at high rates. As a result, higher interest rates raise the overall default risk on a lender's portfolio. In such circumstances, lenders are likely to hold interest rates low, to protect the quality of their lending, and ration loans by other means. If so, there will be consumers who wish to borrow but cannot. There are a number of other possible mechanisms that result in credit constraints and several are reviewed by Hayashi (1987, sect. 4.)

The permanent income hypothesis also has implications for the behavior of assets which either cast doubt on the model itself, or suggest that borrowing restrictions are likely to be an issue, at least eventually. From equation (4.52) recall that for a consumer satisfying the permanent income hypothesis, the change in assets is given by

$$\Delta A_{t+1} = (1+r)s_t = -(1+r)\sum_{i=1}^{\infty}(1+r)^{-i}E_t\Delta y_{t+i}. \qquad (6.22)$$

Take the simplest case where y_t is i.i.d., so that $E_t\Delta y_{t+1} = -\varepsilon_t$ and all later changes are expected to be zero. Substituting into (22), we have

$$\Delta A_{t+1} = \varepsilon_t, \qquad (6.23)$$

so that assets follow a random-walk. As a result, if the consumer lives long enough, assets will exceed any arbitrarily large positive number, or perhaps more to the point, fall below any arbitrarily large negative number, so that consumption will eventually become negative. Either the consumer will voluntarily stop behaving this way, or borrowing constraints will eventually be imposed. With these sorts of dissatisfactions in mind, Schechtman (1976) and Bewley (1977) developed versions of the permanent income hypothesis where borrowing was never allowed, and showed that there were circumstances in which consumption would eventually converge to the mean of a stationary income process, even without access to borrowing. The treatment in the next sections, which is a summary version of Deaton (1991), owes a great deal to this pioneering work.

Assets as a buffer stock

Suppose then that borrowing is impossible, and that asset levels must always be non-negative. Otherwise, the model is exactly the same as before; the consumer maximizes additive intertemporal preferences with a constant rate of time-preference, and a constant real rate of interest paid on assets. The Euler equation for intertemporal allocation is not the same as before, but takes the form

$$\lambda(c_t) = \max\left(\lambda(x_t), \frac{1+r}{1+\delta} E_t \lambda(c_{t+1})\right), \tag{6.24}$$

where, as before, x_t is cash in hand, the sum of assets and current income.

The liquidity constraint means that the maximum the consumer can spend is x_t, so the marginal utility of money cannot be *less* than $\lambda(x_t)$. Of course, the consumer is free to spend up to this amount, so if the desired intertemporal allocation occurs without having to borrow, and the discounted expected future marginal utility is greater than $\lambda(x_t)$, the Euler equation will have the standard form, and the first term in brackets has no effect. However, even when the borrowing constraint is not in effect, so that the Euler equation looks like a standard one, behavior will not generally be the same as for a consumer who is not constrained. The borrowing constraint may bind again in the future, even if it does not bind today, and the expectations of tomorrow's consumption will take this into account, just as tomorrow's consumption will be set taking into account the possibility of binding liquidity constraints in the future. This sounds complicated, but it will be automatically dealt with if we correctly solve the dynamic program. But note again how little is to be learned from the Euler equation by itself; as we shall see, the presence of the borrowing constraints fundamentally alters the way in which consumers behave, even though there will often be few periods in which the constraint is binding. Counting consumers whose marginal utility of consumption is greater than their discounted expected marginal utility will understate the importance of liquidity constraints in modifying behavior.

The precautionary motive for saving, discussed in the previous section, is strengthened by the existence of liquidity constraints. The ability to borrow in bad times is an insurance device for at least some consumers, and if this mechanism is closed off, additional provision must be made for such eventualities. Without the access to external insurance, consumers must provide it for themselves, by accumulating additional assets. As we have seen, the precautionary motive operates through increases in consumption uncertainty increasing expected marginal utility through a convex marginal utility function. If there are borrowing restrictions, high consumption levels are more likely to be disallowed than low consumption levels, so that the expected marginal utility is further increased. Even if preferences are quadratic, and the interest rate and time-preference rates are equal, there will be a precautionary saving motive if borrowing is not allowed. In this case, equation (24) takes the simple form

$$c_t = \max(x_t, E_t c_{t+1}).$$ (6.25)

Increases in future uncertainty lower expected future consumption because, as the spread increases, a greater fraction of the distribution is censored by the inability to borrow.

In order to further characterize the behavior of consumption, it is necessary to make specific assumptions about preferences and about the behavior of incomes. The techniques for solving the Euler equation are parallel to those outlined for precautionary saving in the previous section, so that, in order to take expectations, we need to know what current income implies about the future. I shall also assume that preferences are such that consumers typically *want* to borrow. The exact form of this assumption depends on the income process; if income is known to be growing, consumers are more likely to want to borrow than if it is falling. In the case where income is stationary, I shall assume that $\delta > r$, so that if there were no restrictions, optimal consumption would be falling, a plan that would typically call for borrowing in the early years. When income is growing, a weaker assumption will have the same effect. These assumptions about preferences are made, not because I believe that they are generally valid, but in order to isolate those consumers whose behavior is likely to be affected by the restrictions. Consumers who are patient, and whose incomes fluctuate around a constant mean, are natural lenders, not borrowers, and are not directly affected by the liquidity-constraints. Note however, that in a world where everyone has the same rate of time preference but some fraction of consumers are liquidity constrained, then in equilibrium the excess supply of loans will tend to depress the interest rate below the rate of time-preference.

I proceed in the same way as in the previous subsection, starting with the case where incomes are independently and identically distributed, and then moving on to deal with autocorrelation and non-stationarity. As before, if income is i.i.d., consumption is a function of cash in hand, so that if we substitute $c_t = f_t(x_t)$ into the liquidity constrained Euler equation (24), the functional difference equation is

$$\lambda\left(f_{t-1}(x)\right) = \max\left[\lambda(x), \frac{1+r}{1+\delta}\int\lambda\left(f_t((1+r)(x-f_{t-1}(x))+y)\right)\right].$$ (6.26)

Given that $\delta > r$, and provided that income is always at least as large as some (strictly) positive floor, so that the marginal utility of money remains finite, equation (26) always has a unique time-invariant solution

$$c = f(x) \tag{6.27}$$

(see Deaton and Laroque (1992, Theorem 1) for a proof). Hence, if the agent lives long enough, we can characterize the behavior of consumption in terms of the two equations (6)and (27); the former governs the evolution of cash in hand x_t and the latter translates cash in hand into consumption.

The properties of the function $f(x)$ are illustrated in Figure 6.2; the examples are calculated using the methods described in the previous section, but the properties discussed are general. In all cases illustrated, the felicity functions are isoelastic, and the coefficients of relative risk-aversion are taken to be 2 or 3. Income is i.i.d. normal, with mean 100 and standard deviations 10 or 15, but truncated at 5 standard deviations from the mean. In all cases, the real interest rate is 5% and the rate of time-preference is 10%. In general, the consumption function starts out along the 45–degree line, where everything is spent. At some critical level of cash in hand, the precise value of which depends on the parameters of the problem, it is optimal to keep something for the future, and the fraction of resources so retained increases with the amount of cash in hand. When times are bad, and the consumer has very little, it pays to spend everything; even the last unit of cash in hand is worth more now than it is expected to be in the future. If it were possible, the consumer would borrow, but given the constraint, he or she can do no better than spend what is available. As the consumer's liquidity improves, it becomes desirable to put something away for bad times in the future, and to accumulate assets as a buffer against fluctuations of income and the inability to borrow. The more uncertain is income, the more is saved, and the less is spent; the same is true if we compare more cautious with less cautious consumers, where in this isoelastic example caution is measured by the degree of risk-aversion.

The figure can also be used to get an idea of what happens to assets when the consumer obeys the optimal rule. From the equation governing the evolution of cash in hand, (7), it is easy to show that $x_{t+1} > x_t$ if, and only if,

$$\frac{y_{t+1} - \mu}{1+r} > f(x_t) - \frac{rx_t + \mu}{1+r}. \tag{6.28}$$

The right-hand side is the distance between the function and the upward-sloping straight line in Figure 6.2. This distance is always increasing, so

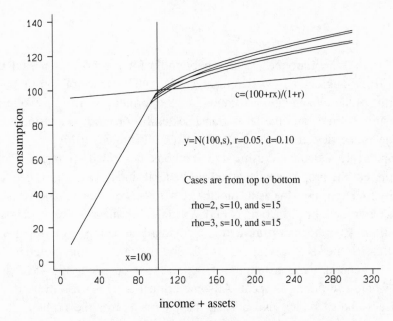

Figure 6.2: Consumption functions for different risk-aversion parameters and standard deviations of income

provided there is an upper limit to income as well as a lower one, cash in hand cannot go on increasing for ever, and will eventually fall. It is harder to show that assets will eventually fall to zero, with cash in hand in the next period equal to income. However, Schechtman and Escudero (1977) show that provided additional restrictions are imposed on preferences, conditions that are satisfied by both quadratic and isoelastic felicity functions, assets are guaranteed to fall to zero in finite time. Like a well designed reservoir, there should be years in which assets run out; the stock of assets, like water in the reservoir, has no value of itself for these impatient consumers, but it does have a derived value in an uncertain world in which there is no access to credit.

Figure 6.3 shows a 200-year simulation of behavior for one of the models shown in Figure 6.2; where the coefficient of relative risk-aversion is 3 and the standard deviation of income is 10. The top panel of the figure shows income, simply 200 independent draws from $N(100, 10)$. The middle panel shows consumption (less 40 to keep the drawings apart from one another), and the bottom panel shows the stock of assets. The first thing to

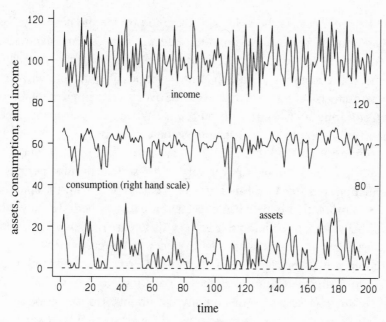

Figure 6.3: Simulations of income, consumption, and assets

note is that consumption is considerably smoother than income. Its standard deviation is only 4.9, which is less than half of that of income. Even without the ability to borrow, and with only themselves to rely on, it is possible for consumers to substantially smooth consumption without recourse to credit, simply by using assets as a buffer. Note too that the distribution of consumption is not symmetric. Over the period of the simulation, there are several downward peaks, but no upward spikes. This is a direct consequence of the asymmetry of the borrowing restriction. The consumer can always save, so that potential upward spikes in consumption can be cut off, and the additional resources saved for the future. Negative shocks to income, by contrast, can be offset by running down assets, if there are assets to run down, but if assets have already been exhausted, nothing can be done, and consumption has to fall. It is instructive to examine such cases in Figure 6.3. The most notable is in year 108, where there is a very large negative income shock at a time when assets, although not zero, are very low, because of low income levels two and three periods before. It is the succession of low incomes, or of low incomes relieved by only mediocre incomes, to which consumers are vulnerable. But note that there are also several cases of poor income draws where consumption is barely affected, because the assets are there to provide the needed protection. Asset-buffering does not provide perfect insurance, and since assets are regularly exhausted, and since incomes are independently distributed over time, it is eventually certain that the worst possible income will occur when there are no assets, so that even the worst consumption outcomes without buffering will occur with buffering. What the asset management scheme does accomplish is to make these outcomes much less frequent.

The figure shows that although assets are zero from time to time, they are usually positive, although never very large, so that in most periods of the simulation, the standard Euler equation is satisfied, with the marginal utility of consumption equated in expectation between periods. Nevertheless, the behavior of consumption is very different from the fluctuations around a falling trend that would be expected if the consumer were permitted to borrow as much as he or she wanted. It is this combination that leads me to doubt the ability of Euler equation tests to detect more than a fraction of the consequences of liquidity constraints. Consumption in this simulation, like income, is stationary, and since assets regularly stock out, there can be no permanent separation between the levels of the two series. Given the degree of consumption-smoothing, and the extent to which consumption is smoother than income, it is remarkable that the average asset holdings are around 7% or less than one standard deviation of income. The data in the US suggest that the median level of household liquid assets in the early 1980s was less than $1,000; such amounts are certainly small, but like the assets in the figure, they may be capable of making consumption a good deal smoother than income.

A question that often arises with strategies such as optimal buffering is whether it is sensible to expect households to calculate these rules for themselves. The dynamic programming techniques that generate the functions in Figure 6.2 require a modest investment in computer technology to calculate, and so are surely beyond the wit of most citizens, though that is not to say that they will not learn to mimic the rules very well, just as a pool player learns to use the laws of physics. However, in the current case, almost the same results as those shown can be generated with simple rules-of-thumb, provided the general outlines of the strategy are understood. For example, suppose that the consumption rules in Figure 6.2 are replaced by the following:

$$c_t = x^* + \alpha(x_t - x^*) I(x_t > x^*). \qquad (6.30)$$

where $I(e)$ is 1 if e is true, and 0 otherwise. This is a simple piecewise linear approximation, and embodies the simple precept of spending everything when times are bad, and saving a fixed fraction of any excess over the amount required to achieve a 'minimum necessity.' If x^* is simply taken to be mean income μ, and α is taken to be 0.3, then the consumption and asset series corresponding to the income series in Figure 6.2 are essentially indistinguishable from those shown in the figure. Any reasonable guess for the parameter α will maker consumption substantially smoother than income. These and other rules-of-thumb are further explored in Deaton (1992b), who also examines the implications for welfare. Not surprisingly given the general modest costs that expected utility theory assigns to consumption fluctuations, there is no detectable welfare cost to replacing the optimal strategy with a sensible version of (30).

Serially correlated incomes

The mathematical convenience of serially independent income processes is greater than their descriptive reality. Except perhaps for farmers in a stagnant economy, a more realistic treatment demands that we look at more general cases. As before, the complications are more computational than conceptual. For an impatient household with serially correlated but stationary income, buffering behavior will be easier or harder depending on the nature of the autocorrelation. Suppose that income is negatively autocorrelated (in levels), as it might be for a tree-crop farmer, since bumper crops tend to 'tire' the tree, and are typically succeeded by mediocre or poor harvests. In such a case, buffering will be both cheaper and more effective than when incomes are i.i.d.. The effectiveness is because high incomes are likely to be immediately succeeded by low incomes, so that the previously accumulated asset stock will frequently be required very soon, and cheaper because it is not necessary to hold assets for very long or in very large quantities. Consumption-smoothing requires the consumer to forgo relatively little consumption.

When incomes are positively autocorrelated, life is more difficult. Good times tend to be followed by more good times, and the amplitude of income 'cycles' is exaggerated by the autocorrelation, so that the consumer needs more assets, and has to hold them longer than is the case when incomes are independent. To illustrate, suppose that income follows a first-order autoregressive process with autocorrelation coefficient $\phi > 0$. The

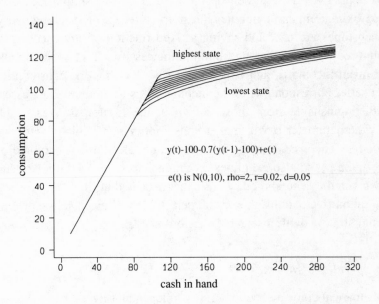

Figure 6.4: Consumption and cash on hand for AR(1) income

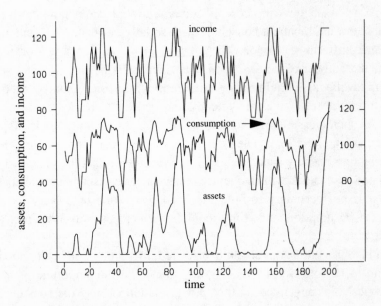

Figure 6.5: Simulations of income, consumption, and income when income is positively autocorrelated

derivation of the consumption function is closely similar to the procedures in the previous section, see equation (17), but with the modification due to the borrowing constraints. Again, given that income has a floor, and that $r < \delta$, the stationary policy function is

$$c_t = f(x_t, y_t). \tag{6.31}$$

The presence of income in the relationship between consumption and cash in hand reflects the need to be more optimistic when income is high, and less optimistic when it is low.

Figure 6.4 shows the case where income can take on ten discrete values, with transition probabilities between them chosen so as to mimic the behavior of an AR(1) with normal errors with autocorrelation coefficient 0.7. For each of the ten income states, the general features of the rule are as before; spend everything up to some critical point, and save a fraction thereafter. However, for the higher draws of income, represented by the higher policy functions in the figure, it is optimal to spend more out of the same amount of cash in hand because the good draw today signals that there will be more tomorrow. Figure 6.5 shows a 200-year simulation using these policy functions, and should be contrasted with the i.i.d. case in Figure 6.3. Because of the serial correlation, income is now more variable, even though the innovation variance is the same as before, and consumption, although smoother than income, tends to track it more closely over the cycles induced by the autocorrelation. Indeed the standard deviation of consumption is now two-thirds of the standard deviation of income, as opposed to half in Figure 6.3. Assets are a good deal larger than before; given the cyclical behavior of income, larger amounts of assets have to be held even to provide the lesser degree of consumption-smoothing. Smoothing is more difficult, requires more assets, and the assets have to be held longer on average. When fortune is persistent, with runs of good and bad luck, insurance is both less effective and more expensive.

Table 6.1 provides a quantitative picture of the relationship between autocorrelation and the degree of consumption-smoothing. The first row shows how the standard deviations of income vary with the autocorrelation coefficient given a constant innovation variance, while the second row shows how the sample standard deviations match up to their theoretical counterparts. The last two rows show the standard deviation of consumption from simulations similar to those in Figure 6.5 and the ratio of the

Table 6.1: Standard deviations of consumption and income for AR(1) income, parameter ϕ

autocorrelation coefficient ϕ	−0.4	0.0	0.3	0.5	0.7	0.9
1. s.d.(y)	10.9	10.0	10.5	11.5	14.0	22.9
2. estimated s.d.(y)	10.8	10.2	10.0	11.4	13.3	27.5
3. estimated s.d.(c)	4.6	5.1	6.7	7.6	10.4	25.9
ratio 3/2	0.43	0.50	0.67	0.67	0.78	0.94

sample standard deviations of consumption and income. As measured by this final ratio, (optimal) smoothing becomes steadily less effective as auto-correlation increases, so that when the autocorrelation coefficient reaches 90%, there is only a 6% reduction in the standard deviation between the two series.

The results in Table 6.1 suggest that when income is a random-walk, there will be no smoothing at all, and that consumption will equal income. In this case, even when preferences are not quadratic, and although the rate of time-preference is greater than the real rate of interest, the presence of the liquidity constraints generates the same solution as the permanent income hypothesis, that consumption should equal income, itself equal to permanent income. Impatient consumers who cannot borrow will still save in order to ride out anticipated or possible temporary shortfalls in income. But when income is a random-walk, all shocks are permanent, and there is no reason to do anything other than adjust consumption immediately to the new, permanent situation. Here is one case, at least, where liquidity con-straints do cause people simply to spend their incomes. Note carefully however that this result comes about, not because income has a unit root, but because income is a random-walk, so that all innovations are persistent. If, for example, income is the sum of a random-walk and white-noise, changes in income will be negatively autocorrelated, income falls are pre-dictable, and there is room for smoothing through buffering.

Aggregation with liquidity constraints

This final subsection is concerned with whether it is possible to use the buffer stock models of consumption and assets to account for at least some of the stylized facts of individual and aggregate behavior in the US. Full-scale estimation of the models of this section remains elusive; the computations needed to calculate the consumption functions would be only one step in any estimation procedure, which is likely to be very costly, especially once the stylized models are enriched to the point where they might reasonably be confronted with the data. My aim here is more modest, to see whether the insights generated by thinking about credit constraints are helpful in interpreting the various pieces of evidence on consumption and income.

One research strategy that will not be successful is to model average behavior as if it were generated by a representative agent who cannot borrow. In the first place, aggregation is always likely to be more difficult where markets are incomplete. If consumers all face the same prices, as in perfectly competitive markets, there is a uniformity across agents that helps make averages resemble the individuals. Of course, as I have repeatedly argued, the representative agent story can be extremely misleading even without borrowing restrictions, but that is certainly no argument for trying to apply it in an even more unlikely context. Second, it is clear from the data that a liquidity-constrained representative-agent model is incapable of explaining the evidence. Aggregate labor income is close enough to a random-walk that the optimal strategy of a liquidity-constrained representative agent would be to save nothing. It would be ironic indeed if, having come so far with theoretical and empirical evidence, the best that we could do would be the hypothesis that consumption equals income! If liquidity constraints play a part in the story of consumption, that part must be elaborated at the level of individual households, and aggregation explicitly taken into account.

All of the evidence, as well as common sense, suggests that not everyone is liquidity-constrained. A sensible starting-point therefore is to accept the standard theory for those consumers, probably a minority, whose patience, thrift, or early inheritances render them immune to the vicissitudes of credit markets. For the rest, there is at best limited access to borrowing. If it were possible to do so, they would borrow to increase their current consumption over what is actually available to them, and they have no desire to accumulate assets over the long term. These are people who would be made worse off if they were forced to (save to) get rich. However, they are subject to considerable income uncertainty; jobs can be lost, new jobs have uncertain pay-offs, there can be temporary lay-offs or changes in the amount of time offered for work, not to mention disturbances from outside the labor market, such as the break up of a marriage, or unanticipated medical bills. In such a world, the precautionary demand for saving is likely to be important, and it will be strengthened if the access to credit is limited when it is most required.

Such a model is consistent with a great deal of what we know about consumption at the microeconomic level. Because assets are only used as a buffer, and because even a few assets can be effective in smoothing consumption, we can explain the very modest liquid asset holdings of most households. Again because assets act as a reservoir, and because the reservoir regularly runs dry, consumption and income are tied together over periods longer than a few years. In the short run, at high frequencies, weeks or months, consumption and income are largely independent, and shocks to income have only a modest effect on consumption. All of the microeconomic evidence on the permanent income hypothesis, from Friedman's own work onwards, provides overwhelming evidence that consumption and income are largely detached in the short run. Over longer periods, at low frequencies, consumption and income move together, as the evidence on 'tracking' shows is in fact the case. The effective planning horizon in the buffer-stock model is the period until assets run out, a period that the simulations suggest is a few years, not a lifetime. Income is smoothed over this much shorter time-frame, not over the lifetimes that are predicted by the life-cycle theory.

The presence of liquidity constraints also explains why predictable increases in income are associated with predictable increases in consumption, both on a short-term year-to-year basis, as well as over the decades during which life-cycle income patterns unfold. The latter is again consistent with the evidence that consumption tracks income, while the evidence on the former depends on how one chooses to read the literature on panel data reviewed in Chapter 5.

It is also possible to construct a model of aggregate consumption using the behavior of liquidity-constrained individuals as the building blocks, and to incorporate the same sort of imperfect information that drives Pischke's (1991) model discussed in Chapter 5.2. The following is certainly not the only way of doing so, but it is perhaps the simplest that is consistent with the main stylized facts from the microeconomic and macroeconomic data. Suppose that the income process of household i is such that its rate of growth is the sum of three stochastic processes:

$$\Delta \ln y_{it} = g + z_{1t} + z_{2it} + z_{3it}, \tag{6.32}$$

where the components are defined as follows:

$$z_{1t} = \varepsilon_{1t} + \beta \varepsilon_{1t-1}, \; z_{2it} = \varepsilon_{2it}, \; z_{3it} = \varepsilon_{3it} - \varepsilon_{3it-1} \tag{6.33}$$

and the ε's are white-noise shocks. The first component, z_{1t}, like the growth rate g, is common to all households, and the parameter β, which is positive, ensures that the aggregate growth process will be positively autocorrelated, mimicking that feature in the aggregate quarterly data. The other two components are idiosyncratic, and average to zero over households, so that average income is the (persistent) MA(1) growth process

$$\Delta y_t = g + \varepsilon_{1t} + \beta \varepsilon_{1t-1}. \tag{6.34}$$

In fact, aggregate income is closer to an AR(1) in first differences, but (34) captures the positive autocorrelation, and the fact that the three components of (32) are all moving averages of degree one or less means that they sum to a moving average of degree one, which makes feasible the calculation of the individual policy functions. The second component of (32) is the first difference of an idiosyncratic random-walk, so that each household has a persistent component of income that is different from each other household. The final component is the first difference of idiosyncratic white-noise; each household has some transitory income.

I assume that the aggregate process is not known to the individual households, so that each observes only the sum of the three components, itself a moving average of the first degree which I write as

$$\Delta \ln y_{it} = g + \eta_{it} - \psi \eta_{it-1}. \tag{6.35}$$

The variance of the η_t and the parameter ψ can be calculated by equating the variance and first autocovariance of (35) and (32), giving

$$\sigma_2^2 = (1 - \psi)^2 \sigma_\eta^2 - (1 + \beta)^2 \sigma_1^2$$
$$\sigma_3^2 = \psi \sigma_\eta^2 + \beta \sigma_1^2. \tag{6.36}$$

The individual household data provide estimates of the process (35) and thus of ψ and σ_η. The aggregate data provide estimates of the macro process, and thus of β and σ_1. Given these four parameters, (36) can be used to calculate σ_2^2 and σ_3^2. For the purposes of the example, I choose the following parameters. From the micro data, and particularly from Ma-Curdy's (1982) study from the PSID, I take $\psi = 0.44$, and the standard deviation σ_η to be 0.15. This seemingly very large number is actually lower than the estimate of 0.235 obtained by MaCurdy, but I have elected to lower it (by an admittedly arbitrary amount) on the grounds that the estimate is likely to be inflated by measurement error. Even so, and since MaCurdy's sample is restricted to white prime-age males, it could be argued that my standard deviation is too *small*. It is certainly smaller than the estimate used by Carroll (1991).

I take the moving average parameter of the aggregate process to be 0.5, which generates an autocorrelation coefficient of 0.4, roughly in line with the estimates reported in Chapter 3. Finally, the standard deviation of the aggregate income innovation is many times smaller than that of the micro process, and I take it to be 0.01, again based on the actual data. From (36), we can see that the fact that σ_1 is much smaller than σ_η means that the idiosyncratic components of income, z_2 and z_3, have to account for nearly all the variance in individual incomes, something that is entirely in accord with the limited role of aggregate factors in explaining the changes in individual incomes. Finally, the rate of growth of income is set at 2% a year.

Once the income processes are set up, I carry out the following experiment. Assuming that each household cannot borrow, and that the felicity functions are isoelastic, with coefficient of relative risk-aversion 2, with $r = 5\%$ and $\delta = 5\%$, I can calculate the optimal policy functions for each household, relating consumption to cash in hand x and the individual income innovations η_{it}. (Even though $r = \delta$, the prospect of positive growth in the future makes agents want to borrow, and guarantees the existence of stationary policy functions). I draw the aggregate growth process first, and then add it to individual independent draws according to (32) and (33) for each of 1,000 households; this number has to be large to ensure that the negatively autocorrelated individual income growths do indeed reliably average to a positively autocorrelated aggregate. For each household, I then use the past history of its own income process and the autoregressive representation of the MA process to calculate the individual innovations. These, together with each household's cash in hand, are used to calculate each household's consumption from the policy functions, and the results added up to give average consumption. As with the previous simulations, the model was allowed to run for 200 periods.

The aggregate consumption and income calculations from this experiment reproduce at least some of the broad features of the aggregate and micro data. The borrowing restrictions at the household level generate a negative correlation between consumption changes and lagged income changes, as originally found in the PSID by Hall and Mishkin. This is reversed at the aggregate level, where the growth rate of aggregate consumption has a coefficient of 0.42 on the lagged growth rate of aggregate income, again mimicking the findings reported in Chapter 3. The saving rate is mildly procyclical in aggregate; the ratio of aggregate consumption to aggregate labor income responds to income growth with a coefficient of −0.17, an effect of the correct sign but only half the coefficient in the data (−0.33). Consumption is smoother than income, but not by much; the standard deviation of the growth of consumption is 0.0114 and that of income is 0.0125. However, note that there are no unconstrained consumers in the experiments, and their presence would smooth the reaction of aggregate consumption to innovations in income. Although each individual has zero assets from time to time, there is sufficient independence between households to guarantee that aggregate assets are positive throughout the simulation. As a result, consumption is a little higher than labor income, with the difference supported by the property income. Again, this result reflects the absence of the patient consumers whom I presume to own most of the assets, and who do most of the saving.

While these results are sufficiently encouraging to make me believe that we are unlikely to understand consumption without allowing for the presence of at least some households who are constrained by their inability to borrow, there remain a number of important points that need further clarification. On the empirical side, we need more and better evidence on household behavior, and we need to understand better what it is that the household data do or do not show. As I argued in Chapter 5, my own reading is that there is evidence, albeit far from overwhelming evidence, that some people some of the time are unable to obtain as much credit as they would wish. But the simple theory of this section also needs a good deal of further development. In particular, although it is true that holdings of liquid assets, bank accounts, stocks and bonds, are typically very small in the US, there are a great many more people who are covered by pension schemes, by social security, and who possess houses and automobiles. None of these assets provides very good insurance against income shocks, but all are held, more or less voluntarily, and the presence of these illiquid and sometimes high-yielding assets needs to be integrated into the model of credit-constrained consumers. There is also a great deal more development that will have to be done before we find a really satisfactory way of confronting these models with the data.

5.3 Precautionary saving versus liquidity constraints

It will not have escaped the reader's attention that there are important similarities, as well as a few differences, between the behavior induced by liquidity constraints, and behavior based on the precautionary motive. Indeed, the model discussed in this section, with a combination of no borrowing and impatience (or at least $\delta > r$), generates buffering behavior that is essentially identical to that predicted by Carroll (1991) with no liquidity constraints, but assuming precautionary saving and a voluntary abstinence from borrowing. At this stage, it is very hard to know how to separate these two models, particularly since both have only been roughly calibrated to the data, and neither has been estimated. Carroll's model, by not relying on liquidity constraints, is relieved of the burden of explaining them. The price is the somewhat far-fetched story of why consumers never borrow; the backward induction argument that is required to generate the result is not robust to the introduction of minimum consumption guarantees, and seems implausible as a motivation for actual behavior. Furthermore, buffering behavior does not always appear as a result in models with the precautionary motive. Not only does it require impatience, but the income process must be quite risky, and must include a finite probability of zero income in each period. The liquidity-constraints model also requires impatience, but will always generate buffering behavior provided only that there is a minimum floor to income. We also have precise conditions on the parameters for this case, conditions that have not yet been developed for Carroll's model. Only further work will show whether the parameters necessary for Carroll's results are supported by the data.

The two buffering models are where precautionary saving and liquidity constraints look most alike. In general, they are capable of producing very different behavior. Borrowing is entirely consistent with the precautionary motive, although prudent consumers will generally borrow less than those who exhibit certainty equivalence. Liquidity constraints also interact with prudence, since the inability to borrow in a tight spot is an additional reason to accumulate precautionary balances. Both models also have a distinct Keynesian flavor; liquidity-constrained models because consumption responds very directly to income with little attention to the future, and precautionary savings models because the future is to some extent discounted. Both models therefore differ very sharply from traditional life-cycle or permanent income models that set consumption equal to the annuity value of total resources, although perhaps less from the original permanent income models of Friedman (1957) and especially (1963), where the future is heavily discounted and the horizon is short.

The links between precautionary saving models and models of liquidity constraints suggest a quite different taxonomy of intertemporal choice models than has been customary in the literature. There is a loose but common usage that describes all models without borrowing constraints as 'permanent income models,' including for example the model with isoelastic felicity functions. These 'permanent income' models are then contrasted with models with liquidity constraints, including rule-of-thumb consumer models, and simple Keynesian models. I have tried to avoid such usage throughout the book, something that is most difficult when describing the empirical work, where several different theories are often being used at once. However, the material in this chapter, as well as some of the empirical work described in Chapter 5, suggests that for some purposes, the models with liquidity constraints and the models with precautionary saving ought to be grouped together, and set in opposition to (formal) permanent income and (conventional) life-cycle models.

CHAPTER 7

Understanding Consumption

It is time to take stock, and to try to summarize what we have learned, and what we have still to learn. Which of the puzzles are resolved, and which are as mysterious as ever? A good point of comparison is a date in the early 1970s, about twenty years ago. The life-cycle and permanent income theories of consumption had been fully absorbed into mainstream economics, they were taught in the textbooks, and were used by econometricians to predict consumption, and in the construction of macroeconomic models to help understand and predict business cycles. The theory was clear and convincing, it matched the evidence, and the consumption function was among the most well behaved and well fitting of all the empirical relationships in macroeconomics. The life-cycle and permanent income models were both rooted in the theory of individual behavior, and both had been tested and found useful on household level data. The microeconomic and macroeconomic data were each consistent with a more or less unified body of theory. From such a perspective, it seems that there has been regress, not progress. The certainties have gone, together with the empirical failure of the macroeconomic models in the mid-1970s. There is much less consensus now than there was then, and much more disagreement about what the evidence shows. Nevertheless, there is no doubt that we have learned a great deal, about theory, about methodology, and even about substance. If we are less confident, it is because we know more, not because we know less.

Let me begin with the issues reviewed in this book, and make some attempt to sort out the substance from the arguments about methodology. I judge substance partly by how much we are helped to explain and understand the empirical evidence, partly by how much we are led to change the way that we think about issues, and partly by the potential consequences for policy.

Much of the theory in Chapter 1 was well understood twenty years ago, but a good deal of it was not. The material is now much better unified, so that the permanent income and life-cycle hypothesis are no longer seen as distinct models, or as the same model in some vague sense, but as well-defined special cases of the general theory of intertemporal choice. The unification is more than convenient because it has led to a much better understanding of the content of the models, what is included and what is excluded, and what are the (previously largely implicit) assumptions that underlie them. At a technical level, there has been enormous progress in the treatment of uncertainty. Dynamic programming techniques are now well understood, and are routinely applied in both theoretical and empirical analysis. Twenty years ago, the lack of a well-based applicable method for dealing with uncertainty left an uncomfortable gap between the models that were being estimated, which typically assumed perfect certainty, or at least certainty equivalence, and an obviously uncertain world in which uncertainty seemed to have major effects on behavior.

I think that the empirical pay-offs to the better understanding of uncertainty are beginning to appear only now, particularly in current work on the precautionary motive for saving. The beguiling simplicity of certainty equivalence has led to a natural overemphasis on permanent income, and a reluctance to confront the computational and analytical complexities of the more general models. As a consequence, it is only recently that we have begun to appreciate the richness of behavior that can be handled by even simple models once certainty equivalence is abandoned. Such models are consistent with behavior that is strikingly different from the predictions of permanent income and conventional life-cycle models. Saving responds positively to uncertainty, and consumption can be made to track income over the life cycle. Fiscal policies that do not change expected lifetime resources can have large effects on consumption, and consumers will typically behave as if they (over-) discount the future. Precautionary motives can account for large wealth holdings, or for zero wealth holdings, and they can explain why people hold mixed portfolios of assets even where some assets dominate others in both mean and variance. We have also learned that prudence and risk-aversion are not the same thing, and Kimball's work has elucidated how to measure the former, and how to separate it from the latter

We are also beginning to explore the consequences of constraints on borrowing, not just as an undeveloped alternative hypothesis to the theory of intertemporal choice in their absence, but as a positive theory in its own right, with its own predictions and characterization of behavior. To the surprise of many of us, behavior with liquidity constraints can look much more like the behavior of prudent consumers in an uncertain world than it looks like behavior under the permanent income or life-cycle hypothesis.

For many economists, the major development in the last twenty years has been the rational expectations revolution, and the treatment of consumption and saving behavior has been one of the areas of economics where the effects have been as dramatic as in any. We have learned a great deal about ways to model expectations, and have come a long way from the mechanical (and frequently internally inconsistent) treatments of the 1970s. We have learned a great deal about time-series analysis, about trends and cycles, and about the difference between unit roots and deterministic trends. We have learned better how to judge the adequacy of econometric models, and how to treat non-stationarity, so that armed with a battery of diagnostic and over-identification tests, we are much more capable of rejecting false models than was the case when econometricians used to mindlessly accept models on the basis of a high R^2 and correctly signed coefficients. It used to be frequently bemoaned that economic theory had nothing to say about dynamics, and was only concerned with the long-run relationship between variables. It is hard to think of a more dramatic refutation of such a position than Hall's (1978) introduction of the random-walk model for consumption. In contrast to twenty years ago, we now have a theory of dynamics, and a theory that incorporates new advances in understanding the role of uncertainty in conditioning behavior.

Of course, we cannot expect progress on substance to be as rapid as progress on theory. Some theories turn out to be wrong, and we frequently need methodological advance in statistical procedures before we can reach agreement on what the data tell us. From that perspective, twenty years is not a great deal of time, and it is unreasonable to expect too much.

The macroeconomic work on excess sensitivity has reached a large measure of agreement that the quarterly consumption change responds to predictable income change with a coefficient in the region of 0.4. Given that this is a time-series finding, it is less clear whether it applies to all predictable income changes, regardless of source, or whether people condition on what they know about the source of the change. There also seems to be broad agreement that similar figures, or at least figures greater than zero, apply in most other countries. It is not entirely clear how we can use this information, or whether it has been worth the considerable efforts that have gone into obtaining it. It certainly contributes to the general goal of understanding, but it would be a good deal more interesting if it did not relate to a mythical representative agent, whose relationship to actual consumers remains at best unclear. For the US, whose political arrangements essentially preclude the timely use of fiscal measures, it is doubtful whether the estimates have any great policy significance. This is less true for countries that are governed differently, and where administrations can (and do) engineer major changes in tax rates overnight. Even if such changes were possible, they would not necessarily be desirable, but the excess sensitivity result points to levers that could potentially be manipulated.

The accumulating microeconomic evidence casts increasing doubt on the life-cycle hypothesis, or at least on the insights that come from the 'stripped-down' version, that saving is largely hump-saving for retirement, that consumption is based on lifetime resources, that aggregate wealth is accountable for by life-cycle saving, and that saving responds positively to productivity and population growth. At least since Mirer (1979), research has queried whether the elderly actually do dissave, and there is still a good deal of debate, partly because it is hard to disentangle the effects of behavior from the effects of selection and attrition among the elderly. Nevertheless, it is certainly the case that the household data typically show no clear evidence of asset decumulation among the old. There are other problems earlier in the life-cycle, and although there is often some hump saving in late middle age, there is also typically a very close articulation of consumption and income over the whole of life. Survey data also show that many households possess little or no wealth, certainly not in financial assets, and many individuals have little beyond social security after they retire. All of this spells trouble for the long held belief that life-cycle wealth can account for most of the wealth in the US, and although Kotlikoff and Summers' (1981) original estimates have not gone unchallenged, it now seems that bequest motives are a good deal more important than we used to think. It is hard to think of issues that are more important than understanding why people are prepared to hold the aggregate wealth stock of the economy.

Another issue on which views have changed is the relationship between saving and growth. Although there is a correlation across countries between saving rates and rates of productivity growth, the evidence presented in Chapter 2 makes it seem unlikely that this correlation can be attributed to the effects of growth on saving, as is predicted by the aggregate version of the life-cycle model. Nor does the life-cycle explanation seem to work within countries. The fall in the saving rate in the US is not attributable to a redistribution of aggregate income towards the old, but comes from an increase in expenditures, particularly expenditures on durable goods, across all cohorts, particularly prime-age cohorts, see Bosworth, Burtless, and Sabelhaus (1991) and Attanasio (1991). The consumption boom in the UK is also not attributable to any fall in the growth rate. Indeed, much of the increase in consumption comes from the younger cohorts, though there is also evidence that financial liberalization has enabled older home-owners to borrow against the equity in their homes, see Muellbauer and Murphy (1990), and Attanasio *et al.* (1992).

The failure of life-cycle predictions on the cross-country evidence tends to favor alternative models in which the causation runs from saving, through investment, to growth, and not from growth to saving. These matters are far from being well understood, and the productivity slow-down in the US is not easily attributed to the decline in the saving rate, since the share of investment to GDP did not fall in line with the saving ratio, and it is surely investment, not saving, that is responsible for growth. Even so, recent research has certainly created an intellectual climate that thinks more positively about the possibilities of increasing growth through policies that favor saving, in both developed and less developed economies. Twenty years ago, we tended to think of growth as being independent of savings, as predicted by the Solow model in the long run, with the correlation between saving and growth explicable by life-cycle aggregation effects. Current thinking would be very different; the life-cycle explanation is not supported by the evidence, and there is a renewed interest both in the transitional dynamics of the Solow model, as well as in non-Solow models in which growth is permanently increased by increasing the saving ratio.

There is also a good deal of evidence against the life-cycle and permanent income predictions that income is irrelevant for consumption once the influence of lifetime resources or permanent income have been allowed for. No one disputes the original permanent income account of high-frequency smoothing, that consumption and income are detached over short periods of time, but there is much less evidence for low-frequency smoothing, with consumers using assets or loans to smooth their consumption in the face of long-term or life-cycle fluctuations in income. The expected value of lifetime resources is certainly not the only variable that determines consumption, and in at least one study, Carroll (1992), expected future income, based on occupational age profiles, had no effect on consumption over and above the effect of current income. If such results come to be accepted, there are major implications for a whole host of policy issues, particularly those that involve the intertemporal reallocation of resources.

Kotlikoff (1992) has written an eloquently argued polemic designed to draw public attention to the intertemporal and intergenerational implications of recent government policies in the US, particularly Social Security and Medicare (medical assistance to the elderly). According to his analysis, the federal government has been and currently is redistributing resources towards the old and away from the young and from future generations. If consumers are aware of these facts, as now they should be, and if their current consumption depends on their total lifetime resources, then the younger generations will be saving now to pay the tax bills and the reduced social security that they are going to receive in the future. In the light of the evidence against low-frequency smoothing, and of the limited relevance of expected future income, especially distant future income, it seems unlikely that they will do so. For exactly the same reasons, Ricardian equivalence will not hold, and government deficits will decrease national saving. The US government may not be able to manipulate its fiscal stance in the short run, but its long-term policies are not so constrained, and their consequences are unlikely to be offset by the clear-sighted and far-sighted actions of permanent income consumers. These essentially empirical conclusions are now well supported by theoretical models, particularly those that recognize either liquidity constraints or precautionary saving.

Although nothing that I have said so far will be accepted by everyone, there are other topics where the disagreements are even larger, and where we know very little. Some of these are very large issues indeed. What is it that determines cross-country variations in saving ratios? If it is not life-cycle effects, what is it? Currently we can do little more than lamely ascribe saving behavior to differences in tastes. Nor do we have a good explanation for the near universal drop in saving rates over the last two decades (see Table 2.1). Once again, the life-cycle story does not appear to yield the answer, but if not that, then what? Growth is surely part of the story, and it is possible to think of explanations other than the life-cycle one for a link, habits being the most obvious example. If consumers are cautious about committing themselves to living standards that they might not be able to maintain, productivity growth gives them a margin of safety, with new income saved at first, and then turned into consumption only when it is safe to do so. A productivity slow-down would threaten such a mechanism. Resources would have to be committed to protecting past living standards, and there would be less room for saving. Although the theory behind such models has been receiving a good deal of recent attention (see the discussion in Chapter 1), the empirical work lags behind.

The links between consumption and finance have also been subject to a great deal of controversy, though a consensus seems to be developing on the failure of representative agent models that attempt to integrate the theories of intertemporal choice and asset pricing. There are also a whole series of puzzles associated with portfolio choice, with why people hold cash in the bank at zero interest, while simultaneously borrowing on credit cards at high rates. The role of Individual Retirement Accounts (IRAs) has also been much debated. These are accounts, with asset composition chosen by the holder, that (for a period) could be bought by almost everyone up to a fixed limit. The contributions were tax deductible, and the assets were accumulated tax free, with tax deferred until withdrawal after retirement. In a series of papers, Venti and Wise (1987*a*, 1987*b*, 1988, and 1991), have used data from various surveys to argue that the existence of these accounts has increased saving in total, generating new saving from those who had not saved before, and not simply causing a reallocation of assets. Carroll and Summers (1987) have also argued that similar policies in Canada may have been responsible for increasing household saving over what it otherwise would have been. Venti and Wise's conclusions have not been universally accepted, largely because of the nature of the cross-sectional evidence. Unless we can track individuals, and have good data on their assets, it is hard to provide a definitive measure of the new saving induced by IRAs, and whether it was large enough to offset the dissaving that comes from the tax losses to the government.

There are a number of other intriguing puzzles associated with IRAs, some of which are much harder to answer than others. The tax deductibility of IRA contributions was removed for most households after 1986, and there has been a very large drop in contributions. Yet tax rates are very likely lower now than they will be in one or two decades from now—see again Kotlikoff (1992)—so that paying the tax up front instead of later should make IRAs more attractive, not less. Another puzzle concerns the timing of IRA contributions, a large fraction of which were made immediately before each year's tax-filing deadline in April, instead of fifteen months before, when the law first allowed. If IRA contributions are being made because of their high rates of return, contributions should be made as early as possible and not at the last minute. Although there has been recent progress in using the precautionary motive to help understand IRAs, see Engen and Gale (1991), it is not clear that these other puzzles are explicable by standard theory. Indeed, such phenomena enhance the appeal of other non-standard or behavioral theories, such as Shefrin and Thaler's (1988) behavioral life-cycle hypothesis in which consumers assign money from different sources to different non-fungible accounts. While I am not unsympathetic to these alternative models of behavior, I am not convinced that our understanding of the standard model is yet complete, nor that it does not have more surprises in store.

I should like to conclude this summary with one of the recurring themes of the book, the importance of aggregation. I believe that future progress is most likely to come when aggregation is taken seriously, and when macroeconomic questions are addressed in a way that uses the increasingly plentiful and informative microeconomic data. Partially aggregated data, such as cohort data, are playing an increasing role, not just in the analysis of consumption, but also in labor economics and elsewhere. Such data are informative about aggregate issues, because they can be matched to the aggregate data; they are constructed from individual data, so they respect the microeconomics, and they allow experimentation with alternative aggregation schemes. They also contain a great deal more information than the already over-used aggregate time-series data. Similar considerations apply to cross-country analyses, where a plethora of recent cross-country regressions has all but exhausted the information in the Penn World Tables and successive issues of the World Development Report. Once again, there are many household survey data sets, and there is a major research program ahead of us in making cross-country comparisons of the internal structures of consumption and saving in each country.

This book has reported a great deal of very high-quality research, and if methodology has frequently dominated over substance, that is the nature of the research process, and I have tried to maintain that flavor in telling the story. Nevertheless, I hope that readers will in the end share my own optimistic view that progress in understanding consumption has been very real, and that there is reason to suppose that even better answers lie ahead.

Bibliography

Abel, Andrew, and Laurence J. Kotlikoff, 1988, 'Does the consumption of different groups move together? A new nonparametric test of intergenerational altruism,' NBER working paper no. 2490 (Jan.), mimeo.

Abowd, John, and David A. Card, 1989, 'On the covariance structure of earnings and hours changes, *Econometrica*, 57, 411–45.

Aghevli, B., James M. Boughton, Peter J. Montiel, Delano Villanueva, and Geoffrey Woglom, 1990, *The role of national saving in the world economy*, Occasional Paper 67, International Monetary Fund, Washington, D.C.

Altonji, Joseph, Fumio Hayashi, and Laurence J. Kotlikoff, 1989, 'Is the extended family altrusitically linked? Direct tests using micro data,' NBER working paper no. 3046 (July), mimeo.

—— and Aloysius Siow, 1987, 'Testing the response of consumption to income changes with (noisy) panel data,' *Quarterly Journal of Economics*, 102, 293–328.

Anderson, Ronald W., 1979, 'Perfect price aggregation and empirical demand analysis,' *Econometrica*, 47, 1209–30.

Ando, Albert, and Arthur B. Kennickell, 1987, 'How much (or little) life cycle is there in micro data? The cases of the United States and Japan,' in Rudiger Dornbusch, Stanley Fischer, and John Bossons (eds.), *Macroeconomics and finance: essays in honor of Franco Modigliani*, Cambridge, Mass. MIT Press, 159–223.

Atkeson, Andrew, and Masao Ogaki, 1990, 'Engel's law and saving,' Univerity of Chicago and University of Rochester (July), mimeo.

Attanasio, Orazio P., 1991, 'A cohort analysis of saving behavior by US households,' Stanford University (Sept.), mimeo.

—— Luigi Guiso, Tullio Jappelli, and Gugielmo Weber, 1992, 'The consumption boom in the UK and Italy in the late 1980s,' Stanford University, Bank of Italy, Universita' di Napoli, and University College London (May), mimeo.

—— and Guglielmo Weber, 1989, 'Intertemporal substitution, risk aversion and the Euler equation for consumption,' *Economic Journal*, 99, (Supplement), 59–63.

—— —— 1991, 'Consumption growth, the interest rate and aggregation,' Stanford University and University College, London (June), mimeo. (*Review of Economic Studies*, forthcoming).

—— —— 1992, 'Consumption growth and excess sensitivity to income: evidence from US micro data,' Stanford University and University College, London (Apr.), mimeo.

Attfield, C.L.F., David Demery, and Nigel W. Duck, 1990, 'Saving and rational expectations: evidence for the U.K.,' *Economic Journal*, 100, 1269–76.

Barro, Robert J., 1974, 'Are government bonds net wealth?' *Journal of Political Economy*, 82, 1095–117.

Barsky, Robert B., N. Gregory Mankiw, and Stephen P. Zeldes, 1986, 'Ricardian consumers with Keynesian propensities,' *American Economic Review*, 76,

676–91.

Bean, Charles R., 1986, 'The estimation of "surprise" models and the "surprise" consumption function,' *Review of Economic Studies*, 49, 497–516.

Becker, Gary S., 1974, 'A theory of social interactions,' *Journal of Political Economy*, 82, 1063–94.

—— 1991, 'Habits, addictions, and traditions,' Nancy Schwartz Lecture, Northwestern University, NORC Discussion Paper 91–8 (Aug.), mimeo.

—— and Kevin Murphy, 1988, 'A theory of rational addiction,' *Journal of Political Economy*, 96, 675–700.

Bertola, Giuseppe, and Ricardo J. Caballero, 1990, 'Kinked adjustment costs and aggregate dynamics,' in Olivier J. Blanchard and Stanley Fischer (eds.), *NBER Macroeconomics Annual 1990*, Cambridge, Mass. MIT Press, 237–95

Bewley, Truman, 1977, 'The permanent income hypothesis: a theoretical formulation,' *Journal of Economic Theory*, 16, 252–92.

Blanchard, Olivier J., 1985, 'Debts, deficits, and finite horizons,' *Journal of Political Economy*, 93, 1045–76.

—— and Stanley Fischer, 1989, *Lectures on macroeconomics*, Cambridge, Mass. MIT Press.

—— and N. Gregory Mankiw, 1988, 'Consumption: beyond certainty equivalence,' *American Economic Review (paps. and procs.)*, 78, 173–7.

Blinder, Alan S., and Angus S. Deaton, 1985, 'The time-series consumption revisited,' *Brookings Papers on Economic Activity*, 465–521.

Blundell, Richard W., Martin J. Browning, and Costas Meghir, 1991, 'Consumer demand and the lifetime allocation of household expenditure,' University College, London, mimeo.

Börsch-Supan, Axel, and Konrad Stahl, 1991, 'Life cycle savings and consumption constraints. Theory, empirical evidence, and fiscal implications,' *Journal of Population Economics*, 4, 233–55.

Boskin, Michael J., 1978, 'Taxation, saving, and the rate of interest,' *Journal of Political Economy*, 86, 3–27.

Bosworth, Barry, Gary Burtless, and John Sabelhaus, 1991, 'The decline in saving: some microeconomic evidence,' *Brookings Papers on Economic Activity*, 183–241.

Browning, Martin J., 1989, 'The intertemporal allocation of expenditure on non-durables, services, and durables,' *Canadian Journal of Economics*, 22, 22–36.

—— Angus S. Deaton, and Margaret Irish, 1985, 'A profitable approach to labor supply and commodity demands over the life-cycle,' *Econometrica*, 53, 503–44.

Caballero, Ricardo J., 1990a, 'Expenditure on durable goods: a case for slow adjustment,' *Quarterly Journal of Economics*, 105, 727–43.

—— 1990b, 'Consumption puzzles and precautionary saving,' *Journal of Monetary Economics*, 25, 113–36.

—— 1991, 'Earnings uncertainty and aggregate wealth accumulation,' *American Economic Review*, 81, 859–71.

Calvo, Guillermo, 1979, 'On the time inconsistency of optimal policy in a monetary economy,' *Econometrica*, 46, 1411–28.

Campbell, John Y., 1987, 'Does saving anticipate declining labor income? An alternative test of the permanent income hypothesis,' *Econometrica*, 55, 1249–73.

—— and Angus S. Deaton, 1989, 'Why is consumption so smooth?' *Review of Economic Studies*, 56, 357–74.

—— and N. Gregory Mankiw, 1987, 'Are output fluctuations transitory?' *Quarterly Journal of Economics*, 102, 857–80.

—— —— 1989, 'Consumption, income and interest rates: reinterpreting the time series evidence,' in Olivier J. Blanchard and Stanley Fischer (eds.), *NBER Macroeconomics Annual 1989*, Cambridge, Mass. MIT Press, 185–216.

—— —— 1991, 'The response of consumption to income: a cross-country investigation,' *European Economic Review*, 35, 715–21.

Carroll, Christopher D., 1991, 'Buffer stock saving and the permanent income hypothesis,' Board of Governors of the Federal Reserve System, mimeo.

—— 1992, 'How does future income affect current consumption?' Board of Governors of the Federal Reserve System (Jan.), mimeo.

—— and Lawrence H. Summers, 1987, 'Why have private saving rates in the United States and Canada diverged?' *Journal of Monetary Economics*, 20, 249–79.

—— —— 1991, 'Consumption growth parallels income growth: some new evidence,' in B. Douglas Bernheim and John B. Shoven (eds.), *National Saving and Economic Performance*, Chicago. Chicago University Press for NBER, 305–43.

Chamberlain, Gary, 1984, 'Panel data,' in Zvi Griliches and Michael D. Intriligator (eds.), *Handbook of Econometrics*, Vol. 2, North-Holland. Amsterdam, 1247–318.

Christiano, Lawrence J., 1987, 'Is consumption insufficiently sensitive to innovations in income?' *American Economic Review*, (*paps. and procs.*), 77, 337–41.

—— and Martin Eichenbaum, 1990, 'Unit roots in real GNP: do we know and do we care?' *Carnegie–Rochester Conference Series on Public Policy*, 32, 7–61.

—— —— and David Marshall, 1991, 'The permanent income hypothesis revisited,' *Econometrica*, 59, 397–423.

Clarida, Richard H., 1991, 'Aggregate stochastic implications of the life-cycle hypothesis,' *Quarterly Journal of Economics*, 106, 851–67.

Cochrane, John, H., 1988, 'How big is the random walk in GNP?' *Journal of Political Economy*, 96, 893–920.

—— 1989, 'The sensitivity of tests of the intertemporal allocation of consumption to near-rational alternatives,' *American Economic Review*, 79, 319–37.

—— 1991, 'A simple test of consumption insurance,' *Journal of Political Economy*, 99, 957–76.

Cogley, Timothy, 1989, 'Is consumption too smooth? Evidence from Canada,' Univeristy of Washington, mimeo.

Constantinides, George M., 1990, 'Habit formation: a resolution of the equity premium puzzle,' *Journal of Political Economy*, 98, 519–43.

Danziger, Sheldon, Jacques van der Gaag, Eugene Smolensky, and Michael Taussig, 1983, 'The life cycle hypothesis and the consumption behavior of the elderly,' *Journal of Post-Keynesian Economics*, 5, 208–27.

Davidson, James E.H., and David F. Hendry, 1981, 'Interpreting econometric evidence: consumers' expenditures,' *European Economic Review*, 16, 177–92.

—— —— Frank Srba, and Stephen Yeo, 1978, 'Econometric modelling of the aggregate time-series relationship between consumers' expenditure and income in the United Kingdom,' *Economic Journal*, 88, 661–92.

Deaton, Angus S., 1974, 'On the empirical implications of additive preferences,' *Economic Journal*, 84, 338–48.

—— 1977, 'Involuntary saving through unanticipated inflation,' *American Economic Review*, 67, 899–910.

—— 1985, 'Panel data from a time-series of cross-sections,' *Journal of Econometrics*, 30, 109–26.

—— 1987, 'Life-cycle models of consumption: Is the evidence consistent with the theory?' in Truman F. Bewley (ed.), *Advances in Econometrics, Fifth World Congress*, Vol. 2, Cambridge and New York. Cambridge University Press, 121–48.

—— 1990, 'Saving in developing countries: theory and review,' *World Bank Economic Review*, Special Issue, Proceedings of the First Annual World Bank Conference on Development Economics, 61–96.

—— 1991, 'Saving and liquidity constraints,' *Econometrica*, 59, 1221–48.

—— 1992a, 'Saving and income smoothing in the Côte d'Ivoire,' *Journal of African Economies*, 1, 1–24.

—— 1992b, 'Household saving in LDCs: credit markets, insurance, and welfare,' *Scandinavian Journal of Economics*, 94, 253–73.

—— and Guy Laroque, 1992, 'On the behavior of commodity prices,' *Review of Economic Studies*, 59, 1–23.

—— and John Muellbauer, 1980, *Economics and consumer behavior*, New York. Cambridge University Press.

—— and Christina H. Paxson, 1992, 'Saving, growth, and aging in Taiwan,' Research program in development studies, Princeton (June), mimeo.

DeLong, Bradford J., and Lawrence H. Summers, 1986, 'The changing cyclical variability of economic activity in the US,' in Robert J. Gordon (ed.), *The American business cycle: continuity and change*, Chicago. Chicago University Press, 679–734.

Diamond, Peter A., and Jerry A. Hausman, 1984, 'Individual retirement and savings behavior,' *Journal of Public Economics*, 23, 81–114.

Dickey, David A. and Wayne A. Fuller, 1981, 'Likelihood ratio statistics for autoregressive time series with a unit root,' *Econometrica*, 49, 1057–72.

Diebold, Francis X., and Glenn D. Rudebusch, 1991, 'Is consumption too smooth? Long memory and the Deaton paradox,' *Review of Economics and Statistics*, 73, 1–17.

—— and Marc Nerlove, 1990, 'Unit roots in economic time series: a selective survey,' in Thomas B. Fomby and George F. Rhodes (eds.), *Advances in econometrics: cointegration, spurious regressions, and unit roots*, Greenwich, Connecticut. JAI Press, 3–69.

Dow, J. Christopher R., 1964, *The management of the British economy, 1945–60*, Cambridge. Cambridge University Press.

Duesenberry, James S., 1949, *Income, saving, and the theory of consumer behavior*, Cambridge, Mass. Harvard University Press.

—— Gary Fromm, Lawrence R. Klein, and Edwin Kuh (eds.), *The Brookings Quarterly Econometric Model of the United States*, Chicago. Rand-McNally.

Engen, Eric M., and William Gale, 1991, 'IRAs and saving in a stochastic life-cycle model,' University of California at Los Angeles (Dec.), mimeo.

Engle, Robert, and Clive W.J. Granger, 1987, 'Co-integration and error correction: representation, estimation, and testing,'*Econometrica*, 55, 251–76.

Epstein, Larry G., and Stanley E. Zin, 1989, 'Substitution, risk aversion, and the temporal behavior of consumption and asset returns: a theoretical framework,' *Econometrica*, 46, 185–200.

—— —— 1991, 'Substitution, risk aversion, and the temporal behavior of consumption and asset returns: an empirical analysis,' *Journal of Political Economy*, 99, 263–86.

Ermini, Luigi, 1989, 'Some new evidence on the timing of consumption decisions and on their generating processes,' *Review of Economics and Statistics*, 71, 643–50.

Evans, Michael K., 1969, *Macroeconomic activity: theory, forecasting, and control*, New York. Harper & Row.

Feldstein, Martin, and Charles Horioka, 1980, 'Domestic saving and international capital flows,' *Economic Journal*, 90, 314–29.

Flavin, Marjorie, 1981, 'The adjustment of consumption to changing expectations about future income,' *Journal of Political Economy*, 89, 974–1009.

—— 1990 'The excess smoothness of consumption: identification and interpretation,' University of Virginia, mimeo.

—— 1991, 'The joint consumption/asset demand decision: a case study in robust estimation,' NBER working paper no. 3802, mimeo.

Friedman, Milton, 1957, *A theory of the consumption function*, Princeton. Princeton University Press.

—— 1963, 'Windfalls, the "horizon" and related concepts in the permanent income hypothesis,' in Carl Christ *et al.* (eds.), *Measurement in Economics*, Stanford. Stanford University Press, 1–28.

Fry, Maxwell, 1987, *Money, interest, and banking in economic development*, Baltimore, Md. Johns Hopkins University Press.

Galí, Jordi, 1990, 'Finite horizons, life cycle savings and time series evidence on consumption,' *Journal of Monetary Economics*, 26, 433–52.

—— 1991a, 'Budget constraints and time series evidence on consumption,' *American Economic Review*, 81, 1238–53.

—— 1991b, 'International evidence on consumption variability,' Columbia University, mimeo.

Gersovitz, Mark, 1988, 'Saving and development,' in Hollis Chenery and T.N. Srinivasan (eds.), *Handbook of Development Economics*, Vol. 1, Amsterdam.

North-Holland, 381–424.

Ghez, Gilbert R., and Gary S. Becker, 1975, 'The allocation of time and goods over the life-cycle,' New York. NBER.

Goodfriend, Marvin, 1992, 'Information aggregation bias,' *American Economic Review*, 82, 508–19.

Gorman, William M., 1959, 'Separable utility and aggregation,' *Econometrica*, 27, 469–81.

Granger, Clive W.J., and Paul Newbold, 1986, *Forecasting economic time-series*, 2nd edn., New York. Academic Press.

Grossman, Sanford J., and Guy Laroque, 1990, 'Asset pricing and optimal portfolio choice in the presence of illiquid durable consumption goods,' *Econometrica*, 58, 25–51.

—— and Robert J. Shiller, 1982, 'Consumption correlatednes and risk measurement in economies with nontraded assets and heterogeneous information,' *Journal of Financial Economics*, 10, 195–210.

Guiso, Luigi, Tullio Jappelli and Daniele Terlizzese, 1991, 'Earnings uncertainty and precautionary saving,' Bank of Italy, Rome, mimeo.

Hall, Robert E., 1978, 'Stochastic implications of the life cycle-permanent income hypothesis: theory and evidence,' *Journal of Political Economy*, 96, 971–87.

—— 1988, 'Intertemporal substitution in consumption,' *Journal of Political Economy*, 96, 339–57.

—— 1989, 'Consumption,' in Robert J. Barro (ed.), *Modern Business Cycle Theory*, Cambridge, Mass. Harvard University Press.

—— and Frederic S. Mishkin, 1982, 'The sensitivity of consumption to transitory income: estimates from panel data on households,' *Econometrica*, 50, 461–81.

Hansen, Lars Peter, and Ravi Jagannathan, 1991, 'Implications of security market data for models of dynamic economies,' *Journal of Political Economy*, 99, 225–62.

—— William Roberds, and Thomas J. Sargent, 1991, 'Time series implications of present value budget balance and of martingale models of consumption and taxes,' in Lars P. Hansen and Thoams J. Sargent, *Rational expectations econometrics*, Boulder. Westview, 121–61.

—— and Thomas J. Sargent, 1981, 'A note on Wiener-Kolmogorov forecasting formulas for rational expectations models,' *Economics Letters*, 8, 253–60.

—— and Kenneth J. Singleton, 1982, 'Generalized instrumental variables estimation of nonlinear rational expectations models,' *Econometrica*, 50, 1269–86.

Hayashi, Fumio, 1982, 'The permanent income hypothesis: estimation and testing by instrumental variables,' *Journal of Political Economy*, 90, 895–916.

—— 1985a, 'The effect of liquidity constraints on consumption: a cross-sectional analysis,' *Quarterly Journal of Economics*, 100, 183–206.

—— 1985b, 'The permanent income hypothesis and consumption durability: analysis based on Japanese panel data,' *Quarterly Journal of Economics*, 100, 1083–113.

—— 1987, 'Tests for liquidity constraints: a critical survey and some new observations,' in Truman F. Bewley (ed.), *Advances in Econometrics: Fifth World Congress*, Vol. 2, 91–120.

——, Joseph Altonji, and Laurence J. Kotlikoff, 1991, 'Risk-sharing, altruism, and the factor structure of consumption,' NBER working paper no. 3834 (Sept.), mimeo.

Heaton, John, 1990, 'The interaction between time-nonseparable preferences and time aggregation,' Sloan School MIT, working paper 3181–90–EFA (June), mimeo.

—— 1991, 'An empirical investigation of asset pricing with temporally dependent preference specifications,' Sloan School MIT, working paper 3245–91–EFA (Feb.), mimeo.

Heckman, James J., 1971, 'Three essays on the supply of labor and the demand for market goods,' Ph.D. dissertation, Princeton University.

—— 1974, 'Life-cycle consumption and labor supply: an exploration of the relationship between income and consumption over the life cycle,' *American Economic Review*, 64, 188–94.

Hendry, David F., John N.J. Muellbauer, and Anthony Murphy, 1990, 'The econometrics of DHSY,' in John D. Hey and Donald Winch (eds.), *A Century of Economics: 100 Years of the Royal Economic Society and the Economic Journal*, Oxford. Blackwell, 298–334.

—— and Thomas von Ungern-Sternberg, 1981, 'Liquidity and inflation effects on consumers' expenditure,' in Angus S. Deaton (ed.), *Essays in the theory and measurement of consumer behaviour in honour of Sir Richard Stone*, Cambridge. Cambridge University Press, 237–60.

Hotz, V. Joseph, Finn E. Kydland, and Guilherme L. Sedlacek, 1988, 'Intertemporal preferences and labor supply,' *Econometrica*, 56, 335–60.

Houthakker, Hendrik S., and Lester D. Taylor, 1970, *Consumer demand in the United States: analysis and projections*, Cambridge, Mass. Harvard University Press.

Hubbard, R. Glenn, Jonathan Skinner, and Stephen P. Zeldes, 1992, 'Precautionary saving and social insurance,' Columbia University, University of Virginia, and University of Pennsylvania (Apr.), mimeo.

Jappelli, Tullio, 1990, 'Who is credit-constrained in the US economy,' *Quarterly Journal of Economics*, 105, 219–34.

—— and Marco Pagano, 1988, 'Liquidity constrained households in an Italian cross-section,' London, Centre for Economic Policy Research, discussion paper no. 257, mimeo.

—— and Marco Pagano, 1989, 'Consumption and capital market imperfections; an international comparison,' *American Economic Review*, 79, 1088–105.

Keane, Michael, P., and David E. Runkle, 1992, 'On the estimation of panel data models with serial correlation when instruments are not strictly exogenous,' *Journal of Business and Economic Statistics*, 10, 1–9.

Kimball, Miles S., 1990, 'Precautionary saving in the small and in the large,' *Econometrica*, 58, 53–73.

—— and N. Gregory Mankiw, 1989, 'Precautionary saving and the timing of taxes,' *Journal of Political Economy*, 97, 863–79.

King, Robert G., and Sergio T. Rebelo, 1989, 'Transitional dynamics and economic growth in the neoclassical model,' NBER working paper no 3185, mimeo.

Kotlikoff, Laurence, J., 1988, 'Intergenerational transfers and savings,' *Journal of Economic Perspectives*, 2, 41–58.

—— 1992, *Generational accounting*, New York. Free Press.

—— and Lawrence H. Summers, 1981, 'The role of intergenerational transfers in aggregate capital formation,' *Journal of Political Economy*, 89, 706–32.

Kreps, David M., and Evan L. Porteus, 1978, 'Temporal resolution of uncertainty and dynamic choice theory,' *Econometrica*, 46, 185–200.

Kydland, Finn, and Edward Prescott, 1977, 'Rules rather than discretion: the inconsistency of optimal plans,' *Journal of Political Economy*, 85, 473–91.

Lawrance, Emily C., 1991, 'Poverty and the rate of time preference: evidence from panel data,' *Journal of Political Economy*, 99, 54–77.

Lucas, Robert E., 1976, 'Econometric policy evaluation: a critique,' in Karl Brunner and Alan Meltzer (eds.), *The Phillips curve and labor markets*, Carnegie–Rochester Conference Series on Public Policy, Vol. 1, Amsterdam. North-Holland, 19–46.

Lusardi, Annamaria, 1992, 'Permanent income, consumption, and precautionary saving: an empirical investigation,' Ph.D. thesis, Princeton University.

McCallum, Bennet T., 1976, 'Rational expectations and the natural rate hypothesis: some consistent estimates,' *Econometrica*, 44, 43–52.

Mace, Barbara J., 1991, 'Full insurance in the presence of aggregate uncertainty,' *Journal of Political Economy*, 99, 928–56.

MaCurdy, Thomas E., 1982, 'The use of time-series processes to model the error structure of earnings in longitudinal data analysis,' *Journal of Econometrics*, 18, 83–114.

Maddison, Angus, 1992, 'A long-run perspective on saving,' *Scandinavian Journal of Economics*, 94, 181–96.

Mankiw, N. Gregory, 1982, 'Hall's consumption hypothesis and durable goods,' *Journal of Monetary Economics*, 10, 417–25.

—— Julio J. Rotemberg, and Lawrence H. Summers, 1985, 'Intertemporal substitution in macroeconomics,' *Quarterly Journal of Economics*, 100, 225–53.

—— and Matthew Shapiro, 1985, 'Trends, random walks, and tests of the permanent income hypothesis,' *Journal of Monetary Economics*, 16, 165–74.

—— and Stephen P. Zeldes, 1991, The consumption of stockholders and non-stockholders,' *Journal of Financial Economics*, 29, 97–112.

Mariger, Randall P., and Kathryn Shaw, 1990, 'Unanticipated aggregate disturbances and tests of the life-cycle model using panel data,' Board of Governors of the Federal Reserve and Carnegie Mellon University, mimeo.

Mehra, Rajnish, and Edward C. Prescott, 1985, 'The equity premium: a puzzle,' *Journal of Monetary Economics*, 15, 145–61.

Merton, Robert C., 1969, 'Lifetime portfolio selection under uncertainty: the continuous time case,' *Review of Economics and Statistics*, 67, 353–62.

Mirer, Thad W., 1979, 'The wealth-age relationship among the aged,' *American Economic Review*, 69, 435–43.

Modigliani, Franco, 1986, 'Life cycle, individual thrift, and the wealth of nations,' *American Economic Review*, 76, 297–313.

—— 1988, 'The role of intergenerational transfers and life cycle saving in the accumulation of wealth,' *Journal of Economic Perspectives*, 2, 15–40.

—— 1990, 'Recent declines in the savings rate: a life cycle perspective,' Frisch Lecture, Sixth World Congress of the Econometric Society, Barcelona (Aug.), mimeo.

—— and Richard Brumberg, 1954, 'Utility analysis and the consumption function: an interpretation of cross-section data,' in Kenneth K. Kurihara (ed.), *Post-Keynesian economics*, New Brunswick, N.J.. Rutgers University Press, 388–436.

—— —— 1979, 'Utility analysis and the consumption function: an attempt at integration,' in Andrew Abel (ed.), *The collected papers of Franco Modigliani*, Volume 2, Cambridge, Mass. MIT Press, 128–97.

Mork, Knut A., and V. Kerry Smith, 1989, 'Testing the life-cycle hypothesis with a Norwegian household panel,' *Journal of Business and Economic Statistics*, 7, 287–96.

Mroz, Thomas A., 1987, 'The sensitivity of an empirical model of married women's hours of work to economic and statistical assumptions,' *Econometrica*, 55, 765–800.

Muellbauer, John N.J., 1988, 'Habits, rationality and myopia in the life cycle consumption function,' *Annales d'économie et de statistique*, 9, 47–70.

—— and Anthony Murphy, 1990, 'Is the UK balance of payments sustainable?' *Economic Policy*, 5, 347–95.

Muth, John F., 1960, 'Optimal properties of exponentially weighted forecasts,' *Journal of the American Statistical Association*, 55, 299–306.

Nelson, Charles R., 1987, 'A reappraisal of recent tests of the permanent income hypothesis,' *Journal of Political Economy*, 95, 641–46.

Nerlove, Marc, 1957, 'A note on long-run automobile demand,' *Journal of Marketing*, 21, 57–64.

Newbery, David M. G., 1989, 'Agricultural institutions for insurance and stabilization,' in Pranab Bardhan (ed.), *The economic theory of agrarian institutions*, Oxford. Clarendon Press, 267–96.

Obstfeld, Maurice, 1990, 'Intertemporal dependence, impatience, and dynamics,' *Journal of Monetary Economics*, 26, 45–75.

Phillips, Peter C. B., and Pierre Perron, 1988, 'Testing for a unit root in time series regression,' *Biometrika*, 75, 335–46.

Phlips, Louis, 1974, *Applied consumption analysis*, Amsterdam. North-Holland.

Pischke, Jörn-Steffen, 1991, 'Individual income, incomplete information, and aggregate consumption,' Industrial Relations Section working paper no. 289, Princeton University, mimeo.

Priestley, M.B., 1981, *Spectral analysis and time series*, London. Academic Press.

Quah, Danny, 1990, 'Permanent and transitory movements in labor income: an explanation for "excess smoothness" in consumption,' *Journal of Political Economy*, 98, 449–75.

Ravallion, Martin and Shubham Chauduri, 1992, 'Tests of risk-sharing in three Indian villages,' The World Bank and Princeton University, mimeo.

Rebelo, Sergio, 1991, 'Long run policy analysis and long run growth,' *Journal of Political Economy*, 99, 91–109.

Romer, Paul, 1990, 'Endogenous technical change,' *Journal of Political Economy*, 98, S71–S102.

Rosovsky, Henry, 1990, *The university: an owner's manual*, New York. Norton.

Runkle, David E., 1991, 'Liquidity constraints and the permanent-income hypothesis,' *Journal of Monetary Economics*, 27, 73–98.

Samuelson, Paul A., 1969, 'Lifetime portfolio selection by dynamic stochastic programming,' *Review of Economics and Statistics*, 51, 239–46.

Schechtman, Jack, 1976, 'An income fluctuation problem,' *Journal of Economic Theory*, 12, 218–41.

—— and Vera Escudero, 1977, 'Some results on "An income fluctuation problem",' *Journal of Economic Theory*, 16, 151–66.

Shefrin, Hersh M., and Richard H. Thaler, 1988, 'The behavioral life-cycle hypothesis,' *Economic Inquiry*, 26, 609–43.

Sims, Christopher A., James H. Stock, and Mark W. Watson, 1990, 'Inference in linear time series models with some unit roots,' *Econometrica*, 58, 113–44.

Singleton, Kenneth J., 1990, 'Specification and estimation of intertemporal asset pricing models,' in Benjamin M. Friedman and Frank H. Hahn (eds.), *Handbook of Monetary Economics*, Vol. 1, Amsterdam. North-Holland, 583–626.

Skinner, Jonathan, 1988, 'Risky income, life-cycle consumption, and precautionary saving,' *Journal of Monetary Economics*, 22, 237–55.

Spinnewyn, Franz, 1981, 'Rational habit formation,' *European Economic Review*, 15, 91–109.

Stiglitz, Joseph E., and Andrew Weiss, 1981, 'Credit rationing in markets with imperfect information,' *American Economic Review*, 71, 393–410.

Stock, James, and Kenneth D. West, 1988, 'Integrated regressors and tests of the permanent income hypothesis,' *Journal of Monetary Economics*, 21, 85–95.

Stone, J. Richard N., 1964, 'Private saving in Britain, past, present, and future,' *Manchester School of Economic and Social Research*, 32, 79–112.

—— 1966, Spending and saving in relation to income and wealth, *L'Industria*, 4, 471–99.

—— 1973, 'Personal spending and saving in postwar Britain,' in H. Bos (ed.), *Economic structure and development: essays in honor of Jan Tinbergen*, Amsterdam. North-Holland.

—— and Derek A. Rowe, 1957, 'The market demand for durable goods,' *Econometrica*, 25, 423–43.

—— —— 1958, 'Dynamic demand functions: some econometric results,' *Eco-*

nomic Journal, 68, 256–70.

—— —— 1962, 'A post-war expenditure function,' *The Manchester School of Economic and Social Studies*, 30, 187–201.

Strotz, Robert H., 1956, 'Myopia and inconsistency in dynamic utility maximization,' *Review of Economic Studies*, 23, 165–80.

Suits, Daniel B., and Gordon R. Sparks, 1965, 'Consumption regressions with quarterly data,' in James S. Duesenberry, Gary Fromm, Lawrence R. Klein, and Edwin Kuh (eds.), *The Brookings Quarterly Econometric Model of the United States*, Chicago. Rand-McNally, 202–23.

Summers, Robert, and Alan C. Heston, 1991, 'The Penn world table (mark 5): an expanded set of international comparisons 1950–1985,' *Quarterly Journal of Economics*, 106, 327–68.

Tauchen, George, 1986, 'Finite state Markov chain approximations to univariate and vector autoregressions,' *Economics Letters*, 20, 177–81.

—— Robert Hussey, 1991, 'Quadrature based methods for obtaining approximate solutions to nonlinear asset pricing models,' *Econometrica*, 59, 371–96.

Thurow, Lester D., 1969, 'The optimum lifetime distribution of consumption expenditures,' *American Economic Review*, 59, 324–30.

Tobin, James, 1967, 'Life-cycle saving and balanced growth,' in W. Fellner *et al.* (eds.), *Ten economic studies in the tradition of Irving Fisher*, New York. Wiley, 327–68.

Townsend, Robert M., 1991, 'Risk and insurance in village India,' NORC discussion paper no. 91–3 (May), mimeo.

Uzawa, Hirofumi, 1968, 'Time preference, the consumption function, and optimum asset holdings,' in J. N. Wolfe (ed.), *Value, capital and growth: papers in honour of Sir John Hicks*, Chicago. Aldine, 485–504.

van der Ploeg, Frederick, 1989, 'Risk aversion, intertemporal substitution and consumption: the CARA-LQ problem,' CentER for Economic Research, Tilburg University, The Netherlands, mimeo.

Venti, Steven F., and David A. Wise, 1987a, 'IRAs and saving,' in Martin Feldstein (ed.), *The effects of taxation on capital accumulation*, Chicago. University of Chicago Press, 7–48.

—— —— 1987b, 'Have IRAs increased US saving? Evidence from consumer expenditure surveys,' *Quarterly Journal of Economics*, 105, 661–98.

—— —— 1988, 'The determinants of IRA contributions and the effect of limit changes,' in Zvi Bodie, John Shoven, and David Wise (eds.), *Pensions in the U.S. economy*, Chicago. University of Chicago Press, 9–47.

—— —— 1991, 'The saving effect of tax-deferred retirement accounts: evidence from SIPP,' in B. Douglas Bernheim and John B. Shoven (eds.), *National Saving and Economic Performance*, Chicago. University of Chicago Press, 103–28.

Visaria, Pravin, 1980, *Poverty and living standards in Asia*, World Bank, Living Standards Measurement Study, mimeo.

Watson, Mark, W. 1986, 'Univariate detrending methods with stochastic trends,'

Journal of Monetary Economics, 18, 49–75.

Weil, Philippe, 1990, 'Nonexpected utility in macroeconomics,' *Quarterly Journal of Economics*, 105, 29–42.

West, Kenneth D., 1988, 'The insensitivity of consumption to news about income,' *Journal of Monetary Economics*, 21, 17–34.

Wilcox, David W., 1987, 'Income tax refunds and the timing of consumption expenditures,' Board of Governors of the Federal Reserve System (May), mimeo.

—— 1989, 'Social security benefits, consumption expenditure, and the life cycle hypothesis,' *Journal of Political Economy*, 97, 288–304.

—— 1991, 'The construction of the US consumption data: some facts and their implications for empirical work,' Board of Governors of the Federal Reserve System, mimeo.

World Bank, annual, *World Development Report*, Washington, D.C.

Zeldes, Stephen P., 1989*a*, 'Consumption and liquidity constraints: an empirical investigation,' *Journal of Political Economy*, 97, 305–46.

—— 1989*b*, 'Optimal consumption with stochastic income: deviations from certainty equivalence,' *Quarterly Journal of Economics*, 104, 275–98.

Index of Names

Index of Subjects